Our Heavenly Father's Manufacturer's Handbook!

Our Heavenly Father's Manufacturer's Handbook!

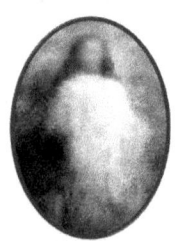

"Disclosure of the Eternal Gift"

Charles E. Dickerson

Neo Nexus Publishing, LLC

COLUMBIA, SOUTH CAROLINA

*

ISBN-10: 0-9846673-8-5
ISBN-13: 978-0-9846673-8-3
Library of Congress Control Number: 2017911257

*

Copyright © Charles E. Dickerson 2 0 1 7
First Edition
ALL RIGHTS RESERVED.
No part of this publication is to be reproduced in any manner without prior written permission from the publisher.

*

PRINTED IN THE UNITED STATES OF AMERICA

Quotations taken from:

Unless otherwise noted...
All Scripture quotations are taken from the following translations of The Holy Bible:

King James Version®,
Copyright © 1611 by Public Domain

American Standard Bible®,
Copyright © 1901 by Public Domain

The Amplified® Bible®,
Copyright © 1954, 1958, 1962, 1964, 1965,
1987 by The Lockman Foundation
Used by permission. (www.Lockman.org)

Contemporary English Version®,
Copyright © 1991, 1992, 1995
by American Bible Society, Used by Permission.

NKJV: New King James Version®,
Copyright © 1982 by Thomas Nelson, Inc.
Used by permission. All rights reserved.

New American Standard Bible®,
Copyright © 1960, 1962, 1963, 1968, 1971, 1972, 1973,
1975, 1977, 1995 by The Lockman Foundation
Used by permission." (www.Lockman.org)

NCV: New Century Version®,
Copyright © 2005 by Thomas Nelson, Inc.
Used by permission. All rights reserved.

New International Reader's Version®,
Copyright © 1996, 1998 Biblica.
All rights reserved throughout the world.
Used by permission of Biblica.

Holman Christian Standard Bible®,
Copyright © 1999, 2000, 2002, 2003 by Holman
Bible Publishers. Used by permission. Holman Christian
Standard Bible®, Holman CSB®, and HCSB® are federally
registered Trademarks of Holman Bible Publishers.

21ˢᵗ Century King James Version®,
Copyright © 1994. Used by permission of Deuel
Enterprises, Inc., Gary, SD 57237. All rights reserved.

New International Version® Anglicized, NIV®,
Copyright © 1979, 1984, 2011
By <a href="http://www.biblica.com/"> Biblica, Inc.® </a>
Used by permission. All rights reserved worldwide.

New Living Translation®,
copyright © 1996, 2004, 2007 by Tyndale House Foundation.
Used by permission of Tyndale House Publishers, Inc.,
Carol Stream, Illinois 60188. All rights reserved.

ESV® Bible (The Holy Bible, English Standard Version®),
Copyright © 2001 by Crossway, a publishing ministry of Good
News Publishers. ESV® Text Edition: 2011. The ESV® text
has been reproduced in cooperation with and by permission of
Good News Publishers. Unauthorized reproduction of this
publication prohibited. All rights reserved.

Additional Quotations & Reference Sources:

Strong's Exhaustive Concordance of the Bible

Dr. Albert Einstein

Carl Sandburg
US Biographer and Poet 1878 – 1967

Van der Gaag
Early Childhood Development:
An Economic Perspective[9]

National Research Council Institute For Medicine
The Science Of Early Childhood Development

TheHuffingtonPost.com, Inc.
HuffPost Healthy Living

Wikipedia Encylopepia

National Catholic Register

Merriam-Webster Dictionary

Encyclopedia Britannica Concise

Our Heavenly Father's Manufacturer's Handbook!

Dedication	ix
Foreword	x
Preface	xv
Introduction	1
Author and scribe	5

The Overview...	A Tablet Moment!	9

Man... God's manufactured product	10
Our Heavenly Father's Manufacturer's Handbook	11
Commissioning of the Manufacturer's Handbook	12
The Holy Bible... Man's guide to spiritual redemption	13
Eden's Spirit Culture	15
The metamorphic process relative to genetic transformation	15
Man's highest state of existence	17
Metamorphosis engenders transformation	17
Image of God	18
Likeness of God	23
Trinitary oneness in God and man	23
Nature of the child	24
Nature of the adult	26
Jehovah and Joseph, *"Master Builder"* and *"minor builder"*	26
Historical significance of the cross	27
Nature of the elder	29
Special relationship between God and man	30
The Garden of Eden	31
War in heaven... Lucifer cast into the Earth as Satan	33
The downfall of man	35
The *"Law of Use"*	36
Forbidden knowledge of God consumed	36
Forbidden knowledge reserved for God alone	37
Forbidden knowledge translates into sin	38
Sin translates into death	38
How many deaths are there?	40
Death to man's spiritual character	41
Death to man's physical body	42

Our Heavenly Father's Manufacturer's Handbook!

Death to man's soul	43
Jesus… Man's seed of salvation	44
Eden's Spirit culture lost	45
Tree of knowledge of good and evil	45
Tree of life	46
Calvary's holy cross	46
Eternal life	47
Eve converses with a walking and talking serpent	48
Understanding freewill first	49
Dual components of freewill	51
Adam's failure to surrender his freewill in place of God's will	52
Adam's non-surrender of freewill, a death sentence for Jesus	53
Free agency, gone wrong	53
Man's authenticity called into question	55
Test of creature authenticity	55
Faith in God, an uncommon characteristic in fallen man	56
Call from the Apostle Paul to renew our common purpose	57
Man's walk with God	58
Faith in God's character	60
The authenticity of man's character	60
Jesus models man's *"spiritual walk"* with God	62
Man's appointed purpose twisted and confused by Satan	64
Spirit of distraction, an enemy to man's appointed purpose	65
God's plan and promise for our lives…	66
Whatever Adam would become, we are	69
Man… God's emissary and ambassador to the Earth	70
Man… God's special creation	71
Man… God's master creation and genuine article	72
Man… The genuine article debased and fallen	72
The inferior element of sin in man	73
Jesus born human to model man's special creation	73
God with us	74
God's commandments governs our *"spiritual walk"*	76
Behavior and conduct, man's offering of blessing	77
All creatures, bound by God's appointed purpose	78
Lucifer's introduction to Eve as the serpent	79

Our Heavenly Father's Manufacturer's Handbook!

Satan approaches Eve in the *"image & likeness"* of a serpent	80
The inventory	80
Proof required as evidence in the absence of faith	82
Sin used as a tool of spiritual subversion to bind man	83
The birth of Jesus foils Satan's masterplan	84
The Holy Spirit, man's Spiritual chauffeur into eternity	86
Our Lord and Savior, Jesus Christ	88

~ First Trinity ~

The shortest poem ever written	90
The precious present	91
My name is Spirit	94
Rich little	96
Thou shall not	98
Daughters	102
I Am That I Am	104
Divine purpose	107
Seven seals	110
Babylon	112
Mother love	115
Cradle of hope	117
So they say	119
The seer	122
Thy kingdom come	124
You are	127
God knows	130

When a chair is not a chair...   A Tablet Moment!   134

~ Second Trinity ~

The greatest name ever spoken	142
The Adam family	143
Thank you Jesus	145
In Your name	148
Carpenter's son	150
Cry of the poet	153
Your Holiness	155

Our Heavenly Father's Manufacturer's Handbook!

The Messiah	158
Christ risen	160
P.E.S.	163
Convicted	166
Resurrected	168
All come	170
Wismatic gesture	172
The good fight	174
The Apostle Paul	176
No questions asked	178
Hands of praise	180
Kingdom keepers	183
In His Image	185
Damascus Road	187
Prodigal Son	189
Perfect Fruit	192
Reason for the season	195

The Eternal Gift...   A Tablet Moment!   198

Reflections of the small child	199
Santa Claus, my childhood philanthropic hero	199
Holiday favorites	200
Early childhood development, the seat of understanding	201
The *"preeminent gift"* of Christ, undermined	201
Jesus, the good and perfect *"Spiritual Gift"*	202
Mythical Santa, believed to be real	203
Every gift, not necessarily a *"good gift"*	204
Jesus... God's gift of "Spiritual Redemption" to the world	205
The authenticity of Jesus Christ	205
Gifts of the wise men imitated, but totally misunderstood	207
Satan and mythical Santa, one and the same	207
Jesus, the *"Good Shepherd"*	207
Jesus Christ, *"Our Lord and Shepherd"*, voice of the Church	209
Tradition, an enemy to the Christian Church and man	211
Will you obey God or will you continue to obey Satan and man?	213
Santa Claus and Satan, *"participating partners of illusion"*	214
Gifts of the wise men... Business gifts thought to be affectual	214

Our Heavenly Father's Manufacturer's Handbook!

Threefold ministry of Jesus	215
The heavenly commission of the young Messiah misunderstood	215
Satan transforms himself into the mythical Santa Claus	216
Satan, Santa Claus and the Early Christian Church	217
Sunday worship, Satan's counterfeit to Sabbath observance	218
Mythical Santa emerges as a fictitious imposter of Saint Nicholas	218
Satan's mission of world-wide deception fulfilled in Santa Claus	219
Damaging effects of *"affectual gifting"* on little children	220
"Effectual gifting" and "EARLY CHILDHOOD DEVELOPMENT"	221
Christ, subliminally upstaged by Christmas carols of Santa Claus	221
Where are the gifts?	222
Choosing Christ over Santa Claus and his host	223
Who was I the little child to trust?	224
The worldly cornerstones of commercialized Christmas	224
Affectual Gifting, the life blood of the Christmas economy	225
The "GREATEST WORLDLY ILLUSION"	226
Lucifer aka Satan, the world's greatest deceiver	228
Gifting, the granddaddy of roots for commercial marketing	228
Residual effects of Christmas toys in later life	229
The formative years of "EARLY CHILDHOOD DEVELOPMENT"	230
Breaking the traditional cycle	231
Age old motive for deception	234
Loyal disciples of Satan, unaware	235
Beware of those who come bearing gifts!	236
How many categories of gifts are there?	236
The greatest business gifts ever given!	241

~ Third Trinity ~

The greatest temple ever created	245
Little bittie seed	246
He lives in me	248
A man	251
Expediency	253
Lessons	255
My dad	257
Ma'at	259
Flashback	262

Our Heavenly Father's Manufacturer's Handbook!

Backslider	264
God's *"do"* diligence	266
Under pens	268
Ring your own bell	270
Orphan	272
Sanctuary	275
Brother's keeper	277
Touched by an angel	280
More than an idol	282
God's best friend	286
What does it mean?	289
Metamorphosis	291
A time to be born and a time to die	294
The wall	297

A *maze in Grace*...   **A Tablet Moment!**   301

Life is like a vapor	302
Time is like a coin	303
Each new day, a spiritual labyrinth	303
Life outside of Christ	304
Jesus made lower than angels	305
The life or death question	306
A *"God Day"* dwarfs the solar measurement of time	306
A *"perceivably long"*, but very short life	307
Time, the only provision that belongs to man	307
The penalty of the Law versus the mercy of Grace	310
Life's spiritual maze	314
The Heavenly Father's will desired in us	316
Readers acknowledgment	318

To every descendant
of Adam Adam and Eve Adam…
This includes all persons born into
the human race since God created the world.

In the beginning all humans were created as God's
personal property and were given the sir name *"Adam"*.
This event occurred prior to Satan's deceitful claim to the Earth,
wherein God's human family became chattel property of Satan and
was spiritually transformed into indentured servants of the devil.

This book was written in special acknowledgment of each of those
humans; the authentic Adam Family of yesterday and today.
It includes every person that lived before and after the birth,
death, resurrection and ascension of Jesus Christ,
in whom the Holy Scriptures refer to as…
"The Last Adam".

*"Male and female created he them;
and blessed them, and called their name Adam,
in the day when they were created."*

Genesis 5:2 - King James Version

*Now & Always… The Adam Family is redeemed!
Our Lord Jesus Christ is the "Last Adam"*

*1st Corinthians 15:45 thru 58
King James Version*

Foreword...

The Holy Bible!

It would be reckless and irresponsible to write and publish a book of reverence paying homage to the Holy Trinity with special acknowledgment being given to Jesus Christ without first providing background reference concerning the source from whence the record of God was taken, thus requiring a preface and overview to be written.

The Bible is the Holy book of God's laws of governance for humanity, containing prophetic disclosure of future world events that are foretold by chosen men of faith on behalf of God. The Bible is proven to be an accurate predictor and forecaster of major earthly events that predate the coming kingdom of Heaven on Earth through the preordained Lordship of Jesus Christ.

The Bible has been packaged as a timeless collection of inspired writings that have been passed down from generation-to-generation beginning around 500 years following the great flood that occurred during the days of the biblical patriarch, Noah. The scriptural content of the Bible is the inscribed record of the Word of God that has been witnessed and recorded by chosen men of God, spanning the whole of creation.

The prophet is a human spokesperson chosen by God, one that makes announcements concerning undisclosed world events that are yet to come. Prior to the birth of Jesus, God used the vocal medium of prophecy and the written law of the Old Testament to communicate His earthly will and judgment to man, this served as a forerunner to the arrival of the gospel of Christ, the King, Redeemer, and Savior of man.

The introduction to God's law came by way of Moses with the deliverance of the Ten Commandments at Mount Sinai in Egypt. Bible prophecy came by way of Enoch, the great, great, great, great grandson of Adam and great, great grandfather of Noah and ended with John the apostle, a contemporary and disciple of Jesus.

The biblical patriarch Enoch initiated the reign of Bible prophecy that lasted for approximately 3,000 to 3,300 years and spanned 35 generations. The reign of holy prophets of the Bible ended with the Apostle John's writing of the book of Revelation, confirmation of this event is recorded in the book of Luke chapter 16, verse 16…

> "The Law and the Prophets were until John; since then the good news of the kingdom of God is preached, and everyone forces his way into it." {English Standard Version}

Enoch's prophecy voiced God's reproach to the practices of ungodliness that entered into the world and hearts of men through the reckless disobedience of Adam and Eve, which has persisted throughout the course of human history until the present day. Enoch's prophecy makes reference to the coming of the promised Messiah that would culminate in the *birth, mission, ministry,* and *second coming of Jesus Christ, our Lord.* The total sum of all events issuing out of prophecy are but a shadow or precursor to the *"second coming of Christ"* and the *"day of judgment"* for those who fail to heed God's warnings to accept Jesus Christ as their Redeemer, Lord and Savior.

The crucifixion and resurrection of Jesus is the clarion call from God to a lost world concerning the approaching end to Satan's earthly rule, which exist and thrive in the *"sin culture"* of the present day world. This final call, which is recorded in the book of Jude chapter 1, verses 14 through 16 is fulfilled and established upon generations of warnings and admonishments to man:

> "And Enoch also, the seventh from Adam, prophesied of these, saying, 'Behold, the Lord cometh with ten thousand of His saints to execute judgment upon all, and to convince all who are ungodly among them of all their godless deeds which they have godlessly committed, and of all the harsh speeches which godless sinners have spoken against Him.'" {21st Century King James Version}

The preordained acts of Jesus' birth, death, and ascension are the prophetic fulfillment of the Law and the Prophets, which is signified through His crucifixion and resurrection. These Heaven and Earth shaking events were the prophetic fulfillment to the voice of prophecy that birthed the gospel of Christ. This very gospel, which was received by the world nearly 2,000 years ago in the form of the *"Good News"*, is responsible for bridging the Old Testament and New Testament ages and is being taught, preached, and published in hundreds of languages throughout the world today.

The Bible is man's Holy Grail of life from which the fruit of eternal life is served. Jesus is the vine from which the branches unto eternal life is derived and we the *"faithful"* and *"chosen"* are the fruits of witness for the unredeemed of a lost world, whom are literally dying to be saved. The irony and shame is that Jesus has already journeyed from Heaven to Earth and surrendered His life on Calvary to die the *"Adam-death"* that God disclosed in the original covenant.

This premiere publication takes the reader on a spiritual journey that began in the Garden of Eden with the world's original humans being tied to the Lord in common purpose before being drawn away by the rebellious archangel Lucifer, *also known as the serpent, the dragon, the devil, the beast, and Satan (Rev. 20:1-2)*. Satan would influence the first male and female humans to disobey the "FOUNDATIONAL COMMANDMENT" of God, causing them to abandon the *"image"* and *"likeness"* of God in which they had been purposely created. Upon breaking away from God, they became "bankrupt in character", "void of purpose", and "lacking the natural desire to please God".

This singular event would breach the "ETERNAL LIFE COVENANT", which had been established by God to nourish and preserve the human family throughout eternity, causing the first humans to be expelled from their utopian home in paradise. "Our Heavenly Father's Manufacturer's Handbook" chronicles the chain of events that caused the first male and female humans to break away from God, requiring the "ultimate blood sacrifice" by Jesus, whom would be born into the world to die a horrific death by crucifixion to restore humanity's right to "ETERNAL LIFE".

The author utilizes "The Holy Scriptures", "commentary", "poetry" and "prose" to tap into a *"biblical thread"* that chronicles 4,000 years of death, trials and deception that man would endured in order for the intimate relationship that once existed between God and Man to be restored. The author presents an extremely compelling, interwoven biblical narrative that climaxes with the death, resurrection and ascension of Jesus, Who triumphs over the powers of Satan to restore man's "God-like character", "spiritual desire" and "appointed purpose".

The author has succeeded in taking seemingly difficult to digest biblical material that can be considered confusing to many and carefully packaged it in a series of topics that are interwoven into a biblical narrative that connects the overall sequence of biblical events leading up to Christ, causing "Our Heavenly Father's Manufacturer's Handbook" to read like a novel. This unique publication makes it possible for "EVERYONE" to understand and be blessed by the Lord's "MYSTICAL BOOK OF SPIRITUAL AND HUMAN BEHAVIOR" that is known to all as the Holy Bible. The read is easy and informative, causing all that have read it to experience awe-inspiring eureka moments!

The details of this book began with man being intimately joined and spiritually linked with God in *"Eden's spirit culture"*, only for our lives to become mired in the godless acts of human behavior that permeates the *"sin culture"* of today's world that brings displeasure to God and death to man. The words of this book are used to magnify and illuminate the thoughts of God that are present in *"His Word"*. All humans share a *"common purpose"* that has been draped in obscurity until now. **The goal of this book is to reacquaint believers and nonbelievers alike with their "appointed purpose" of pleasing God!!!**

"*Our Heavenly Father's Manufacturer's Handbook*" pursues a nontraditional, yet biblical approach to providing long awaited answers to many of the complicated and ambiguous questions that have puzzled readers of the Bible since the earliest of times. This is a long awaited *"**book of biblical explanations**"* concerning many things written in the Holy Scriptures that have been misinterpreted or yet to be revealed, until now. "*Our Heavenly Father's Manufacturer's Handbook*" is the preeminent **"*how-to-book of understanding... that teaches us how to fulfil our "appointed purpose" of pleasing God!!!*"**

It is my sincere hope that the knowledge presented in this book will be received as truth and revelation to chasten, educate, and enlighten all that read it. May God bless the writing of this material and cause all that receive it to be spiritually awakened and positively moved.

> *"Blessed is the one who finds wisdom,*
> *and the one who gets understanding,"*
> Proverbs chapter 3, verse 13 {ESV}

Preface...

The Spiritual Tablets!

Included herein are sixty-two *"Spiritual Tablets" ("poems of praise")* and four *"Tablet Moments" (147 pages of "thought provoking commentary")* that have been broken down into a **"series of linear topics" versus "chapters"** and footnoted with Scriptures taken from thirteen biblical translations. Many of the titles are rooted in the real life experiences of the *"scribe"*, while others find their roots in the *"scribe's"* reflections on matters of *"temporal life"* and *"life eternal"*. The *"scribe"* is referred to as *"author"* for publishing reasons only.

There is a deeply held belief by the scribe that all human experiences are but life's spiritual lessons stored within us, wherein many are buried by the mind and later forgotten in the name of *"error"* as we journey down the road of life. The undiscovered wisdom that has been embedded in our lives since we were born is systematically stifled by a protective mechanism of the mind that causes us to avoid pain and seek pleasure. This process is termed the *"Pleasure Principle";* a psychoanalytical term coined by the renowned psychiatrist Sigmund Freud, whom foundered the Psychoanalytic School of Psychology in Vienna, Austria in the 1890s.

Our minds were designed to analyze, compute and store data that arise out of our *experiences, thoughts, perceptions, feelings, memories, will and imagination.* Beyond the processes of *thinking, reasoning and applying knowledge,* our minds have become fertile dumping grounds for all of the things that have gone wrong in our day-to-day living; when in fact the things that have gone wrong and caused us pain, hold the *"spiritual keys"* to our perpetual joy. The old saying... *"No pain... no gain..."* is literally true and it is for this reason that our personal mistakes are silently begging to be *"spiritually exhumed".*

It is to this end that the scribe views the Bible as *"a purposed tool for unraveling the mega-massive crime scenes of our minds"* that have gone undisturbed since childhood. The Bible identifies and interprets the various types and models of *sinful behavior* that make up our *sin nature,* which is encoded into our DNA by Satan prior to our births, only to become *targeted, defined and reinforced* during childhood.

If you were to ask the majority of folks to identify the most dangerous and harmful place in life, they would more than likely name a *geographical location, urban community* or *war zone*. When in fact, the most dangerous and harmful place in life is not a place or physical location at all, it is the *"human developmental zone"* known to all as *"childhood"*. Satan uses this zone to *mark, brand and classify* us by those who have already been *emotionally marked, spiritually branded and sin classified* by his loyal and devoted servants. Very few, if any pass through the zone of childhood without coming out emotionally bruised or permanently scarred and this is true for the majority of people. Sadly, few have the spiritual foundation and human courage that is needed to know and then tell the truth… *"And you shall know the truth, and the truth shall make you free." {John 8:31-32}*

This is why studying the Bible is essential and vital to our understanding God's plan and purpose for our lives. God's Word spiritually empowers us to live beyond the borders of the *"sin classifications"* assigned to us by Satan when we were little children. A consistent practice of biblical indulgence on a routine basis provides the spiritual nourishment and empowerment for a peaceful, prosperous, well-adjusted life. To this end were 62 poems *("Spiritual Tablets")*, four thought provoking commentaries *("Tablet Moments")* written and accompanied by 500 plus Scriptures to speak wisdom to our carnal minds, with the aim of deepening our spiritual understanding. The Apostle Paul recorded the following in Romans chapter 12, verse 2…

> *"Do not be conformed to this world, <u>but be transformed by the renewal of your mind, that by testing you may discern what is the will of God</u>, what is good and acceptable and perfect." {English Standard Version}*

The abundance of Scriptures that compliment this body of works was purposely chosen to provide deeper insight and spiritual clarity to the reader. *The scribe's desire is for the reader to be attracted to this book for the sole purpose of exploring the title, only to read the "Spiritual Tablets" and "Commentaries" that are referred to as "Tablet Moments" and be guided back to the Bible for additional reading and in-depth study.* Reading and studying the Bible is essential, if we are to receive and understand the spiritual revelations covering the many *"timeless models of spiritual and human behavior"* that God has packaged in the Holy Scriptures for our life-long benefit.

Jesus promised that if we would only believe in Him that the Father would send back the *"Comforter"* to teach and remind us of *all things* spoken of by Him. If we have not read God's Word, it is impossible for the Comforter to remind us of things that we have not heard, thus causing us to miss out on the teachings that have been provided in the *"gospel of the kingdom"* by Jesus to increase the *"fruitfulness of our spiritual understanding"*. As we increase in God's Word, we increase in faith, which is required for us to counteract and overcome the trials of Satan. The following is recorded in Romans chapter 10, verse 17... *"So then faith comes by hearing, and hearing by the Word of God."*

We are to study God's Word to equip ourselves for the work that will be done in us by the Holy Spirit. When we are faithful in seeking God through diligent study, *God's Word is stored within us in the form of a "spiritual antidote" that functions to counteract the demonic thoughts, ideas and suggestions of Satan, when temptations and hardships arise. When armed with the Word, which is the essence and source of our faith, the Holy Spirit activates the spiritual principles embodied within the Holy Scriptures based upon the measure of faith that we have in God the Father through Jesus, our Lord and Savior.*

When we love the Lord with all of our hearts and souls, having unwavering faith in His commandments, Our Heavenly Father will supply our needs in times of trouble (Deuteronomy 4:29-31). He alone has the "POWER" to enable us with what we need to counteract the trials and tribulations that we alone are powerless to endure.

Once the Holy Scriptures have been activated by our Comforter (Holy Spirit), the *"Spirit of Christ"* comes alive in us to strengthen our *"inner man"* in the areas where we are spiritually weak, thus causing Satan and his demons to flee from the presence of the Lord Who is alive and operating in us through the power of our faith in His Word.

Our Heavenly Father is a God of increase and short of miraculous intervention *(which in many cases is..."a result without a process");* God uses mere seeds to supply all of our needs. The following is stated by King David in the book of Psalms chapter 119, verse 130...

> *"The unfolding of your words gives light; it imparts understanding to the simple." {English Standard Version}*

God's greatest seed of blessing is the *"seed of understanding"*, which nourishes and increases our spiritual awareness. Jesus understood this all too well as shown and communicated by the Apostle John in John chapter 14, verse 26, wherein it is written...

> *"But the Comforter, which is the Holy Ghost, whom the Father will send in my name, He shall teach you all things, and bring all things to your remembrance, whatsoever I have said unto you." {King James Version}*

To this end were the selected Scriptures chosen to serve as *"spiritual seeds of anchor"* for the particular poems with which they have been so diligently paired. Included among the selected Scriptures are those taken from the King James Version of the Authorized Bible. The King James Version utilizes Old English pronunciations such as *'shalt'* for shall, *'mayest'* for may, *'searcheth'* for search, *'knoweth'* for know, *'Holy Ghost'* for Holy Spirit, etc. I am well aware of the fact that Old English terminology has its challenges and is not desired by most for an easy read. Special considerations were taken wherein twelve additional translations were utilized with the intent of providing interpretive balance for the best possible read.

The following biblical translations were utilized with this specific purpose in mind...

> *American Standard Version, Contemporary English Version, The "Amplified" Bible, English Standard Version, Holman Christian Standard Version, New American Standard Version, New Century Version, New International Version, New International Reader's Version, New King James Version, New Living Translation and 21st Century King James Version.*

The King James Version was used after several comparisons deemed it necessary to provide the best interpretive fit with regard to the particular subject matter being discussed.

𝒴ou are invited to explore this premiere publication that grew out of a larger body of works composed of *commentary, poetry* and *prose*. The chosen titles have been carefully selected and paired with Scriptures that footnote and accentuate the spiritual principles that are embodied in Scripture. The poems are inscribed…*"spiritual tablets"*.

𝒯he spiritual tablets unite poetry and Scripture in such a way that it causes the mind's eye to become open to what the Lord is saying to us in His Word. The phenomenal insight reflected in this work provides a refreshing look into the spiritual interpretation of the Word of God on a level that is simple to digest and easy to understand.

𝒯he spiritual tablets were written in acknowledgment of the Holy Trinity, honoring *God the Father, God the Son, and God the Holy Spirit*. Upon being combined with four thought provoking commentaries inscribed *"Tablet Moments"*, the completed work was brought together in a three-part composition entitled <u>*"Our Heavenly Father's Manufacturer's Handbook : Disclosure of the Eternal Gift"*</u>.

𝒯his publication serves as a reminder of a commonly overlooked fact with regards to living. So let us not forget that life with all of its difficulties, nuances and intricacies has for itself the results of the experiential distance traveled, which is oftentimes interpreted and expressed differently by those who have reached their final destination. Some may view the distance traveled as a *"journey"*, wherein others might well view the distance traveled as only a *"trip"*. I believe life to be a *"journey defined by shared experiences"*, wherein the *"trip is defined by the destination sought"* and the experiential distance is often traveled alone. <u>*Enjoy the read; experience the spiritual journey!!!*</u>

𝒟ear Heavenly Father, I thank You for granting me the sacred art of writing that was blessed upon me as a precious gift of salvation. Jesus, I thank You for steadying the course while the Holy Spirit imparted the *divine wisdom, inspirational knowledge,* and *spiritual understanding* needed to develop and complete this long awaited publication. I thank the Holy Trinity for fashioning me into a "CREATURE OF THIRST" that I might be inspired as a pupil to eat the "Holy Book" and learn of You!!!

Introduction...

~ The Mantra ~

An Unfamiliar Verse!

Several years ago I embarked upon my daily commute to work and not far into the journey I was mentally struck with what appeared to be a biblical verse of scripture. What I received was a simple combination of words that quickly morphed into a lyrical chant. I can vividly remember repeating the *"unfamiliar verse"* at least two hundred times or more within the space of a ten miles journey. The verse swirled around in my head repeatedly as I drew closer and closer to my destination. By the time I arrived at my place of work, what had initially been received as a biblical verse of "HOLY SCRIPTURE" had soon become a mantra. Wikipedia Encyclopedia defines "mantra" in the following way… *"A mantra is a sound, syllable, word, or group of words that is considered capable of "creating transformation".* This simple combination of words was so powerful and moving that immediately upon arriving at my desk, I logged onto my computer and created the following 3D text screensaver…

"In the Anointing of the Gift… there is Praise!"

Day after day for approximately ten years this unfamiliar verse tumbled and swirled about in my head *while illuminating every thought that it would convey* as it mimicked the matching text that tumbled and swirled about on my computer screen. The synchronization linking the two processes mimicked the perpetual motion of a supremely crafted Rolex watch. What is even more intriguing and mystifying is that the verse lacked the benevolence and grace to reveal its true meaning. Immediately it became apparent that the verse was of incredibly great importance and that God had deposited the verse into my spirit for a very significant reason. I knew not the purpose of the verse at the time, and more over, I had no idea what its intended meaning was. I initially believed the verse to be a biblical verse of Holy Scripture, prompting me to perform several days of computerized searches of the Bible that would all come up empty. After a very long and exhaustive process of combing the King James Bible and the Strong's Exhaustive Concordance of the Bible, the Lord blessed me with the following understanding of the verse that I had so enthusiastically received…

The Holy Spirit's revelation to me was that all are blessed with special gifts, even though there are many who live their entire lives unaware of being the bearers of such gifts. Gifts that are intentioned by God to be used as *"tools of special purpose"* in the desired works of exposing His coming kingdom to the lost and unredeemed on Earth. Many of those whom are blessed to discover their gifts realize that humble acknowledgment of God's presence and outward praise of the Lord's purpose and anointing is evidenced by God's appointed gifts in their lives, which in many cases have gone undisclosed from birth.

In my particular case, the gift of *"poetry"* and *"verse"* that was very much a part of my spiritual essence was evidenced through my embrace of rhyme, lyric and verse, which were endowed in me long before my birth and remained undisclosed until my spiritual awakening and conversion to Christ at the age of twenty-three. It was here at this juncture that I accepted Jesus as my Lord and Savior. Within days of my conversion, I received *"poetry"* and *"verse"* as my *"appointed gifts of blessing"* and *"tools of special purpose"* to aid in fulfilling the earthly assignment conferred upon me by God. My appointed gifts serve as constant companions that have complemented my *"spiritual walk"* with the Lord throughout the past forty plus years of my life.

My yearning to understand an array of baffling and enigmatic experiences began to crystallize into poems that would shed light on the many daunting and perplexing issues of life that compromised the moral fabric of the world surrounding me. The poems were later revealed to me as *"spiritual tablets"*. This is just one of many such instances wherein God has shown Himself faithful to reveal and anoint the *"gifts of blessing"* that are vested within us, when we diligently seek first His kingdom and His righteousness *(Matthew 6:33)*.

God's commission for the *"gifted"* is to use their naturally appointed gifts to attract the masses that come seeking after the *carnal fruits of expression* flowing from those gifts, only to receive a *"fervent believer's confession of faith"* that can be found in the Good News that is manifest in Jesus Christ. The Gift of Christ to the world is the Holy Father's *"Anointed Gift of Eternal Blessing"*. Unfortunately, few of the *"naturally gifted"* among us understand the reason for having *freely received* their appointed gifts in the first place. The following is recorded by the Apostle Peter in 1st Peter chapter 4, verse 10...

> *"Each of you should use whatever gift you have received to serve others, as faithful stewards of God's grace in its various forms."* {New International Version - UK}

*I*nterestingly enough, this brings us to the heart and soul of this publication. I entertained several themes and titles along the way, once I became serious about writing this book. After about five years into the process, I began to entertain the *"unfamiliar verse"*. Yet up until the final moment, I had not settled on a title. Then it dawned upon me that God had given me the *"foundational theme"* to this publication ten years in advance of the book being written.

*Y*ou see... "God knew that I would write this book long before I did. To be perfectly honest, God is the *"True Author"* and I'm just the appointed scribe. In fact, I am nothing more than a designated ghostwriter for God. One, having been recruited by the Holy Spirit to use the naturally appointed gifts of *"prose"* and *"verse"* to draw people unto God the Father, to receive salvation by way of His only begotten Son, Jesus Christ. The words of this book are purposed to magnify and illuminate God's thoughts that are present in "HIS WORD".

*S*o it was here at this spiritual juncture that I realized the true purpose for my having received the *"unfamiliar verse"*, which was predestined from the very beginning to become the heart and soul of a book that had not yet been conceived nor written. This humble awakening birthed a series of *"internal poetic reflections"* having been deposited into my human spirit over several decades by the Holy Spirit. The poems were later compiled as a personal gift and testimony to God and are herein reintroduced as *"spiritual tablets"* as coined by one of God's appointed brokers of thought; Brother Sam Rhodes.

*G*od... in His infinite wisdom and Supreme Majesty has proven to me that He is the "AUTHOR" and "CREATOR" of all things. I, the least among many am just a scribe chosen by God to document but a mere fraction of His "DIVINE CREATION". In the name of our Lord and Savior Jesus Christ, I Charles E. Dickerson joyfully present to you...

"Our Heavenly Father's Manufacturer's Handbook"

About...

The scribe!

In preparing to write this book…

I searched the breadth and depth of my being,
reminiscing back to the threshold of my conscious existence,
only to discover four things that were most prevalent to me;
the pain of *emptiness, grief, death and despair.*

It appeared as though I had witnessed
the countless faults of my life laughing out at me,
glaring out from deep within the ever widening cracks
of an ages-old looking glass.

My early life was sorely reminiscent
of a gigantic jigsaw puzzle,
one fragmented and broken into
millions and millions of assorted pieces,
only for me to receive *"last pieces first"*.

I can vividly remember being spiritually awakened
one bright and sunny April's afternoon…
out of what appeared to be a devil's trance,
from a myriad of voices conversing in a violent storm.

My life… once simple, respectable and good,
had become tarnished and riddled with habitual stench.
My soul was exhausted and fatigued from idle roaming,
leaving my heart paralyzed by reckless abandonment.

I had grown aimlessly lost and totally confused,
dwelling among many of whom I no longer knew, nor trusted.
I was suffering from extreme paranoia and spiritual exhaustion,
brought on by my paradoxical and nonsensical existence.

Unbeknownst to myself…

I had wantonly and carelessly squandered
the greatest and most precious of life's gifts.
God's fundamental gifts of eternal blessing…
which are… love, joy, peace and happiness!

By age twenty-three, I had engaged two countries,
five states and several cities;
only to find that I could no longer escape
the haunting memories of my being.

Nonetheless, there came a time, when I…
One who had consciously forsaken God,
heard, witnessed, and envisioned things
that a corrupt mind and spiritless soul could not bear.

It was here at this peaceful juncture
that I acknowledged, confessed
and accepted Jesus Christ as Lord
and Savior of my life.

Thank You Heavenly Father
for my unabbreviated being,
as perceived by those whom doubted Your blessings
of earthly longevity and divine purpose in my life.

The doubts and hopes of many
concerning my life choices
would have been correct,
had it not been for Your unconditional love.

Eternal thanks to You, our Heavenly Father
in the name of Your precious Son Jesus
for allowing Your Holy Spirit
to establish permanent residency in me!

*God's abundant peace and
"Eternal Blessing" to you…
Relax and enjoy the read!!!*

*Passionately penned by the scribe…
Charles E. Dickerson*

Overview...

Our Heavenly Father's Manufacturer's Handbook!

$\mathcal{I}$ am simply surprised and amazed at the number of people that lay claim to Christendom whom would love to know God better, but when it comes to God's will, plan, and purpose for their lives, many are lacking the practical concept needed to better understand, interpret, and receive God's Word. The Bible intimidates many of us for various reasons. For some the Bible is considered too difficult to understand, while others believe it mystical and impossible to decode, and there are those whom consider it too complicated to digest and comprehend. In simple terms, many of us fail to understand our personal relationship with the Bible or God *(the Bible's true author)* and consequently believe it to be optional in our lives. In practical terms, the Bible provides total care and maintenance for God's *"Master Creation"*. The Bible is a personal companion guide that explains the *use, care and benefits of God's manufactured product, which is man!*

Man, God's manufactured product...

$\mathcal{I}$n the book of Genesis man is regarded as a special creation in comparison to the rest of the creatures. Unlike the terrestrial and celestial creations, man was not spoken into being. Man was handmade *(Genesis 2:7, Psalm 119:73, Job 10:8)* and uniquely fashioned by special design. Man was *"manufactured"* in accordance with the trinitary powers emanating from the Holy Trinity. The term "TRINITARY" has been coined to note the uniqueness of character and persona that man shares with God in his *"Special Creation"* as a creature comprised of three persons in one living entity. Evidence of this special creation is recorded in Genesis chapter 1, verse 26...

> *"And God said, Let us make man in our image, after our likeness: and let them have dominion over the fish of the sea, and over the fowl of the air, and over the cattle, and over all the earth, and over every creeping thing that creepeth upon the earth." {King James Version}*

$\mathcal{T}$his one particular Scripture when viewed in relationship to the other 31,102 verses of Scripture is by far one of the most important and critically binding to man, yet it is commonly overlooked. This is especially true for the ones of us who are bold and believing enough to adopt a new vision of ourselves as *"handmade products"* and accept a modified view of the Holy Bible as the *"Manufacturer's Handbook"*. If we are to receive all of the benefits and safeguards made available to us from birth to death under the blood covenant of Jesus, we must begin to view God as our Heavenly Manufacturer, thereby realizing that we are God's *"personal property"* and *"Master Creation"*. In the book of Job chapter 10, verses 8 thru 9 we have biblical proof of our unique and special creation in the form of *"manufactured products"*...

> *"Your hands shaped me and made me. Will you now turn and destroy me? Remember that you moulded me like clay. Will you now turn me to dust again?" {New International Version}*

"Our Heavenly Father's Manufacturer's Handbook"

The Holy Bible is man's *"spiritual life-guide"*, wherein humanity can attain a better life on Earth leading to an afterlife with God in eternity. The Holy Bible is the Creator's *"Manufacturer's Handbook"* that was prepared especially for man. Fitting enough, the root word in *"manufacturer"* is *"man"*. Once we begin to view ourselves as *"handmade products"* manufactured by the *"Creator"* rather than just mere *"creatures"* that entered into life by chance and accept the Bible for what it is, we will begin to see the Holy Bible as an owner's manual provided by our Heavenly Creator. God is responsible for the creation of all things in heaven (2nd heaven *cosmic space*) and Earth (1st heaven *planetary sphere*) and He prepared an *"inspirational companion guide"* to usher His *"Master Creation"* into their appointed place of destiny.

The Bible is nothing more than the *"Creator's owner's manual"* and the *"Lord's Book of Spiritual Instruction"*. The Bible was authored by God Himself and inscribed by man, especially for man, which took 40 men a period of about 1500 years to complete it *(1400 B.C. - 90 A.D.)*. Man is God's creation, making man God's *"personal property"* and *"manufactured product"*. Few are willing to think of themselves as products and certainly not as property, but that is exactly what we are to God. The Bible was purposed and designed to serve as a companion guide for instructing humans in all areas of mortal preservation. The instructional content of the Bible is based upon countless... *"spiritually inspired human behavioral narratives"* known as Bible stories, which are central to its teachings, theme, and focus.

The Bible is without doubt an owner's manual. In fact, the Bible is in many ways identical to the large majority of owner's manuals that accompany the life experiences of many of today's leading commercial products. If one were to compare the Bible to a common owner's manual, he or she would quickly discover that the Bible shares very similar *usage, upkeep, warranty, and replacement characteristics of the majority of manmade products.*

If one were to use an automobile as an example, one would find that the following areas are covered: The automobile's... ***a.*** *interior, body and core components,* ***b.*** *operating specifications,* ***c.*** *care and maintenance,* ***d.*** *parts replacement,* ***e.*** *designated place of repair,* ***f.*** *manufacturer's lifetime warranty,* ***g.*** *total vehicle replacement.*

The Bible provides the same coverage for humans. ***a.*** <u>God's Word</u> provides spiritual coverage for our mind, body, and soul, ***b.*** <u>God's commandments</u> are the operating specifications for a healthy, productive, fruitful life, ***c.*** <u>Christ-like conduct</u> provides spiritual sobriety, emotional health, and wellness, ***d.*** <u>spiritual conversion</u> salvages our flawed hearts, corrupt minds and lost souls, ***e.*** <u>Church</u> is our designated place of spiritual repair, ***f.*** <u>redemption</u> is our unlimited warranty guaranteeing abundant life on Earth, ***g.*** <u>salvation</u> guarantees immortality and eternal life with our Lord Jesus Christ in the afterlife.

Commissioning of the Manufacturer's Handbook...

The Bible is a wonderful compilation of inspired Holy Scriptures that has been passed down from generation-to-generation for more than three and one half millenniums and has been revealed to the world and the Church as the Holy Bible. Certainly all should agree that the practice of managing our lives would be much easier if we were to accept the Bible for what it is, an owner's manual provided by our Heavenly Manufacturer and Creator for the proper care and treatment of ourselves as God's property and personally manufactured products.

Let us make a comparison between two sets of products, a simple hammer and nail versus the sophistication and complexity of a computer or other highly technical machinery. If one were asked to determine which group of products comes with an owner's manual… <u>which would you choose</u>? It is obvious that a hammer and nail does not require an owner's manual, and for very good reason. Unlike a computer or similar products, both a hammer and nail are simplex. They both lack the extreme complexity and sophistication in function that would suggest a high probability of failure, which applies to very complex machinery and technical equipment.

In that man was created in the "IMAGE" and "LIKENESS" of GOD, his functionality and complexity far exceeds any manmade product, thus requiring the need for an owner's manual. Therefore, God commissioned a host of spiritual journalists (<u>prophets</u>, <u>kings</u>, <u>Old Testament judges</u>, <u>apostles</u>, and <u>other notable appointed men of faith</u>) to write an instructional handbook to compliment the life experiences of every human birthed on Earth, whom were made to live outside of the Garden of Eden where the "TREE OF LIFE" was known to exist.

If Adam had obeyed God's commandment, man would have been allowed to remain in the Garden of Eden and eat from the "TREE OF LIFE" throughout eternity and the Bible as we know it today would have consisted of only 58 verses, beginning with the book of Genesis chapter 1, verse 1 and ending with Genesis chapter 3, verse 1.

The Holy Bible, man's guide to spiritual redemption…

The Holy Bible is a *"Personal Companion Guide"* and *"Lifetime Manufacturer's Handbook"* that explains how one can find their inner path to repentance and spiritual redemption. The Apostle Paul recorded the following in the book of Romans chapter 10, verses 9 thru 10…

> *"That if you confess with your mouth, Jesus is Lord, and believe in your heart that God raised him from the dead, **<u>you will be saved</u>**. For it is with your heart that you believe and are justified, and it is with your mouth that you confess*

and are saved." *{New International Version – UK}*

To gain a better understanding of God's need for commissioning the writing of the Bible, it is imperative that we take a closer look at the original human products *(man & woman)* whom were patented by God as His *"Human Intellectual Property"* and given the greatest of all physical addresses on Earth *(Genesis 2:8 & Genesis 2:15)*, which is the Garden of Eden. *The Garden of Eden is where* man's fall *and* journey toward recovery *began and the Bible is at the very heart of the story.* The best way to understand the human story is to allow the Bible to tell its own story, as only the Bible can. Once inside the story the reader can relax and allow the story to tell itself as all good stories do.

Contrary to popular belief, the Bible does tell its story quite well, once we get beyond the mystique and symbolism with which it has been shrouded. Sadly enough, our approach to interpreting the *"symbolisms" of the Old Testament and "manifestations" of the New Testament* have been treated much like the Egyptologists standard approach to understanding the *age, origin*, and *true builders* of the magnificent Sphinx, and Great Pyramids of Giza. Unfortunately, there are many who have made it a practice of interpreting the existing biblical facts to fit their foregone conclusions, while ruling out any new and undisclosed revelation that would challenge the foundation of what they believe to be *"THE TRUTH"*. This is especially true in view of the long standing misinterpretation of the *"Creation account"* that is recorded in the first chapter of Genesis *(later discussed - pp. 22, 23)*.

The Holy Bible when viewed in simple terms is nothing more than the *"Creator's Owner's Manual"*, which was authored by God and inscribed by a series of *"inspired spiritual journalist" (Patriarchs, Judges, Apostles, and Disciples)* before being packaged in the form of a *"spiritual handbook"* especially written for man. The Holy Bible was personally drafted and dictated by God Himself through the Holy Spirit to accompany man's journey outside of the Garden of Eden following Adam and Eve's expulsion from their eternal home in paradise. God having fashioned and created the celestial and terrestrial bodies of the Universe was well aware of the Earth's propensity toward natural violent reaction, environmental upheaval and atmospheric calamity. God took these factors into account when He chose Eden as the most suitable location to establish man's earthly domain. God in His divine mercy, grace, and infinite wisdom was quite mindful of these environmental factors when He formed the garden and placed it in the heart of the Earth to serve as man's eternal home.

Eden's Spirit Culture...

The Garden of Eden afforded Adam and Eve the eternal luxury of residing in a spirit-filled culture that was perpetually steeped in the divine essence of God. *Culture is unique in that culture cannot exist without environment and environment cannot exist without culture. Culture and environment are eternally linked and synonymous with one another. Culture has for itself the duty of elevating the creature to its highest level of creative potential, regardless of the environment in which the creature finds itself.* I am utterly convinced that...

<u>*Preparation for transition is the true role of culture!!!*</u>

Culture has a great deal to do with preparation for transition from a lower state of *"creature consciousness"* into the highest state of *"actualized existence"*, causing humans to transition into *"actualized beings"*. This is true for all creatures, whether a caterpillar, tadpole, or a mere human embryo. Culture is the spiritual brew that prepares one to rise to its highest level of creative functionality, based upon the uniqueness of one's natural creation relative to culture. It is to this end that the faithful are admonished *"...not to forsake the assembling of ourselves together"* (Hebrews 10:24-25). In the aftermath of man's banishment from the Garden of Eden, the Christian Church is the *"last bastion of divine spirit culture"* remaining on Earth until the second coming of Christ. On that final day the existing Earth's *"atmosphere* [1st heaven]*"*, *"physical environment"* and *"societal culture"* will be transformed into the *"new heaven"* and *"new Earth"* (Rev. 21:1-2).

The metamorphic process relative to genetic transformation...

There is a long established natural law regarding culture. To gain a better understanding of the process, we need only look to nature and examine the metamorphic processes relative to the genetic transformation of the toad and the butterfly. The toad starts out as a tadpole in its natural state, before spending a prolonged period of time in the grungy and murky pond water, which causes it to morph into its highest state of *"actualized existence"* as a toad. Upon transitioning the toad no longer *"thinks"* or *"behaves"* like a tadpole, for its *"mental image"* and *"functional likeness"* has morphed and is permanently changed!

The same is true for the butterfly that starts out as larva before developing into a caterpillar and spending a prolonged period of time in a dark and dampened cocoon, which causes it to morph into its highest state of *"actualized existence"* as a butterfly. Upon transitioning the butterfly no longer *"thinks"* or *"behaves"* like a caterpillar, for its *"mental image"* and *"functional likeness"* has morphed and is permanently changed!

If for some reason, the tadpole is removed from the grungy and murky pond water it never morphs into a toad, because the transformative properties of the toad resides in the natural environment of the pond water that houses the essence and attributes of the tadpole's native culture.

The same is true for the caterpillar, if the caterpillar is removed from the dark and dampened recesses of the cocoon it never morphs into a butterfly, because the transformative properties of the butterfly resides in the natural environment of the dark and dampened cocoon that houses the essence and attributes of the caterpillar's native culture.

Man's highest state of existence...

The metamorphic process applies to man also, _relative to spiritual transformation or lack thereof_. The Garden of Eden engendered the essence and attributes of God in whom man was fashioned to emulate in thought *(mental image & imagination)* and trinitary behavior *(functional likeness)*. Upon removal from the Garden of Eden's *"spirit filled native culture" (Gen. 3:24)*, _man ceased to function as the God-like creatures that God had purposed them to be from their creation!!!_ Man naturally and without compulsion freely emulates and exudes the character and mannerism of God, when operating at his highest state of *"actualized existence"*.

When pondering the question of... *What is the highest state of "actualized existence" for humans?* We need only examine the metamorphic processes of the toad and the butterfly and then compare those results to the coming transition spoken of by the Apostle Paul in the book of 1st Corinthians chapter 15, verses 52 thru 54...

> *"In a moment, in the twinkling of an eye, at the last trump: for the trumpet shall sound, and the dead shall be raised incorruptible, and we shall be changed. For this corruptible must put on incorruption, and this mortal must put on immortality. So when this corruptible shall have put on incorruption, and this mortal shall have put on immortality, then shall be brought to pass the saying that is written, Death is swallowed up in victory." {King James Version}*

Metamorphosis engenders transformation...

The Apostle Paul describes the metamorphic process by which man is transformed from a _terminal state of sinful existence_ as a mortal with a _carnal disposition that is Satan-like_, into his highest state of spiritual existence, wherein man is eternally translated into a _spiritual_ *disposition that is God-like (1Cor. 15:52-54)*. The evidence of man's spiritual transformation is realized at Christ's second coming, which is accompanied by the creation of the *"new heaven"* and *"new Earth" (Revelation 21:1-2)*. The sin culture of the present day Earth and its polluted atmosphere issuing from the *"tree of knowledge of good and evil"*, shall be transformed into the *"Spirit culture"* that man originally enjoyed in the Garden of Eden prior to Adam's original sin. Spirit culture emanates from the *"tree of life"*, which was centrally located in the Garden of Eden prior to man's fall and expulsion. *The "tree of life" is restored at Christ's second coming during the "coming kingdom transition period", when the "New Jerusalem" aka "Holy City" descends from God in Heaven (Rev. 3:12 & 21:2)*. When the Apostle John refers to the Holy City as the *"New Jerusalem"*, he describes it as the *"paradise of God" (Revelation 2:7)*.

Man was naturally influenced by Eden's Spirit culture while residing in the Garden of Eden prior to Adam and Eve's collusion with Satan. Arbitrarily, man outside the Garden of Eden is unnaturally influenced by the world's sin culture on a moment-by-moment basis. Spirit culture is comprised of the divine nature embodied in *"God the Father"*, *"God the Son"* and *"God the Holy Spirit"* that is biblically known as the *"Holy Trinity"*, wherein the Apostle Paul identifies Jesus as the *"Godhead"*. Jesus is the human manifestation of this holy union *(Colossians 2:9-10)*, which works in mutual agreement to reshape man back into the *"mental image"* and *"functional likeness"* of God.

Image of God…

The *"image of God"* is a *"semblance of God's Spirit"* that is *manifested in the nature and person of Jesus Christ (Colossians 1:15)*. God's image was bestowed upon man at the time of his creation and is intrinsic to one's *"authentic self"* and *"personage"*. A question was put to Jesus by one of the Pharisees and legalist of His day concerning the greatest commandment in the Law. Jesus answered by citing the first commandment, which identifies the *heart, soul* and *mind* as being the essential components of one's *"total being" (Matthew 22:36 & 37)*.

From among the three, the *"mind of God"* is the creative model from which the *"mind of man"* was fashioned and is undoubtedly man's mirror. When in need of spiritual reflection, we need only look into the Word of God to receive a *"spiritual snapshot"* or *"spiritual image"* of ourselves. The process is identical to the practice of people in modern societies that utilize manmade mirrors in their surroundings to receive a reflection of their *"physical image"* at the start of each day.

When it comes to spiritual matters, the process and the results are the same. We simply look into the mind of God to view a reflection of our spiritual selves and if what God reflects back to us is different from what we see, a mental and spiritual adjustment is required. We have the choice of accepting Jesus Christ as our Lord and Savior in order to be transformed back into the *"mental image"* and *"functional likeness"* of God, which constitutes the *"character of God"* in man. Man is the trinitary likeness of God in his persona *(1Thess. 5:23)*.

So let us start by pointing out that the word *"image"* is the root word for *"imagination"*. It is very important to note that of all the terrestrial creatures, only one of those creatures was endowed with the *"power of imagination"*, which was accompanied by the power of God's *"spoken word"*. When we evaluate each of those creatures, be they *sea creatures, wing creatures, cattle, creeping things, beasts, and man*, we find that man is the only creature that was gifted and blessed with the *"power of imagination"*.

Merriam-Webster Dictionary defines *"imagination"* as the ...

> *"The act or power of forming a mental image of something not present to the senses or never before wholly perceived in reality (creative ability)."*

The Scriptures make initial reference to man having *"imagination"* shortly after the great flood, when Noah's offsprings were building the Tower of Babel. The following is recorded in the book of Genesis chapter 11, verses 4 thru 6...

> *"And they said, "Come, let us build us a city and a tower whose top may reach unto heaven; and let us make us a name, lest we be scattered abroad upon the face of the*

whole earth."

And the LORD came down to see the city and the tower, which the children of men built. And the LORD said,

Behold, the people are one and they have all one language, and this they begin to do; and now nothing will be withheld from them which they have <u>imagined</u> to do." {21st Century King James Version}

Imagine birds of the sky having imagination, they certainly would not flap their wings for thousands of miles to fly south for the winter, when they could just as easily do like man and build aircrafts in the *image and likeness of themselves* that are comparable to Boeing's 747 and fly first class on A380 Airbuses made by birds to their destinations.

Imagine birds of every kind flocking into gigantic airports built and staffed by birds. Imagine countless numbers of birds boarding aircrafts piloted by bird captains that are staffed by bird crewman and bird flight attendants. Imagine birds being seated in first class resting and relaxing their wings while watching popular bird movies featuring their favorite bird celebrities and stars. Imagine birds reclining in their cushioned seats eating bird seeds and enjoying themselves as they are leisurely and effortlessly transported to their localities and climates of choice. <u>Unfortunately, birds unlike humans lack imagination!!!</u>

The same would be true for certain types of fish, they certainly would not flap their fins and swim hundreds of miles to spawn, they too could easily do like man and build luxury cruise liners in the *image and likeness of themselves* and travel first class in ships made by fish that are as graceful and elegant as man's modern day MSC Meraviglia cruise ship which far exceeds the legendary Titanic.

Imagine fish of all breeds, shapes and sizes swimming into aqua-ports that are built and staffed by fish, while boarding gigantic cruise liners captained by fish whom were employed to navigate safe passage to their destination. Imagine fish deckhands, water sports instructors and fitness trainers assisting and serving other fish as they relax and lounge in onboard fish-made Jacuzzis. Imagine fish entertaining themselves while watching popular fish movies featuring their famous fish celebrities and stars. Imagine common and exotic breeds of fish eating their favorite fish foods, while being leisurely and effortlessly transported to their respective localities to mingle and spawn.

Unfortunately, fish unlike humans lack imagination!!!

Man having been *"created in the image of God"* refers to the *mental image" (Colossians 3:9-10)* that endows man with unlimited creativity, power, and ability, which sets humans apart from the other earthly creatures. The imagination component affords man the mental capacity and intellectual ability to create anything that he or she can envision. Unlike the rest of the patented creatures of God, man *"before the fall"* shared the *spirit, mind, vocabulary,* and *language of God*.

*M*an was naturally endowed with the language of God from creation. Unfortunately, man's unbridled imagination caused God to replace that original language with the *"diversity of foreign tongues"* when the building of the Tower of Babel was interrupted by God during its construction *(Genesis 11:1-5).*

Artistic rendering of the Tower of Babel

*T*he Scriptures refer to this event *as "confounding their language".* The details of this event is duly noted and recorded in the book of Genesis chapter 11, verses 6 thru 7...

> *"And the LORD said, "Behold, the people are one, and They have all one language, and this they begin to do; and now nothing will be withheld from them which they have imagined to do.*
>
> *Come, let Us go down, and there confound their language, that they may not understand one another's speech." {21st Century King James Version}*

*W*e are provided with a brief snapshot of Adam in the Garden of Eden at the very outset of creation. It is here that we have witness of Adam being directed by God to utilize the linguistic tools of that original language to carry out the initial assignment of naming all of the living creatures pursuant to God's instruction. Moses recorded the following in the book of Genesis chapter 2, verse 19...

"And out of the ground the LORD God formed every beast of the field, and every fowl of the air; and brought them unto Adam to see what he would call them and whatsoever Adam called every living creature, that was the name thereof." {King James Version}

Likeness of God...

Man was *"created in the likeness of God"* in many ways *(Gen. 1:26 & 5:1)*, but there is one unique characteristic that is predominate among all the others, which is the *"trinitary presence"* and *"character of God"* that was endowed in man at the time of his creation.

The personality of man is composed of the *"child"* in the <u>first person</u>, the *"adult"* in the <u>second person</u> and the *"elder"* in the <u>third person</u>. When the trinitary nature of the child, the adult and the elder are fused, the synthesis that occurs becomes the total embodiment of behavior that characterizes man's *"human nature"*. <u>Human nature uninterrupted is the guiding light of consciousness for every living person, but when flawed it becomes a stumbling block of fate</u>. When brought under subjection to God by the Word of the Lord, our human nature that became flawed in Adam is kindled in God's divine nature by the Holy Spirit and our journey of spiritual transformation is complete.

Trinitary Oneness in God and man...

There are three divisions in human nature that are essential to man's persona and character. Though individual in function, the three are unified in the governance of an individual's conduct, in addition to playing an essential role in framing an individual's character, and chronological behavior. We see evidence of this fact with regards to the tri-fold nature of our *mental, emotional, and spiritual behavior*, relative to our special relationship to *God the Father, God the Son, and God the Holy Spirit* in the way that we comport ourselves among men.

We have scriptural evidence of this *"sameness in trinitary oneness"* that is present in God and also present in man. The following is recorded in the book of 1st John chapter 5, verses 7 thru 9...

> "*For there are three that bear record in heaven, the Father, the Word, and the Holy Ghost: and these three are one. And there are three that bear witness in earth, the Spirit, and the water, and the blood: and these three agree in one.*" {King James Version}

This "*sameness in trinitary oneness*" that is present in God in Heaven functions to unify the human likeness of man with the spiritual likeness of God in Earth for humans to walk *("behave self")* in one spirit *(Philippians 1:27)*, with one mind *(Romans 15:6 & Philippians 2:2)* stayed on God. One simple question can be asked of a man at each of the three stages of man's chronological development and three completely different answers will be given. The *child* thinking and behaving as a child in the *"first person"* will give a <u>child's answer</u>. The *adult* thinking and behaving as an adult in the *"second person"* will give an <u>adult answer</u>. The *elder* thinking and behaving as an elder in the *"third person"* will give an <u>elderly answer</u>. The Apostle Paul recorded the following in 1st Corinthians chapter 13, verse 11...

> "*When I was a child, I spoke as a child, I understood as a child, I thought as a child; but when I became a man, I put away childish things.*" {New King James Version}

Nature of the child...

Interestingly enough, the nature of the child is *creative in function* and when given simple blocks to play, the child will build something. This behavior, which is native in the child, is resident in God the Father, Whom used the *"Spoken Word"* that was commissioned in Christ *(Ephesians 3:9)* to fashion and create the world. By the *"Word made flesh"* was the Universe created in its three dimensional form issuing from *"darkness"*, *"Spirit"*, and *"water" (Gen 1:2)*. These primal entities are the root source that comprises the *"primordial building blocks"* of the heavens and the Earth aka "THE UNIVERSE".

These primal entities are eternal and without origin. This is evident based upon the fact that they <u>were not</u> included in the *"fifteen patented acts of creation"* recorded in Genesis chapter 1, verses 3 thru 27...

"God said, let there be [(1)] *light,* [(2)] *heaven,* [(3)] *earth,* [(4)] *vegetation,* [(5)] *plants,* [(6)] *trees,* [(7)] *sun,* [(8)] *moon,* [(9)] *stars,* [(10)] *sea creatures,* [(11)] *wing creatures,* [(12)] *cattle,* [(13)] *creeping things and* [(14)] *beasts". "Then God said, Let Us make* [(15)] *man in Our image, according to Our likeness;"*

These *"patented creations"* filled the *"formless void"* that is in Genesis 1:2 and they were either spoken into existence by the *"Word of the Spirit" (John 1:1-3)* or formed by *"God's hands" (Psalm 119:73 & Job 10:8-9)*. When combined, the celestial and terrestrial hosts of the Universe that are *"theorized to have replaced NOTHING"* were brought into existence. The presence of "NO THINGS" existing prior to "CREATION" was introduced to the world as "NOTHING". The mere existence of "NOTHING" would qualify "NOTHING" as "SOMETHING", which is inconceivable based upon the *"laws of existence"*.

According to the Merriam-Webster Dictionary the word "NOTHING" was introduced into the modern lexicon in the 12th century A.D. originating from the Old English word *"nān" (for "no")*. *"nān"* was later conjoined with *"thing"* to create the word "NOTHING". Nothing is the absence of something!!! The existence of *"NOTHING"* is a *"PERFECT IMPOSSIBILITY"* based upon the existence of entities water, Spirit, and darkness that are identified in "GENESIS 1:2" by Moses.

> *"And the earth was without form, and void; and* **darkness** *was upon the face of the deep. And the* **Spirit** *of God moved upon the face of the* **waters***." {Gen 1:2}{King James Version}*

Prior to the foundation of the world *(Psalm 18:15)*, entities *water, Spirit and darkness* existed composing the "FORMLESS VOID" *(Gen 1:2)*. God filled the formless void with the "PATENTED THINGS" that He had spoken into existence, in addition to man in which He had formed and the Universe with its myriad of solar systems, milky ways and galaxies came to be. If *water, Spirit, and darkness* did not exist prior to the creation of the Universe; where did these entities come from?

These PRIMAL ENTITIES were *"NOT CREATED"*; they are found in the 1st

trinitary phase of "Infinity" that is known as "Existence", which precedes the 2nd and 3rd trinitary phases of "Infinity" that are known to man as "Time" and "Eternity". When viewed objectively outside of the realm of so-called *"NOTHINGNESS"*, all of the information recorded in the *"Genesis Creation Narrative"* points to *"darkness"*, *"Spirit"*, and *"water"* being the *primal entities* upon which the *"foundation of the world"* is established. This interpretation is supported by the Apostle Peter who makes this point known in 2nd Peter chapter 3, verses 5 thru 6. Peter provides a record of the Lord having spoken the heaven*s* (*^{1st} Earth's atmosphere, ^{2nd} outer space, ^{3rd} Holy City of God*) and Earth into being, whereby the entire Universe was formed out of the *water* referenced in Genesis chapter 1, verse 2…

> *"But they deliberately forget that long ago by God's word the heavens came into being and the earth was formed out of water and by water. By these waters also the world of that time was deluged and destroyed." {NIV - UK}*

Nature of the adult…

The nature of the adult is *restorative in function*. The adult goes about the mission of restoring that which was built and torn down by the child. This behavior, which is native in the adult, is resident in God the Son, Whom gave His life to correct the imperfection of the world that was physically destroyed *(torn down)* by Father God, Jehovah *(Genesis 6:5-8)*, resulting from the sin and imperfection caused by Adam. Father God, Jehovah destroyed the world that He had commissioned His Son to create, by allowing the great flood to completely cover the face of the Earth during the time of Noah. Jesus made the following statement in Matthew chapter 5, verse 17 when teaching His apostles on the subject of discipleship and the world…

> *"Think not that I came to destroy the law or the prophets: I came not to destroy, but to fulfill". {21st Century KJV}*

Jehovah and Joseph, "Master Builder" and "minor builder"…

It is here that Jesus the divine offspring of Father God, Jehovah and earthly son of Joseph, a builder among men *(Matthew 13:54-57)* makes known His mission of restoring the world to its *"former state of spiritual balance" (comparable to the Garden of Eden, prior to the fall of Adam - Revelation 21:1-5)*. When we study the life, mission and ministry of Jesus it is not surprising to find that His Heavenly Father, Jehovah and Joseph, his earthly parent were both builders. Father God, Jehovah was the Master Builder, Fashioner, and Creator of the Universe and Joseph was a carpenter and minor builder among men.

If one had to guess which of the carpenter's tools were best suited to represent Joseph's trade, many would believe it to be the hammer, when in fact the *"carpenter's level"* is the most important tool in the carpenter's toolbox. Ironically the carpenter's level, which is formally known as the *"spirit level"* is used to determine whether a surface or foundation is horizontally level and vertically plum. Given the eternal foundation of God's Word, the *"carpenter's level" aka "spirit level"* conforms to the vertical and horizontal relationships that characterizes both the *"Holy Cross"* and *"Ten Commandments"*, providing a firm foundation for the righteous *(Psalm 11:2 -4 & Exodus 20:3-17)*.

Historical significance of the Cross...

The spiritual symbolism expressed in the vertical and horizontal relationship that is characteristic of the *"cross of crucifixion"* was present centuries before the Roman Empire or the historical Jesus...

The earliest known record of the use of the cross as a spiritual symbol goes back to ancient Egyptian culture where the *"Ankh"* was represented as the *"symbol of life"*. The Merriam-Webster Dictionary provides the following definition for *"Ankh"*:

> *"a cross having a loop for its upper vertical arm and serving especially in ancient Egypt as an emblem of life."*

The following is recorded in the Concise Encyclopedia provided by Merriam-Webster:

> *"Ancient Egyptian* HIEROGLYPH *signifying life, consisting of a cross surmounted by a loop. In tomb inscriptions, gods and pharaohs are often pictured holding the ankh, which forms part of the hieroglyph for concepts such as health and happiness. It is used as a cross in the* COPTIC ORTHODOX CHURCH.*"*

The spiritual essence and religious symbolism of the cross was revealed during the time of Moses, wherein the order and ranking of the Ten Commandments revealed their *"vertical relationship"* to God *(1 thru 4)* and their *"horizontal relationship"* to man *(5 thru 10)*.

Commandments one through four symbolize the <u>vertical relationship</u> between *"God in Heaven"* and *"man on Earth"*. Wherein, commandments five through ten symbolize the <u>horizontal relationship</u> between *"man"* and his *"fellowman" (Exodus 20:3-17)*. Coded into the Ten Commandments are the *"tenets of the law"* that are present in the Old Testament Dispensation issuing from Moses and the *"tenets of the prophets"* beginning with Enoch up through Elijah. Also coded into the Ten Commandments are the *"tenets of the two great commandments"* that are present in the New Testament Dispensation of the gospel of grace under the blood of Jesus; *Jesus being the "fulfillment and righteousness of the law" (Romans 3:21 & 10:4)*.

The vertical and horizontal relationships *(once broken between God and man)* were intersected and crisscrossed in Jesus' death on the cross, representing the *"fulfillment of the Law and the Prophets"* through the establishment of God's grace in Christ Jesus. It is here that we bear witness of Jesus, *the human son of a carpenter* and *the divine Son of God* taking upon Himself the builder's attributes of His Heavenly Father, Jehovah and those of His earthly parent Joseph. Jesus became the *"Spirit Level"* for Father God and the *"Carpenter's Level"* for man. Jesus surrendered His life for the sins of man in order for the *"vertical relationship"* between *"God and man"* and the *"horizontal relationship"* between *"man and man"* to be balanced and restored.

Our Lord shed His *"divinity as God"* to walk the Earth as *"Jesus *the unfallen man*" in order to sacrifice his life by dying on a tree *(Galatians 3:13) "for the remission of sin"*. These things were done in order for our heavenly and earthly relationships to be made *"vertically plum"* with God and *"horizontally level"* among men *(Jews and Gentiles // man and fellowman)*, conforming to the characteristics of the *"Ten Commandments"* that are symbolized by the *"Holy Cross"*.

The birth, ministry, death, resurrection and ascension of Jesus are the prophetic fulfillment of the *"two great commandments"*. If it were not for the transgression of Adam, there would not have been a need for the *"law"* and the *"prophets"* that were fulfilled in Jesus. The two great commandments highlight and illuminate the broken relationships that existed between *"God and man"* and *"man and man"* prior to Jesus paying the ultimate price for our redemption on Calvary's cross. Jesus drank the *"cup of sin and death"* that Adam filled *(Romans 8:2)* to restore the *"covenant relationship"* broken by Adam that the law and the prophets alone could not fix. The following is recorded in Matthew chapter 22, verses 35 thru 40 and chapter 17, verses 1 thru 3...

> *"One of them, an expert in the law, tested him with this question: 'Teacher, which is the greatest commandment in the Law?' Jesus replied: '"Love the Lord your God with all your heart and with all your soul and with all your mind."*
>
> *This is the first and greatest commandment. And the second is like it: "Love your neighbour as yourself." All the Law and the Prophets hang on these two commandments.'"*
> *{New International Version - UK}*

Throughout Scripture, Moses is shown to represent the *"Law"* and the prophet Elijah is shown to represent *"Prophecy"*...

> *"Six days later Jesus took with Him Peter and James and John his brother, and led them up on a high mountain by themselves. And He was transfigured before them; and His face shone like the sun, and His garments became as white as light. And behold, Moses and Elijah appeared to them, talking with Him." {New American Standard Bible}*

Nature of the elder...

The nature of the elder is *instructive in function*. The elder goes about the mission of teaching from the experiences encountered in life to make the lives of others better. This behavior, which is native in the elder, is resident in the Holy Spirit Whom Jesus promised would return if He were to ascend to the Heavenly Father following His resurrection. The elder regardless of infirmity or habit seeks to teach what he or she has learned from life's experiences, *not realizing that outside of Christ, life functions as our "worldly teacher", when in Christ the Holy Spirit is our "Heavenly Teacher"*. This behavior, which is native in the elder, is resident in the Holy Spirit Whom Jesus referred to as *"the Comforter"*. Jesus told His disciples in John chapter 14, verses 25 thru 26 that if He were to go away the Father would send back the Comforter Who would teach *all things* and bring into remembrance all of the things that He taught during His 3½ years of ministry.

> *"These things have I spoken unto you, while yet abiding with you. But the Comforter, even the Holy Spirit, whom the Father will send in my name, he shall teach you all things, and bring to your remembrance, all that I have said unto you." {American Standard Version}*

Upon receiving Christ into our lives as Lord and Savior, life ceases to function as our teacher. The Comforter that the Heavenly Father sent instructs us that God is our teacher. The wisdom of God informs us that the world is our classroom and life's experiences is the syllabus from which God teaches us *"what not to do"* versus taking it upon ourselves *in the absence of God* to figure out *"what to do"*. When we surrender ourselves to the Lord, the Holy Spirit instructs us in *"what to do"* as our Trinitary Elder and orders our steps accordingly. This is evidenced in Psalm chapter 119, verse 133 and chapter 37, verse 23...

> *"The steps of a good man are ordered by the Lord: and he delighteth in his way." {King James Version}*

The special relationship between God and man...

The special relationship that exists between God and man is

evidenced by God distinctively setting man apart from the other earthly creatures in mental make-up and functional design. All of the original creatures entered into the world in one or two ways. They were either spoken into being by the Word of God or fashioned into being by the works of God's hands. When God created the earthly creatures they were all spoken into being accept man. The following is recorded in the book of Genesis chapter 1, verses 20 thru 26…

> "God said, let us make man in our image, after our likeness." "God said, let the waters bring forth the wing creatures and sea creature…"; "God said, let the earth bring forth the cattle, creeping things and beasts…" {King James Version}

The Garden of Eden…

For one to fully grasp and understand what it means to operate in the "*mental image*" and "*functional likeness*" of God, one must first understand the significance of the "*environment*" and "*culture*" in which God placed man to fulfill His appointed purpose. God placed man in the Garden of Eden to be nourished and maintained as the "*God-like creatures*" that God purposed man to be, **which pleases God**.

The environment inside the Garden of Eden differed greatly from the environment outside of the Garden of Eden by a ratio of 180 degrees to one. The environment and culture within the Garden of Eden was entirely different from the environment and culture of the Earth outside the garden in many respects.

For one, the Garden of Eden was endowed with a *perpetually yielding environment* that was steeped and nurtured in the supernatural, which enabled man to be an *absolute reaper* and not a sower. This factor alone constituted man to be supremely blessed above all creatures. The Garden of Eden yielded vegetation, fruits and herbs of every kind on a perpetual basis with no attention being required by man for production. Managing the abundance of overflow was more than likely the fundamental priority for man as "*keeper of the Garden*" (Genesis 2:15). The Garden of Eden was quite unlike the

Earth's natural environment of *sin culture* outside of the garden, which requires ongoing tilling, sowing and cultivation to yield at a marginal level *(Gen. 3:17-19 & Gen. 5:29)*.

For need of comparison without just similarity, one might consider comparing the *Rain Forest of the Amazons* to the Garden of Eden in an extremely rudimentary sense, yet the Rain Forest would not suffice in comparison by any stretch of the imagination. For one, the culture within the Garden of Eden was one of balance, peace and tranquility, unlike the violent Earth that lie without. The Earth outside continues to be plagued with *earth-quakes, volcanoes, wildfires, floods, hurricanes, blizzards, cyclones, tornados, tsunami's, and the like*.

When we look to the Middle Eastern region of the globe where the Bible places the Garden of Eden, we find a land area that is virtually free of the many environmental hazards of nature that plague the rest of the world. Aside from the tremendous effects of the heat, occasional floods and locust swarms, the only storms that affect this region of the world are sand and dust. The earthquakes, volcanoes, wildfires; and the like that affect the rest of the world are simply nonexistent.

The geographical description provided in the book of Genesis chapter 2, verses 10 thru 14 places the Garden of Eden in a centralized area of the world that is in or near the present day countries of Saudi Arabia, Iran and Iraq.

> *"From Eden a river flowed out to water the garden, then it divided into four rivers. The first one is the Pishon River that flows through the land of Havilah, where pure gold, rare perfumes, and precious stones are found. The second is the Gihon River that winds through Ethiopia. The Tigris River that flows east of Assyria is the third, and the fourth is the Euphrates River." {Contemporary English Version}*

When we view this region today, we find an area with a hot climate that undergoes very little weather phenomena, resulting in a relatively stable environment. It is obvious that the Earth's environment outside of the Garden of Eden was very dissimilar to the environment of the Garden of Eden that lies within, in a variety of contrasting ways. The

Earth's natural environment outside of the garden was composed of every brutal element of nature known and unknown to man; which fueled the perils that flourished abundantly in its untamed environment. The Earth's environment in its natural state is rugged, unbridled, uncultivated, and unbalanced, making it virtually unsuitable for early human habitation, wherein man would have to undergo major adaptation and ongoing adjustments in order to survive. God was well aware of these factors when he made the decision to expel man from the Garden of Eden. The harsh and brutal environment required God to prepare coats of skin for Adam and Eve in order for them to survive. The following is recorded in the book of Genesis chapter 3, verse 21…

> *"And the LORD God made for Adam and for his wife garments of skins and clothed them." {English Standard Version}*

Life inside the Garden afforded man total provision, maximum care and ease of comfort for a spiritually secure and non-threatening physical existence. The *"tree of life"* that was planted in the midst of the garden was there to preserve man throughout eternity in a *"perfected state of youthful existence"*, thus rendering man needless of *"health maintenance"* of any kind. For this reason the Garden of Eden is referred to as *"Paradise" (2nd Cor. 12:1 & 4, Luke 24:43, Rev. 2:7)*.

The unfolding *"heavenly drama"* that was referenced earlier would result in Adam and Eve being permanently separated from the tree of life that existed in Eden's garden of unique Spirit culture. God planted the tree of life to nourish and preserve the family of Adam throughout eternity. In the aftermath of Adam and Eve's expulsion, the tree of life was taken up to heaven and planted in the city of the New Jerusalem. The following is recorded in the book of Revelation chapter 22, verses 1 thru 2…

> *"Then he showed me the river whose waters give life, sparkling like crystal, flowing out from the throne of God and of the Lamb.*
>
> *Through the middle of the broadway of the city; also, on either side of the river was the tree of life with its twelve*

> *varieties of fruit, yielding each month its fresh crop; and the leaves of the tree were for the healing and the restoration of the nations" {Amplified Version}*

War in Heaven... Lucifer cast into the Earth as Satan...

*U*nfortunately for man, an angelic war broke out in Heaven and the outcome had a devastating effect on man and his *spirit-filled utopian environment* on Earth. One third of God's angels banded together with the angel Lucifer in an ill-fated attempt of overthrowing the rule of God in Heaven with the intent of seizing control of the Universe. The outcome of the war resulted in Lucifer and his rebel force of angels being defeated by Michael the archangel, only to be cast out of Heaven into the Earth. The details of this event are documented in Revelation chapter 12, verses 7 thru 9 and Isaiah chapter 14, verses 12 thru 17...

> *"And there was war in heaven: Michael and his angels going forth to war with the dragon; and the dragon warred and his angels; And they prevailed not, neither was their place found any more in heaven.*
>
> *And the great dragon was cast down, the old serpent, he that is called the Devil and Satan, the deceiver of the whole world; he was cast down to the earth, and his angels were cast down with him." {New King James Version}*
>
> *"How you are fallen from heaven, O shining star, son of the morning! You have been thrown down to the earth, you who destroyed the nations of the world.*
>
> *For you said to yourself, 'I will ascend to heaven and set my throne above God's stars. I will preside on the mountain of the gods far away in the north. I will climb to the highest heavens and be like the Most High.'*
>
> *Instead, you will be brought down to the place of the dead, down to its lowest depths. Everyone there will stare at you and ask, 'Can this be the one who shook the earth and made the kingdoms of the world tremble?*
>
> *Is this the one who destroyed the world and made it into a*

wasteland? Is this the king who demolished the world's greatest cities and had no mercy on his prisoners?" {New Living Translation}

𝒰pon entering into the Earth realm, the *"fallen angel"*, Lucifer resurfaced in the Garden of Eden as *"Satan"* after having entered into the serpent, which served as a fitting and compatible *"bodily host"*. It is here in the Garden of Eden at the very outset of creation that we find God's rebellious archangel Lucifer having undergone a radical transformation from that of a commanding angelic host of Heaven into *"Satan"*, the eternal archenemy of God and spiritual nemesis of man.

The downfall of man…

𝒯he following Scriptures provide a detailed account of this event, which took place at the very outset of creation <u>leading to the downfall of man and the need for a *"instructional manual"* to be written that would accompany man on his journey outside of the Garden of Eden</u>: The following is recorded in the book of Genesis chapter 2, verses 16 thru 17, chapter 2, verses 8 thru 9 and chapter 3, verses 1 thru 6…

> *"The LORD made a garden in a place called Eden, which was in the east, and he put the man there. The LORD God placed all kinds of beautiful trees and fruit trees in the garden. Two other trees were in the middle of the garden.*
>
> *One of the trees gave life… the other gave the power to know the difference between right and wrong."* {Contemporary English Version}
>
> *"And the LORD God commanded the man, saying, Of every tree of the garden thou mayest freely eat: But of the tree of the knowledge of good and evil, thou shalt not eat of it: for in the day that thou eatest thereof thou shalt surely die."* {King James Version}
>
> *"Now the serpent was more cunning than any beast of the field which the LORD God had made. And he said to the woman, "Has God indeed said, 'You shall not eat of every tree of the garden'?"*

And the woman said to the serpent, "We may eat the fruit of the trees of the garden; but of the fruit of the tree which is in the midst of the garden, God has said, 'You shall not eat it, nor shall you touch it, lest you die."

Then the serpent said to the woman, "You will not surely die. For God knows that in the day you eat of it your eyes will be opened, and you will be like God, knowing good and evil." {New King James Version}

"And when the woman saw that the tree was good for food, and that it was pleasant to the eyes, and a tree to be desired to make one wise, she took of the fruit thereof, and did eat, and gave also unto her husband with her; and he did eat." {King James Version}

The law of use...

Something happened when man ate the fruit from the *"tree of knowledge of good and evil" (Gen. 2:16-17)* that until this day has not been sufficiently explored or adequately explained, based upon its epic importance to the downfall and dreadful saga of man. I find it interesting that what one *eats, drinks or ingest in any given manner* is entirely different from what one *consumes...*

- One can *eat* bread, but *consumes* yeast.
- One can *eat* fish, but *consumes* mercury.
- One can *eat* potatoes, but *consumes* starch.
- One can *eat* eggs, but *consumes* cholesterol.
- One can *drink* coffee, but *consumes* caffeine.
- One can *eat* bananas, but *consumes* potassium.
- One can *smoke* tobacco, but *consumes* nicotine, etc.

Forbidden knowledge of God consumed...

The previous examples were noted to demonstrate a very important, but critically overlooked fact regarding the kind of fruit that was eaten by Adam and Eve. Eve was tempted by the serpent and out of *willful disobedience* and *carnal desire* she took the fruit from the tree of knowledge of good and evil and ate it, she then gave it to Adam to eat *(Genesis 3:6)*. It is very important to note that it was Eve who tempted Adam with the forbidden fruit and not the serpent, as we shall see later. It is a well-known fact that no one knows the actual kind of fruit that was eaten, although myth has typified the apple as being the fruit spoken of in the Bible, yet there is no Scriptural evidence of support.

This legendary myth has been perpetuated and preserved down through the centuries, contributing to the belief that the laryngeal cartilage that is located in the throat of the male human *(commonly referred to as the "Adam's apple")* is the fruit referenced in the Bible. In fact, no one can truthfully say what kind of fruit was grown on the tree of knowledge of good and evil, although many speculations exist. However, there is one thing that we know for certain, which is… *what one eats is entirely different from what one consumes*. What particular fruit Adam and Eve ate we know not, but we know for a certainty that what they consumed was the *"forbidden knowledge of God"*.

Forbidden knowledge reserved for God alone…

When Eve picked the forbidden fruit from the tree of knowledge of good and evil and then gave it to Adam, they consumed knowledge that was reserved for God and God alone. Only God has "ABSOLUTE POWER" over His creation; God created the tree and the fruit thereof. *It is a well-known fact that if one does not have power over what they consume, then what they consume will have power over them*. This is a *"natural law of use"* that has existed since the beginning of creation, one in which large numbers of people today are well acquainted and grapples with on a daily basis. Having consumed the forbidden knowledge, man was now required to have "SUPERNATURAL POWER" to exercise *"dominion"* over what they were "NOT SUPPOSED TO KNOW". The *"law of use"* applies to all things and knowledge is no exception. Even the angels were subject to this law. *Lucifer's radical departure from God, now the fallen angel, Satan is clearly understood.*

In short, man was forbidden to eat from the tree of knowledge of good and evil for a very good reason. God having created man knew that he lacked the "SUPERNATURAL POWER" required to rule over the things that would become resident in his flesh. Man was not spiritually equipped to control the things that lie beyond the boundary of human creation, nor was Lucifer equipped beyond that of the angelic realm.

Man did not possess the *"supernatural power"* required to exercise power over sin and the evil spoken of in the Ten Commandments. History has shown that sin renders man susceptible to *killing, adultery, stealing, lying, covetousness, and all manners of lewd behavior that sows seeds of destruction for man and brings great displeasure to God.*

Forbidden knowledge translates into sin...

The Apostle Paul in whom the Holy Spirit made known the unrelenting power of sin and evil that is resident in the flesh, states the following in the book of Galatians chapter 5, verses 19 thru 21 and Romans chapter 6, verses 21 thru 23...

> *"Now the works of the flesh are evident, which are: adultery, fornication, uncleanness, lewdness, idolatry, sorcery, hatred, contentions, jealousies, outbursts of wrath, selfish ambitions, dissensions, heresies, envy, murders, drunkenness, revelries, and the like; of which I tell you beforehand, just as I also told you in time past, that those who practice such things will not inherit the kingdom of God." {New King James Version}*

> *"Therefore what benefit were you then deriving from the things of which you are now ashamed? For the outcome of those things is death. But now having been freed from sin and enslaved to God, you derive your benefit, resulting in sanctification, and the outcome, eternal life.*

> *For the wages of sin is death, but the free gift of God is eternal life in Christ Jesus our Lord." {New American Standard Version}*

Sin translates into death...

The death that God disclosed to Adam in Genesis chapter 2, verse 17 is believed by many to be the physical death of the human body, *but is this really what God meant?* The Scriptures state...

> *"but you must not eat from the tree of the knowledge of good and evil, for on the day you eat from it, you will certainly die." {Holman Christian Standard Version}*

Did Adam and Eve *physically die on the day that they ate the forbidden fruit* from the tree of knowledge of Good and evil? *Of course not!* If that were the case, Adam certainly would not have lived approximately 900 years after his transgression and Methuselah would not have lived long enough to be regarded as the world's longest lived human. The Scriptures tell us that *"God is not a man, that He should lie;" (Numbers 23:19)* so there has to be a scriptural explanation.

The following is recorded in the book of Genesis chapter 5, verse 27 concerning the years of Adam and Methuselah:..

> *"So all the days that Adam lived were nine hundred and thirty years, and he died." {Genesis chapter 5, verse 5}*

> *"So all the days of Methuselah were nine hundred and sixty-nine years, and he died." {New American Standard Version}*

The Scriptures bear record of the fact that both men lived well into their relative old age and then died like everyone else with the exception of Noah's grandfather, Enoch *(Genesis 5:24)* and the Prophet Elijah *(2nd Kings 2:1-9)*, whom were both taken up to heaven without experiencing death. When a person *"died"* during the Old Testament era they were considered *"physically dead"*, but this long established belief would change during Jesus' 3½ years ministry. The birth of Jesus produced the *"Lord of the resurrection"* as witnessed in His death and resurrection, whereby He among others was raised from the dead. The following is recorded in the book of John chapter 11, verse 25...

> *"Jesus said unto her, I am the resurrection, and the life: he that believeth in me, though he were dead, yet shall he live:" {King James Version}*

The Scriptures provides a record of Jesus waking people from physical death on more than one occasion. Jesus used the raising of Lazarus and the rulers young daughter to demonstrate that death as we know it is not permanent, *but merely the departed soul lying in a "suspended sleep state" awaiting resurrection and final judgment*. The following statements were spoken by Jesus in the book of John chapter 11, verses 11, 38, 39, 17 and 14 concerning physical death...

> *"After saying these things, he said to them, 'Our friend Lazarus has fallen asleep, but I go to awaken him.' Then Jesus told them plainly, 'Lazarus has died,..."* {English Standard Version}

> *"Jesus, once more deeply moved, came to the tomb. It was a cave with a stone laid across the entrance. 'Take away the stone,' he said.*

> *'But, Lord,' said Martha, the sister of the dead man, 'by this time there is a bad odour, for he has been there four days.'"* {New International Version – UK}

> *"And when Jesus came to the ruler's house and saw the flute players and the crowd making a commotion, he said, 'Go away, for the girl is not dead but sleeping.' And they laughed at him."* {English Standard Version}

Prior to Jesus, one would have been considered insane to believe physical death to be sleep and not permanent separation, regardless of the source. Yet, the miraculous works and resurrection of Jesus Himself provided proof to substantiate Jesus' assertion that death is a *"suspended sleep state"* while one awaits *physical resurrection.*

Considering the fact that humanity has continued to live on and reproduce for thousands of years following Adam and Eve's transgression calls into question what God meant when He commanded Adam and Eve... *"In the day you eat of the tree you shall surely die"*. The fact that Adam and Eve did not die *within 24 hours* of eating the fruit from the tree serves as infallible proof that the death in which God commanded was not physical in nature. And if the death spoken of by God was not physical... **then what type of death was it?**

How many deaths are there?

*U*pon revisiting the biblical account surrounding Adam and Eve's transgression we find *"three death experiences"* that would come upon man with the *first death manifesting itself in two parts*. When we examine Adam and Eve's behavior in the aftermath of their transgression, we see a different picture emerging in light of our new understanding of death based upon the *miracles, teaching* and *resurrection of Jesus*. We know that there are at least three distinct deaths that resulted from Adam and Eve's disobedience to God, wherein parts *"a"* and *"b"* of the first death are separate from the second death that is recorded in the book of Revelation *chapters 2:11, 20:6, 20:14 & 21:8*.

Death to man's spiritual character...

*T*he Scriptures provide infallible proof that on the day that Adam and Eve ate from the tree of knowledge of good and evil that their *"God-like character"* ceased to exist. This was in fact the *"first part"* of the *"first death"* that occurred on the exact day that they ate from the tree of knowledge of good and evil in which God had commanded them not to eat. The knowledge that was derived from eating the forbidden fruit expanded their realm of consciousness beyond their naturally prescribed boundaries destroying their innocence.

*P*rior to eating the forbidden fruit that is recorded in the book of Genesis chapter 2, verse 25 Adam and Eve were naked and were not ashamed. Immediately upon eating the forbidden fruit that is noted in the book of Genesis chapter 3, verse 7 they became aware of their nakedness and made coverings for themselves indicating they were now *"sin conscious"* and *"ashamed"*...

> *"And they were both naked, the man and his wife, and were not ashamed." {American Standard Version}*

> *"Then the eyes of both of them were opened, and they knew they were naked; so they sewed fig leaves together and made loincloths for themselves." {Holman Christian Standard Version}*

We have further proof of death to their *"God-like character"* that is readily apparent in the behavior models of today. Our moral behavior is inconsistent with the *"mental image"* and *"functional likeness"* of God that was fashioned in the *"authentic man and woman"* at the time of their creation. Evidence of *disobedience, hiding, fear, shame, blame, and failure to accept responsibility* is provided in the following Scriptures that are recorded in the book of Genesis chapter 3, verses 8 thru 13…

> *"Then the man and his wife heard the sound of the LORD God walking in the garden at the time of the evening breeze, and they hid themselves from the LORD God among the trees of the garden. So the LORD God called out to the man and said to him, "Where are you?"*
>
> *And he said, "I heard You in the garden and I was afraid because I was naked, so I hid." Then He asked, "Who told you that you were naked? Did you eat from the tree that I commanded you not to eat from?" Then the man replied, "The woman You gave to be with me - she gave me some fruit from the tree, and I ate."*
>
> *So the LORD God asked the woman, "What is this you have done?" And the woman said, "It was the serpent. He deceived me, and I ate." {Holman Christian Standard Bible}*

Death to man's physical body…

The Scriptures also provide proof of physical death being manifested in all humans hundreds of years later, barring exception to the prophets Enoch and Elijah, whom were taken into heaven by God before dying. The Scriptures provide credible proof that physical death did not come upon Adam and Eve on the *calendar day* that they ate of the tree from which God had commanded them not to eat, but did in fact occur within the *God Day* spoken of by the Apostle Peter. This is the *"second part"* of the *"first death"* that occurred centuries into the *"Day of 1,000 years"* that is recorded in 2nd Peter chapter 3, verses 8…

> *"But do not forget this one thing, dear friends: with the*

Lord a day is like a thousand years, and a thousand years are like a day." {New International Version - UK}

In fact Scriptural evidence points to man's separation from the *"tree of life"* as being the singular cause for their physical death in the aftermath of their banishment from the Garden of Eden. Adam and Eve's expulsion was not meant for punishment; it was God's way of shielding them from the *"tree of life"*, which would have allowed them to <u>live forever in a fallen state</u> *(Genesis 3:22-24)*. If they had been allowed to remain in the garden, they would have become *"eternal and immortal sinners"* along with *"Satan"* and the *"fallen angels"*. Their expulsion was God's *"fullness of grace"* and *"provision of redemption"*, which would go into effect upon Jesus' resurrection.

There is a widely held belief that physical death came upon man for eating the fruit from the tree of knowledge of good and evil. This idea is erroneously rooted in the fact that many believe man to have been <u>created immortal</u>, when in fact man was subject to death from the time of their creation. Unlike the angels, man is mortal. We have record of Jesus *("Son of God")* being made subject to death as a result of being born a man; the following is recorded in Hebrews chapter 2, verse 9...

"But we see Jesus, who was made a little lower than the angels <u>for the suffering of death</u>, crowned with glory and honour; that he by the grace of God <u>should taste death for every man</u>." {King James Version}

Man was created mortal and was granted eternal life contingent upon his adherence to the "ETERNAL LIFE COVENANT" entered into between God and Adam, known also as the *"Adamic Covenant"*.

The direct cause of man's physical death resulted from Adam and Eve's separation from the "TREE OF LIFE" that had been planted in the Garden of Eden to holistically sustain man throughout eternity. It is an undeniable fact that the overwhelming majority of people live longer than one calendar day during the course of their lifetimes. The proof of life lasting longer than one day is readily apparent... <u>the human race is still here!</u> This is the *"second part"* of the *"first death"*.

Death to man's soul...

The Scriptures refer to a *"second death"* in the book of Revelation *(Rev. 2:11, 20:6 & 14, 21:8)*, causing many to believe that there are only two deaths. However, the scriptures are very clear regarding the second death, leaving very little room for ambiguity or doubt concerning what the second death is. **The *"second death"* results in permanent spiritual separation from God and His kingdom (1st Corinthians 15:50),** allowing no opportunity for spiritual reconciliation. The second death terminates the existence of the fallen based upon their failure to accept Jesus Christ as God's eternal gift of salvation. The names of the *"spiritually lost"* are omitted from the *"Book of Life"* as if they never existed *(Matthew 7:23)*. **The *"second death"* results in everlasting destruction, whereby the soul is consumed by fire.** The following is recorded in Revelation chapter 20, verses 15 and chapter 21, verses 7 thru 8 regarding the second death...

> *"And whosoever was not found written in the Book of Life was cast into the lake of fire." {21st Century King James Version}*

> *"Those who are victorious will inherit all this, and I will be their God and they will be my children. But the cowardly, the unbelieving, the vile, the murderers, the sexually immoral, those who practice magic arts, the idolaters and all liars – they will be consigned to the fiery lake of burning sulphur. This is the second death." {New International Version – UK}*

Jesus... Man's seed of salvation...

The *Omniscient* and *Omnipotent Christ* was birthed into the world as man's *"seed of salvation"*. He was planted by way of crucifixion to die for humanity's sins in order to restore humanity's right to the tree of life *(Romans 6:4-5)*. Jesus accepted death and rose from the dead in order for the Comforter to come on the day of Pentecost to anoint the "FAMILY OF ADAM" with the *"Supernatural Power of the Holy Spirit"* in order for humanity to *"have dominion"* over the things that man was... "NOT SUPPOSED TO KNOW!" Jesus is the *"Messiah"* and *"lamb slain from the foundation of the world"*.

The *"Anointing Power of God"* restores man's *"Spiritual Dominion"*, through it we receive and exercise *"God's Authoritative Power"* over the forbidden knowledge that we were made conscious of through the disobedience of Adam. *Satan does not limit himself to using our "bad" against us, but he uses our "good" against us also.* Moses records the following in Genesis chapter 3, verses 22 thru 23...

> *"And the LORD God said, The man has now become like one of us, knowing good and evil. He must not be allowed to reach out his hand and take also from the tree of life and eat, and live forever. So the LORD God banished him from the Garden of Eden to work the ground from which he had been taken." {New International Version – UK}*

Unfortunately, man was left spiritually powerless to maintenance himself without intervention or personal direction from God following Adam and Eve's expulsion from the Garden of Eden. Man having fallen, no longer had the *"God-given natural power that once resided in their human spirit"*. Man in his fallen state required a *"Spiritual Life-guide"* for survival that would lend spiritual direction in the absence of the presence of God that had been withdrawn. Over the many centuries of separation, man has learned from God's absence that one of the greatest lessons learned by man is the need for "GOD'S PRESENCE" and "GOD'S POWER" in our lives. *The "Power of God's Presence" is "HIS GLORY"; the "Presence of God's Power" is "HIS MIGHT". In order for us to live victorious, we need the Power and Glory of Almighty God!!!*

Eden's spirit culture lost...

Adam and Eve's expulsion from the Garden of Eden permanently separated man from *"Eden's Spirit culture"*, in addition to centuries of separation from God, necessitating the writing of the Bible that served as a *"companion life guide"* and *"substitute"* in God's absence.

Tree of knowledge of good and evil...

There were many trees planted by God in the Garden of Eden, but in the center of the garden there were two special trees that produced very unique fruits *(Gen. 2:9)*. One of the trees produced fruit providing "EVERLASTING LIFE" and the other tree produced fruit yielding *"forbidden knowledge"* and *"destruction to God's spiritual character"* in man, resulting in *"spiritual death"*. The *"tree of knowledge of good and evil"* yielded fruit that was endowed with the demonic essence and spiritual attributes of the devil, "that supplies the knowledge of good and evil to destroy innocence". The Merriam-Webster Dictionary defines innocence as…

> *"Lack of knowledge: freedom from guilt or sin through being unacquainted with evil".*

Upon eating the forbidden fruit, Adam and Eve became conscious of the fact that the forbidden fruit far exceeded their human ability to *"think"* and *"behave"* naturally, so they covered themselves with fig leaves and hid themselves among the trees of the garden *(Genesis 3:7-8)*. A change in Adam and Eve's character was reflected in their mental and spiritual attitudes based upon the guilt and shame they experienced after having eaten the fruit. The Scriptures record the following in the book of Genesis chapter 2, verse 25…

> *"And the man and his wife were both naked and were not ashamed." {English Standard Version}*

Tree of life…

The *"tree of life"* yielded fruit that was endowed with the supernatural essence and spiritual properties of God that granted mortal man eternal life long before the birth of Jesus. The following is stated by Jesus in the book of John chapter 10, verse 10…

> *"…I have come that they may have life, and that they may have it more abundantly." {New King James Version}*

The Scriptures record only two ways for man to receive eternal life and they differ in respect to the Old Testament and the New Testament. At the outset of the Old Testament period the Bible tells us in Genesis that the *"tree of life"* which was planted in the Garden of Eden would cause man to *"live forever"* if allowed to eat of its fruit *(Gen 3:22)*.

Calvary's Holy Cross...

The gospel informs us that Calvary's cross of crucifixion symbolizes the only way for one to receive eternal life in the New Testament era. Therefore, it is not surprising to learn that *"Calvary's cross"* is biblically referred to as a *"tree"* coinciding with the *"Tree of Life"*...

> *"The God of our fathers raised Jesus whom you killed by hanging Him on a tree." {Acts 5:30} {Revised Standard Version}*

Calvary's cross of crucifixion was the *"Old Testament's tree of death"* for Jesus, along with many of His apostles and disciples, only to become the *"New Testament's tree of life"* for us. If it were not for the blood that was shed by Jesus on Calvary's cross as an atoning sacrifice for our sins, we would not have the right to *"eternal life"* today. Our old sin nature was crucified with Jesus, allowing a *new spirit* to be born in us based upon our resurrection and rebirth in Christ. The following is recorded in Romans chapter 6, verses 5 thru 7...

> *"For if we have become united with Him in the likeness of His death, certainly we shall also be in the likeness of His resurrection, knowing this, that our old self was crucified with Him, in order that our body of sin might be done away with, so that we would no longer be slaves to sin; for he who has died is free from sin." {New American Standard}*

Eternal life...

Many are familiar with the following Scripture that is recorded as a testament to Jesus Christ for being our New Testament source of "ETERNAL LIFE" through faith; John chapter 3, verse 16...

> *"For God so loved the world, that He gave His only begotten Son, that whoever believes in Him shall not perish, but have eternal life."*

Few are aware of the following Scriptures being recorded as a testament to the *"Tree of Life"* for being our Old Testament source of "ETERNAL LIFE" through obedience; Genesis chapter 3, verse 16 -17...

> *"And the* LORD *God commanded the man, saying, "Of every tree of the garden you may freely eat; but of the tree of the knowledge of good and evil you shall not eat, for in the day that you eat of it you shall surely die."{New King James Version}*

Eve converses with a walking and talking serpent...

The serpent approaches Eve with the following *"life and death question"*... **"Did God actually say, 'You shall not eat of any tree in the garden'?"** Eve' response to the serpent should have been... "You need to speak with my husband Adam, for it was he that had the "covenant conversation" with God concerning the "tree of knowledge of good and evil" from which we are not to eat, for God had not yet created me." "The only tree in the midst of the garden that concerns me is the tree of life, from whence I love to eat." The following is recorded in the book of Genesis chapter 3, verses 1 thru 4...

> *"Now the serpent was more crafty than any other beast of the field that the LORD God had made. He said to the woman, 'Did God actually say, 'You shall not eat of any tree in the garden?' And the woman said to the serpent,*
>
> *'We may eat of the fruit of the trees in the garden, but God said, 'You shall not eat of the fruit of the tree that is in the midst of the garden, neither shall you touch it, lest you die.' But the serpent said to the woman, "You will not surely die." {English Standard Version}*

If this had been done, Adam and Eve's expulsion from the Garden of Eden, the prophets, the Law of Moses, the Holy Bible, including the birth, death and crucifixion of Jesus, nor the day of judgment would have been required. The intimate relationship that Adam and Eve shared with God in the Garden of Eden at the outset of creation would have continued uninterrupted for all eternity had Eve understood, trusted, and believed in their *"covenant relationship with God"*.

The Garden of Eden was *"man's place of spiritual covenant"*, a place selectively chosen by God as *man's eternal domicile located in paradise*. Eden constituted the supreme embodiment of spirit culture, requiring no detailed set of instructions other than divine reverence and absolute obedience to God. The Bible was not intended to substitute or replace the "TREE OF LIFE", nor was it intended to replace the spiritual relationship that man shared with God in *"paradise" (Luke 24:43, Revelation 2:7, 2nd Corinthians 12:1 & 4)*.

The Bible, independent of an *"intimate relationship"* with the Lord is incapable of providing the spiritual transformation needed to receive eternal life. It is through *"our confession of faith"* and *"belief in Jesus' death and resurrection for our sins" (Romans 10:9-10)* that we are able to live without the *nature of sin* being the dominant force in our lives. The price for our redemption from sin was paid when <u>Jesus shed His blood</u> on Calvary *(Matt. 26:28)* in order for us to once again *"walk like God"* and *"talk like God"* as a *"remade Genuine Articles in Christ"*. So the question is… <u>what is God's will and intended purpose for our lives?</u>

Understanding freewill first…

To understand freewill we need only look to the place of man's origin, relative to man's *"appointed purpose"* and *"special creation"*. Figuratively speaking, Adam and Eve were the first manufactured products to come off of God's assembly line, prior to being placed in the Garden of Eden where they were to be optimally maintained throughout eternity *(Genesis 2:8)*. Unlike the other creatures, Adam and Eve were personally handcrafted by God *(Genesis 2:7)* and were uniquely endowed with *"freewill"* to function as God's personally appointed representatives and *"<u>Power of Attorney</u>"* in the Earth realm. This one critical factor afforded man the liberty to make decisions independent of God *(good and bad)*, thus rendering all humans subject to failure, thereby creating the potential and provision for ultimate replacement. Without freewill, Adam and Eve would have been equivalent to a set of *"glorified human robots"* that were programmed to automatically respond to commands for every given task and situation. The American Heritage Dictionary defines freewill as…

> *"The powers, attributed especially to human beings, of making free choices that are unconstrained by external circumstances or by necessity".*

The freewill component endowed in Adam and Eve at the time of their creation equipped them to function without hindrance as God's personally appointed stewards over the administrative affairs of the Earth. If Adam and Eve and their descendants were to effectively manage the affairs of the planet, it was paramount that they possess the *unlimited ability, capacity,* and *absolute authority* to act *spontaneously, responsively, and independently* without need of heavenly consultation when taking action on crucial decisions along the way. Albert Einstein stated the following regarding the human mind…

> *"The intuitive mind is a sacred gift and the rational mind is a faithful servant. We have created a society that honors the servant and has forgotten the gift."*

The Encyclopedia Britannica defines *"intuitive"* as follows…

> *"a: having the ability to know or understand things without any proof or evidence : having or characterized by intuition, b: based on or agreeing with what is known or understood without any proof or evidence : known or understood by intuition, c: agreeing with what seems naturally right."*

The Encyclopedia Britannica defines *"rational"* as follows…

> *"a: "having reason or understanding, b: relating to, based on, or agreeable to reason :REASONABLE".*

Without doubt, the element of freewill was essential to man's dominion in the Earth, it was an integral part of man's stewardship.

Let us not forget that man was created in a *"saved state of spiritual authority"*, which was *"perfected in his form of God-like creation "before the fall"*. Only *"after the fall"* was man in need of *"repentance"* and *"spiritual redemption"*. This *"special creation"* endowed man with God-like powers and authority, which granted them *(both male and female)* dominion over all the creatures of the Earth, <u>including the serpent</u>. Freewill afforded man the ability and capacity to act and function *independently* and *spontaneously* as God's agent with *unlimited power of authority* on behalf of God.

Without freewill, man's power of dominion would have been severely compromised. When sin entered into man, so did the spirit of Satan, causing man's freewill to become subordinate to <u>Satan's will</u>. The following is recorded in John chapter 2, verses 24 thru 25…

> *"But Jesus, on His part, was not entrusting Himself to them, for He knew all men, and because He did not need anyone to testify concerning man, <u>for He Himself knew what was in man</u>." {New American Standard Version}*

The mind of man which had been sealed from the time of creation with the glory of God was now open to the fallen angel *(Lucifer aka Satan)* due to sin, allowing the *thoughts, ideas,* and *suggestions* of Satan, which are the *"virtual tools of the tempter"* to freely enter.

Man was created single minded in function and purpose allowing for the highest state of mental clarity, functional execution and oneness in earthly authority. <u>As the definition for freewill shows, "man's ability to make independent choices and decisions were not to be constrained by need or circumstances arising from any sources other than himself"</u>. The element of freewill was designed by God to grant humans the freedom and independence to make choices and decisions without need for outside direction *(including Himself)*. When sin entered into man as did Satan's spirit, man became doubled minded in function and was resigned to the fate of attempting to serve two masters *(God and Satan)*. The Apostle Matthew wrote the following in Matthew chapter 6, verse 24…

> *"No one can serve two masters. The person will hate one master and love the other, or will follow one master and refuse to follow the other… You cannot serve both God and worldly riches." {New Century Version}*

Dual components of freewill…

There are two underlying principles that constitute freewill, the first is the grant of *"FREEDOM"* and the second is the right of *"MORAL AUTHORITY"*. There's the *"freedom component" that* grants an individual the unconstrained liberty to exercise independent action. There's the *"moral component" (often times overlooked) that* sanctions the individual boundaries of behavioral authority relative to one's actions of *"expressed thought"*, *"speech"*, and *"physical execution"*. Stated another way... we have the undeterred freedom to do, but we do not always have the inherent right to do!

God grants each of us the unconstrained liberty to do as we choose, but there are moral boundaries for the things that we are to *think, say, and do* in respect to our *"personal will and walk with God"*, which impacts our covenant relationship with God and personal relationships with our fellowman. Freewill affords us *"freedom of choice"* as an *"inherent right to action"* in the *"pursuit of purpose"*, which should come naturally.

The Merriam Webster Dictionary defines the word *inherent* in the following way... *"involved in the constitution or essential character of something : belonging by nature or habit"*.

Adam's failure to surrender his freewill in place of God's will...

Scripture shows Adam functioning as a *"free agent"* when he transferred his vested power of authority as steward over the managerial affairs of the Earth to Satan. It is here that we find Eve functioning as Satan's proxy *(Genesis 3:6)* in persuading Adam to eat the forbidden fruit that would result in the *"transference of Earthly authority to Satan"*. Satan references this transfer of authority when he tempted Jesus following Jesus' forty days of fasting in the wilderness. The following is recorded in the book of Luke chapter 4, verse 6...

> *"The devil said to Jesus, 'I will give you all these kingdoms and all their power and glory. It has all been given to me, I can give it to anyone I wish.'" {New Century version}*

Once again we see Jesus doing what He would later do in the Garden of Gethsemane when He chose not to exercise His own freewill, in order for the Heavenly Father's will to be done in Him. _This is the exact opposite of what Adam did._ The following is recorded in the book of Matthew chapter 26, verses 36 thru 42...

> *"Then Jesus came with them to a place called Gethsemane, and said to the disciples, "Sit here while I go and pray over there." And He took with Him Peter and the two sons of Zebedee, and He began to be sorrowful and deeply destressed.*
>
> *Then He said to them, "My soul is exceedingly sorrowful, even to death. Stay here and watch with Me." He went a little farther and fell on His face, and prayed, saying, "O My Father, if it is possible, let this cup pass from Me; nevertheless, not as I will, but as You will."*
>
> *Then He came to the disciples and found them sleeping, and said to Peter, "What! Could you not watch with Me one hour? Watch and pray, lest you enter into temptation.*
>
> *The spirit indeed is willing, but the flesh is weak." Again, a second time, He went away and prayed, saying, "O My Father, if this cup cannot pass away from Me unless I drink it, Your will be done." {Holman Christian Standard Version}*

Adam's non-surrender of freewill, a death sentence for Jesus...

The cup in which Jesus is referring is the *"cup of sin and death"* that Adam filled when he failed to surrender his freewill in order for the Heavenly Father's will to be done in him. Adam could have chosen not to eat the *"forbidden fruit"* from the *"tree of knowledge of good and evil"*, but he did not. The penalty of death that was clearly Adam's would be imputed to Jesus *(Rom. 6:23)... "For the wages of sin is death, but the gift of God is eternal life in Christ Jesus our Lord."* Jesus was made sin and died a tragic death in our place in order for us to forego the *"second death"* and be granted the right to eternal life.

So, one would think that Adam's motive for colluding with Satan by exercising his freewill to disobey God was due to his undying love for Eve. Perhaps that is the case, but we shall never know. However, this we do know... freewill was endowed in man at the time of his creation as a means of enabling man to function exclusively on behalf of God in carrying out *"God's will"* on Earth through the *"willful actions"* of man on God's behalf. To comprehend this, we need first understand the foundation upon which freewill is established. The presence of freewill in humans enables them to act on their own behalf as *"UNCONSTRAINED MORAL-FREE AGENTS"*.

Free agency, gone wrong...

Scriptural evidence clearly shows that man became a *"free agent"* and *"steward for hire"* when Adam and Eve entered into collusion with Satan. Adam's participation in the eating of the forbidden fruit violated the "ETERNAL LIFE COVENANT" that had been established by the Lord for the purpose of granting and guaranteeing man *"spiritual dominion"* and the blessing of *"eternal life"*. In return for their collusion, Adam and Eve received the *"eye opening awakening"* promised by Satan to expand their realm of consciousness.

Their newly acquired *"sense of expanded consciousness"* and *"heightened awareness"* would cause them to *"know the virtues of good"* and *"the pleasures of evil"*. Their knowledge of good would lead to *"vanity"* and *"a sense of self-righteousness"*, which has proven throughout human history to be the gateway to self-destruction. The knowledge of evil would blot out the *"good imagination"* in man leaving only vestiges of godly thoughts, causing them to *"think"* and *"behave"* more and more like devils. The following is recorded in the book of Genesis chapter 6, verse 5 and Psalm chapter 73, verse 7 concerning the impact that evil has on the hearts and imaginations of man...

> *"And God saw that the wickedness of man was great in the earth, and that every imagination of the thoughts of his heart was only evil continually." {King James Version}*

> *"From their callous hearts comes iniquity; their evil imaginations have no limits." {New International Version - UK}*

Disclosure of the Eternal Gift | 55

*M*ore importantly, Satan promised Eve that if she were to eat the forbidden fruit that they would *"be like God"*. This fact alone implies that Eve was definitely not aware of having been created in the *"image"* and *"likeness"* of God in the first place. There is a distinct possibility that Eve having been created from the rib of Adam viewed herself as being created in the *"likeness of Adam"* rather than being created in the *"likeness of God"*. If this were the case, this could explain Eve's actions in collaborating with Satan by eating the fruit and then encouraging Adam to do likewise, but we shall never know.

Man's authenticity called into question...

*I*t is here that we witness the first instance of Satan offering man something that he already owns and possesses as a *precious gift from God*. Satan offers man the *"Likeness of God"* as a *bargaining chip*. Starting here, we find Satan going about the business of chipping away at man's sense of *"authenticity of being God-like"* and the vision of himself as a *"child of God"*. Satan had begun to lay the foundation of eroding the element of "FREE WILL" that was essential to man's *"individual makeup"* and *"spiritual character"*, by challenging man's knowledge of the ability vested in himself to operate and function in *"God's likeness"* without need of outside direction and intervention.

*W*e see a second instance of this with Jesus, when Satan offers Jesus all of the *"kingdoms of the world"* in exchange, if Jesus would bow down and worship him. *Here again, Satan is attempting to chip away at Jesus' "authenticity of being the Son of God" and "Creator of the heavens and the Earth'", commonly referred to as the "Universe".* The following is recorded in the book of Matthew chapter 4, verses 8 thru 9...

> *"Again, the devil took him to a very high mountain and showed him all the kingdoms of the world and their splendor. 'All this I will give you,' he said, "if you will bow down and worship me.'" {New International Version}*

*S*cripture clearly shows in the book of Colossians chapter 1, verses 16 that the world was created by Jesus and for Jesus...

> *"For by him were all things created, that are in heaven, and that are in earth, visible and invisible, whether they be thrones, or dominions, or principalities, or powers: all things were created by him, and for him:" {King James V.}*

Test of "creature authenticity"...

There is a familiar adage, which is presented in the form of a litmus test or "TEST OF AUTHENTICITY" for determining whether a creature is genuine and of true character or simply an alloy. The adage states...

> "*If it walks like a duck and quacks like a duck, it's a duck!*"

This means the duck should think and behave like a duck, in order for its conscious thoughts and natural behavior to be consistent with a duck's patented creation. When the duck functions in the *"image"* and *"likeness"* of a duck, this lends credence to its authenticity, thereby granting the duck the "CREATOR'S HEAVENLY SEAL OF APPROVAL". This applies to all creatures including man. 2nd Timothy chapter 2, verses 19 thru 21 records the following as a testament to this fact...

> *"But God's firm foundation stands, bearing this seal: "The Lord knows those who are his," and, "Let everyone who names the name of the Lord depart from iniquity."*
>
> *Now in a great house there are not only vessels of gold and silver but also of wood and clay, some for honorable use, some for dishonorable.*
>
> *Therefore, if anyone cleanses himself from what is dishonorable, he will be a vessel for honorable use, set apart as holy, useful to the master of the house, ready for every good work." {English Standard Version}*

This is true for man, Whom God fashioned after Himself in accordance with *Genesis chapter 1, verse 26*. Therefore, man should walk like God *("behave self")* and talk like God *("think")* in order to be considered a man of authenticity like Enoch, whom lived and functioned in God's *"image and likeness"* for 365 years before being translated from a mortal into an immortal without experiencing death.

God's "image and likeness" constitutes God's character!!!
Restoration of God's character constitutes spiritual resurrection!!!

Faith in God, an uncommon characteristic in fallen man...

When we examine our broken relationship with God the Father that was restored through the death-sacrifice of Jesus, we can attribute the downfall of man to a *"lack of faith"*, pointing to man's distrust in the integrity of God's character. The Merriam Webster Dictionary defines *"character"* in the following way...

> *"Character is the way someone thinks, feels, and behaves: someone's personality".*

In essence, the totality of one's *thoughts, feelings and behavior* constitutes one's "CHARACTER" and becomes a living construct for one's "PERSONALITY". Therefore, when we live without an intimate relationship with God based upon His Word, it is impossible to relate to how *God thinks, feels, and behaves toward us*. Once we understand the meaning and significance of *"walking with God"*, we can better appreciate the mercy and grace of God that impact our daily lives.

I find it interesting that the word *"faith"* is recorded in the Bible 231 times, but is only found in the Old Testament twice *(Habakkuk 2:4 & Deuteronomy 32:20)*. This lends special significance to the following scriptural passage recorded in the book of Habakkuk...

> *"Behold, his soul which is lifted up is not upright in him: but the just shall live by his faith."*

The Apostle Paul states the following in 2nd Corinthians chapter 5, verse 7... *"For we walk by faith, not by sight:"* When Adam and Eve sinned due to a lack of faith, man's *"walk with God"* was corrupted, causing *"spiritual death"* to humanity. Adam's and Eve's actions caused humanity to lose its ability to function in Gods *"mental image" (thought life)* and *"functional likeness" (conscious behavior)* resulting in death to man's *"spiritual character"* leading to separation from God.

Call from the Apostle Paul to renew our appointed purpose...

The Apostle Paul knew the heart of God and was more keenly astute concerning the spiritual frailties of men than the other apostles. The following was recorded by Paul in 1st Thessalonians chapter 4, verse 1 concerning the renewal of one's "APPOINTED PURPOSE" in Christ...

> "Finally then, brothers, we ask and encourage you in the Lord Jesus, that as you have received from us **how you must walk and please God**, as you are doing, do so even more." {Holman Christian Standard Version}

Paul was well aware of man's failure of *"God-like character"* and loss of *"appointed purpose"* being fulfilled, when God's *"image"* and *"likeness"* is imperfect in our *"spiritual walk"*. Our renewed spiritual walk was conferred upon us by the grace of Jesus Christ, resulting from His living example which was modeled for our spiritual benefit.

Man's *"renewed spiritual walk"* was made possible by the atoning sacrifice of Jesus, wherein there is no excuse for those *"...whose names **have not** been recorded in the "Book of Life" (Revelation 3:5, 20:12 & 20:15) by the Lamb slain from the foundation of the world."*

The moment-by-moment morphing process that maintained man's *"spiritual walk"* and *"God-like character"* ceased when man was removed from the Spirit culture of the Garden of Eden. This solitary act required Jesus' birth, death, and resurrection as *"Savior"* and *"lamb slain from the foundation of the world"* in order for man to be restored to his *"former state of spiritual dominion"*. Spiritual dominion in Christ is man's state of spiritual salvation. I am utterly convinced that man was created in a *"saved state of spiritual authority"* (*dominion without need of spiritual redemption*) and man would have remained therein, *had they continued to live and function in the image and likeness of God that was ascribed to them at the time of their creation.*

PLEASING GOD IS MAN'S APPOINTED PURPOSE!!!

Man's appointed purpose is to *live* and *walk* in God's *image* and *likeness*, which is to "think" and "behave" like God by operating and functioning in a Christ-like manner. **This pleases God!!!**

"Then God said, 'Let Us make man in Our image,

according to Our likeness; let them have dominion over the fish of the sea, over the birds of the air, and over the cattle, over all the earth and over every creeping thing that creeps on the earth." *{Genesis 1:26}*

Man's walk with God...

The transformative effect of sin fatally altered man's natural *"God-like character"*, affecting man's *"walk with God"*. Sin had a devastating effect on man's personality causing him to immediately begin to comport himself in the *"image"* and *"likeness"* of Satan, rather than the *"image"* and *"likeness"* of God. The *"death"* that God warned Adam and Eve of prior to their eating the forbidden fruit was death to their *"spiritual character"*. *Spiritual character emanates from God and defines our "way of thinking" and our "way of behaving".*

Our walk with God literally translates into how we *"behave ourselves spiritually in the presence of God"* and *"comport ourselves in the presence of man"*. The Strong's Exhaustive Concordance of the Bible provides the following Hebrew translation for the word *"walk"* when used in the context of man *"walking spiritually"* with God:

> *"halak: to go, come, walk, Original Word:* הָלַךְ, *Part of Speech: Verb, Transliteration: halak, Phonetic Spelling: (haw-lak'), Short Definition: go"*

> *"Akin to yalak; a primitive root; to walk (in a great variety of applications, literally and figuratively) -- (all) along, apace, behave (self)...."*

The renowned Matthew Henry *(1662-1714)*, a Presbyterian minister and English commentator on the Bible records the following in his Concise Commentary regarding Enoch's and Noah's walk with God...

Enoch...

> *"To walk with God is to set God always before us, and to act as those that are always under his eye. It is to live a life of communion with God both in ordinances and providences. It is to make God's word our rule and his glory our end in all our actions. It is to make it our*

*constant care and endeavour in every thing to **please God**, and nothing to offend him. It is to comply with his will, to concur with his designs, and to be workers together with him.*"

Noah...

"*He walked with God, as Enoch had done before him. He was not only honest, but devout; he walked, that is, he acted with God, as one always under his eye. He lived a life of communion with God; it was his constant care to conform himself to the will of God, to **please him**, and to approve himself to him.*"

Faith in God's character...

Our *"God-like character"* which is rooted in faith, provides the spiritual foundation for *"**pleasing God**" (Hebrews 11:6)*. This is our *"appointed purpose"*, though few of us are aware of this important, yet simple fact. Many are seeking to **PLEASE GOD** by focusing solely on the *"works"* that are performed in the service of God believing their works to be their *"appointed purpose"*, while failing to understand that their *"works"* are the toils of their *"spiritual and corporate assignments"*. This is the literal meaning of *"faith without works is dead" (James 2:19-21, 2:14-16, 2:24-26)*. Our common purpose is exercising faith in *"God's character"* by embracing His commandments and imitating Jesus in Word and individual deed.

"*Now without faith it is impossible to please God!!! (Heb. 11:6)*"

The authenticity of man's character...

𝒟eath to Adam's and Eve's *"God-like character"* caused all humans to lose their natural willingness and desire to *"operate"* and *"function"* in the *"image"* and *"likeness"* of God. From the very moment that Adam and Eve ate the forbidden fruit from the TREE OF KNOWLEDGE OF GOOD AND EVIL, they began to *"think"* and *"behave"* like Satan, resulting in man *"imitating Satan"* rather than God. Adam and Eve took upon themselves the *"sin-like character"* of the fallen angel Lucifer *(aka Satan),* which replaced the *"God-like character"* that was bestowed in them at the time of their creation. Their transformation in spiritual character confirmed what God had told them would happen in Genesis chapter 2, verse 17. Adam and Eve's character transformation validates *"NATURE'S LAW OF AUTHENTICITY".*

The *"authenticity of character"* that is found intact in all of the "ORIGINAL CREATURES" at the time of their creation was verifiable. We know this to be true from observations of the following creatures found in Genesis chapter 1, verses 20 thru 26 *(including the angels)*...

- *"If it walks upright and exercises imagination and dominion like a man, it's a man"!*
- *"If it is a ministering spirit and a messenger to man, it's an angel!*
- *"If it screams and soars like an eagle, it's an eagle!*
- *"If it swims like a whale and sings like a whale, it's a whale!*
- *"If it hums like a bee and stings like a bee, it's a bee!*
- *"If it gallops like a horse and snorts like a horse, it's a horse!*
- *"If it purrs like a cat and claws like a cat, it's a cat!*
- *"If it's shrewd and cunning like a serpent, it's a serpent!*

At the outset of creation this was true for the winged creatures, sea creatures, cattle, creeping things, beasts, and man. But not far into the creation narrative recorded in Genesis, we have record of a catastrophic incident taking place in Heaven between the angels of God that had a devastating effect on the *"behavior"* and *"character"* of the entire family of man, including the serpent species. The following account is recorded in the books of Revelation and Isaiah...

Revelation chapter 12, verses 7 thru 9:
"And there was war in heaven:
Michael and his angels going forth to war with the dragon;
and the dragon warred and his angels;

And they prevailed not,
neither was their place found any more in heaven.

And the great dragon was cast down, the old serpent,

he that is called the Devil and Satan,
the deceiver of the whole world;

he was cast down to the earth,
and his angels were cast down with him."
{American Standard Version}

<u>*Isaiah chapter 14, verses 12 thru 17*</u>:
"How art thou fallen from heaven,
O Lucifer, son of the morning!

How art thou cut down to the ground,
who didst weaken the nations!

For thou hast said in thine heart,
'I will ascend into heaven,
I will exalt my throne above the stars of God;
I will sit also upon the mount of the congregation,
in the sides of the north.

I will ascend above the heights of the clouds;
I will be like the Most High.'
Yet thou shalt be brought down to hell, to the sides of the pit.

They that see thee shall narrowly look upon thee
and consider thee, saying,

'Is this the man that made the earth to tremble,
that did shake kingdoms,

Who made the world like a wilderness
And overthrew its cities,
Who did not allow his prisoners to go home?'"
{21st Century King James Version}

In the aftermath of this incident all of the heavenly and earthly creatures were faced with the "TEST OF AUTHENTICITY" that validated their true identity and relationship to God. When put to the test, only the <u>angels loyal to Lucifer</u>, <u>serpent</u>, and <u>man</u> would fail the "AUTHENTICITY TEST" that identifies "UNCHARACTERISTIC BEHAVIOR".

Of the terrestrial and celestial creatures, only man was created in the *"image"* and *"likeness"* of God, which should have caused man to behave like the Son of God. So the question for man is…

<u>*Does it walk like God and talk like God? If so, it's a child of God!!! But if it walks like a devil and talks like a devil… It's a child of Satan!!!*</u>

Jesus models man's "spiritual walk with God"…

God the Father dispatched the "WORD" into the Earth in the person of Jesus in order for Christ to walk among humanity as *"Emmanuel"* *(Matthew 1:23)*. A critical assignment in Jesus' mission was to demonstrate how man is to *"think"* in God's *"mental image"* and *"behave"* in God's *"functional likeness"*, thus realigning man with his appointed purpose of **pleasing God**. Satan would have us believe that our *"purpose"* is something other than what the Lord has stated in His Word. Satan dupes us into believing that we have *"individual purposes"* that are to be sought out during the course of our lifetimes, while waiting on God to make the grand disclosure. Many of us are waiting around for God to set an appointment to discuss our futures, when in fact nowhere in Scripture or human history do we have record of man approaching God for an assignment and receiving an interview. God chooses man according to *God's purpose;* man does not choose God for man's purposes, this would be sacrilegious and satanic.

God created man in the human form of Adam and Eve. They were representative of all humanity *(present and future)* at the time of their creation. The following is recorded in Genesis chapter 5, verse 2…

> *"Male and female created he them; and blessed them, and called their name Adam, in the day when they were created.*
> *{King James Version}*

God created the *"Adam family"* with the intent of man *"walking with Him"* as Enoch did. Enoch's *"walk with God"* demonstrated how the family of man was to operate and function in the *"spiritual image"* and *"functional likeness"* of God. *"Enoch's walk"* **pleased God** so much that Enoch did not experience death *(Hebrews chapter 11, verse 5)*. God's divine purpose for man is vested in the creative provision that ensures man the *"dominion"* granted by God over all the Earth and every creature created therein! Man's "EARTHLY DOMINION" is a divine grant of *"Spiritual Authority"* that is established upon man's ability to operate in *"God's image"* and function in *"God's likeness"*, which translates into our having the *"natural ability"* and *"human will"* to *"think"* and *"behave"* like God, thereby equipping us to do God's will. We have proof of this in the book of Colossians chapter 1, verse 10...

> *"That you may walk (live and conduct yourselves) in a manner worthy of the Lord, **fully pleasing to Him** and **desiring to please Him in all things**, bearing fruit in every good work and steadily growing and increasing in and by the knowledge of God [with fuller, deeper, and clearer insight, acquaintance, and recognition]." {Amplified Version}*

When we fail to operate in *"God's image"* and function in *"God's likeness"*, we are rendered powerless and incapable of exercising dominion over the fallen angels and subordinate creatures of the Earth, wherein we imitate Satan and resort to dominating one another. We see first proof of this with Adam and Eve's acquiescence to the serpent by eating the fruit that had been forbidden by God. Later we have record of Cain exercising dominion over his brother Abel by murdering him *(Genesis 4:1-9)*.

Man's "appointed purpose" twisted and confused by Satan...

Far too many Christians confuse their "APPOINTED PURPOSE" with their "MISSIONARY ASSIGNMENTS". Satan does this through the teaching of false doctrines, whereby we are left spiritually confused and lacking the realization that *"all humans share a common purpose"* *(Romans 8:28)*, which was disclosed at the time of man's creation.

All things of a given type are formed with the intent of functioning in a unique manner, conforming to the laws of *"intelligent design"*. In all areas of intelligent design, *"form follows function"* and as a general rule purpose comes first. Every natural creation is God's intellectual property, similar to inventions, patents, and copyrights for publishing that are created by man. All things conform to this law without deviation. This is true for every design, be it an automobile, airplane, or a pair of scissors. Everything in existence is formed in accordance with the purpose that it was intended to fulfill and man is no exception *(Rom. 8:28)*. *It would be utterly futile to create and produce something with the intent of deciding its purpose after it has been brought into existence.* <u>THIS IS SIMPLY LUDICROUS AND MAKES NO SENSE!!!</u>

Our *"missionary assignments"* vary from person to person and are not limited to a spiritual calling as one might think. There are many societal roles that we honor in life in addition to a myriad of secular vocations that qualify as *"corporate assignments"*. There is also the obligation involving special relationships toward our neighbors, wherein we all are assigned to be our *"brother's keeper"*, <u>although many would believe this to be something other than an assignment</u>.

If one is called by God to preach, prophesize, or evangelize, Satan tells us these assignments are their appointed purpose. The same is true for those in the secular realm of entertainment, sports, business, medicine, law, etc. When in fact these assignments are conferred upon individuals by God, based upon their natural gifts and talents for the purpose of servicing the institutions upon which society is structured.

In fact, this scenario perfectly describes the foundation upon which *"Darwin's Theory of Evolution by Natural Selection"* is established. Darwin's Theory advances the notion that *"production comes first"*, leaving *"purpose"* to be determined by the environment in the aftermath, rather than by *"a creator"* at the time of conception. Darwin observed the reproductive unfolding of *"God's Master Creations"* and the process was dubbed *"Evolution"*, *a theory that teaches all life originated from a single cell organism.* When in fact all forms of life, even as simple as a twig of plant life versus animal and human life resulted from *"intelligent design"*, supporting the natural law that in all cases *"form follows function"* and *"purpose comes first"*.

When God said… *"Let Us make man in Our image, according to Our likeness…"* man's purpose had already been established and was not left to chance, pending future determination. Our "COMMON PURPOSE" as set out in the beginning was very clear, though our "INDIVIDUAL ASSIGNMENTS" are diverse and uniquely different. The differences in our individual assignments are based upon the *natural talents* and *spiritual gifts* that God has vested in each of us for the desired purpose of carrying out particular *missionary* and *corporate* works during our brief stay on Earth and those assignments can vary by individual.

Spirit of distraction, an enemy to man's appointed purpose...

Often times we are led astray by Satan when we submit ourselves to a *"spirit of distraction"* that tells us to wait on our purpose rather than *"modeling the creature that God created for the rest of the world to see"* and this is why Jesus had to be born to walk the Earth as a man. Sadly enough, once distracted we go in search of what Satan tells us God wants us to be, void of what God has already stated in His Word. When this happens, we fall prey to the ever increasing and subtle devices of Satan that work in tandem with the world to reshape us into the *"image and likeness of Satan"* rather than the divine *"image and likeness of God"* that Jesus lived and died to model for our example. The following is recorded in the book of 1st Corinthians chapter 7, verse 35...

> *"This I say for your own benefit; not to put a restraint upon you, but to promote what is appropriate and to secure undistracted devotion to the Lord." {New American Standard Bible}*

If we are to understand God's intended purpose for our lives, it is imperative for us to understand what it means to be *"created in the image and likeness of God"*, which is recorded in Genesis chapter 1, verse 26. Once understood, we can begin to exercise the *"God-given dominion"* blessed upon us as "CHILDREN OF GOD", when we begin to "SPIRITUALLY BEHAVE OURSELVES" in accordance with the commandments of God. For example, Saul of Tarsus was predestined and chosen to become the Apostle Paul in order for the Heavenly Father's will and purpose to be communicated to *all men* in the aftermath of Jesus' walk with us. Of all the apostles, Paul was supremely blessed and anointed to receive and comprehend the "DIVINE MYSTERY" and heavenly gift of Jesus Christ as One Who had come to model the *"divine character of God"* in man. The following is recorded in the book of 1st Thessalonians chapter 4, verse 1…

> *"Finally then, brothers, we ask and encourage you in the Lord Jesus, that as you have received from us **<u>how you must walk and please God</u>**, as you are doing, do so even more." {Holman Christian Standard Bible}*

God's plan and promise for our lives…

The Lord will always lead us into His perfect *"Time"* and *"Season"* in the things promised, which will always come to past because God said it. Far too many times we receive an announcement from God as did Abraham and Sarah *(Genesis 17:1 thru 21:3)*, but in many instances we are not patient enough to wait on God to decree what He has made known to us in advance. The biblical account of Abraham and Sarah details a promise from God that Abraham and Sarah would give birth to a child in their old age.

This wonderful patriarchal story should serve as a good example to all of us concerning the promises that we receive from God concerning future hopes and dreams in our lives. Often times we confuse the *"announcement of the promise"* with a *"promise unfulfilled"* that is yet to come to past. God's promises… like all things of God do not come to past until God speaks them into being and then they are so.

Therefore, when we are thinking about the things that God purposes to happen in our lives we are to remember and be guided by *"Numbers 23:19"*, realizing that God does nothing without making an announcement first and God never fail on His promises…

> *"God is not a man, that he should lie, or a son of man, that he should repent. Has he said, and will he not do it? Or has he spoken, and will he not fulfil it?"*

To better understand how God brings things to past, we only have to look at the method and creative model used by God to create the world. The whole of all things brought into existence were either spoken by the Word of the God *(Genesis 1:1-14)* or formed by God's hands *(Psalm 119:73 & Job 10:8-9)*. There were 15 acts of creation performed by God in 6 days resulting in the creation of the world and along with all of the creatures, wherein 14 of those acts of creation were spoken into being except man *(Genesis 1:3 thru 27):*

> "God said <u>let there be</u>... light, heaven, earth, vegetation, plants, trees, sun, moon, stars, sea creatures, wing creatures, cattle, creeping things and beasts." "Then God said, <u>Let Us make Man</u>..."

Then God fashioned man with His hands before He rested on the 7th day. In essence, everything in existence was spoken into being except man, whom He fashioned. God is the "HEAVENLY SPEAKER"... In the moment that He speaks, that which is spoken comes to past!!!

We are to listen to those that God has placed around us to serve

as arbiters in our lives, but ultimately we are to "HEAR HIM"!!!

Often times we listen to others and take a *"right now"* approach with God, wherein we want God to move at the speed of our desires, as if our wants should produce a miraculous result. Miracles are a *"result without a process"*, which means they happen instantaneously, wherein all other things result by means of a process. There's an old adage that was spoken in times past... *"Rome was not built in a day"*. God's scriptural response is neither was the world that was created by Him in 6 days. God is in the process of building us into the persons and spiritual vessels that He created us to be for Him, in order to bring about changes in future times and places. God brings things to past in *"His space & time"* that have been preordained to effect changes in *"His due season"* and He employs laws of governess to bring about desired results.

Disclosure of the Eternal Gift | 69

God's established laws have been put into place to harmonize the Universe, including us. In *"special times"* God will suspend certain laws temporarily in order to perform miracles for the uplifting of *"His Kingdom"* and in doing so, He brings honor unto Himself. God has put forth *"laws of progression"* that governs each of our futures relative to the things that He has planned for us. Only God knows when the work is to begin and when it will be completed. In the meantime, He may accelerate the *"law of progression"* in our lives and produce a miracle that only He can understand. Until then patience should prevail in order for us not to end up like Abraham & Sarah...

Whatever Adam would become, we are...

All creatures were endowed with the *"seed-of-self"* principle at the time of creation. This reproductive attribute enabled each creature to replicate itself in accordance with the patented *"image"* and *"likeness"* conferred upon it by God.

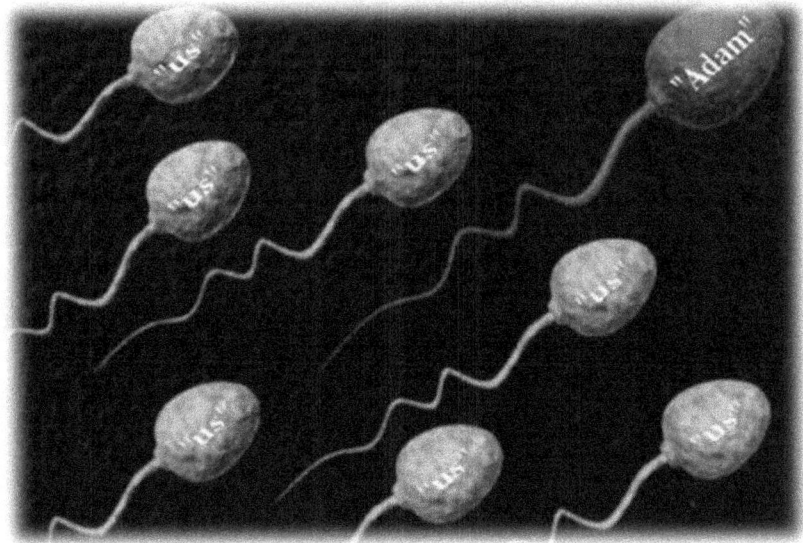

This inherent feature was encoded into each of the master creatures. This process was the means by which each of those creatures *(male and female)* would reproduce in the *"image"* and *"likeness"* of their own kind. After God created the *winged creatures, sea creatures, cattle, creeping things, beasts, and man,* He allowed procreation to abound based upon the *"seed-of-self principle"* that was genetically encoded in each of those creatures. The Holy Scriptures record the offsprings of those creatures entering into the ark of Noah two-by-two prior to the commencement of the great flood *(Genesis 7:1-3)*.

By virtue of this unique design and reproductive attribute, every creature issuing from the *"original"* or *"master creature"* of its kind would inherit the genetic information and hereditary characteristics of the first. This feature defines the *"character"* and *"common purpose"* within its own kind. This awesome design feature, although masterful would result in… <u>**Whatever Adam would become, we are!!!**</u>

Man… God's emissary and ambassador to the Earth…

At the very outset of human creation, Adam and Eve were securely tucked away in the sanctity of God, being eternally sealed in the glory and innocence blessed upon them by God. The divine nature of God clothed their hearts, souls, and minds. Man having been created in the *"image"* and *"likeness"* of God was established as God's emissary, ambassador and steward to the Earth.

<u>**The supreme role and duty of man was to administer the "Kingdom of Heaven" in the Earth.**</u>

The *sea creatures, wing creatures, cattle, creeping things, beasts* and *serpent* were all subject to man's dominion, stewardship and spiritual authority prior to the fall *(Luke 4:5-7)*. The family of Adam was created in a *"saved state of spiritual authority"*, endowing them with the blessing of earthly dominion that was conferred upon them at the very outset of creation in conformance with their purpose.

The process of making man was unlike any other in creation. God appears to have saved His creative best for last, when He chose to create man on the sixth day after the other works of creation were finished. The fashioning of man involved the greatest of godly care and creative detail, especially when considering the vital and critical role that man was to play in managing the "UNFOLDING OF GOD'S MASTER CREATIONS". Unfortunately, the *"unfolding of creation"* is being academically taught and presented to the world as "Evolution". The role of steward required man to perform at the highest creative and managerial level, so God fashioned man in His *"mental image"* and *"functional likeness"* and endowed him with *"freewill"* with this specific purpose in mind.

Man... God's special creation...

Man being created in the *"mental image"* and *"functional likeness"* set man apart from the rest of the creatures, thereby positioning man in a place of preeminence and dominion that was all his own. The creation of man must have been a very simple feat relative to that of the other creatures for the simple reason that God used Himself as a creative model for man, wherein He had to exercise greater imagination to form the *wing creatures, sea creatures, cattle, creeping things,* and *beasts,* simply because their creative models were nonexistent.

I imagine the sixth day being the most special of all the days in creation, one cushioned with anticipation, grace and ease. A relatively mild day compared to the rest, wherein *celebrated expectation* and *partial relaxation* was all rolled into one. A day bound in splendid perfection, wherein man would become God's crowning earthly achievement. The creation of the heavens and the Earth that had taken place in six days *("six spaces of creative activity")* was now finished. God was well pleased and poised in final preparation for retirement to the seventh space of the Sabbath, wherein rest would abound for eternity. Yet, unbeknownst and quite unfortunate for man, drama was unfolding in heaven that would result in deadly consequences on Earth.

Man... God's Master Creation and genuine article...

Adam created special as God's *"Master Creation" and "Genuine" Article"*, prior to the creation of Eve. Adam is the *"model"* and *"master copy"* of all humans that would come after him. From the loins of Adam would all humans be born as replicas of Adam's DNA.

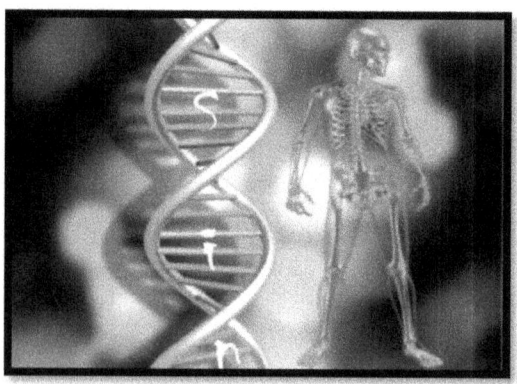

The DNA of Adam would determine his offspring's hereditary characteristics by providing the genetic information for instructing the human body, mind and spirit in its reproductive design, form and function for each generation of offsprings that would succeed him.

Man... The genuine article debased and fallen...

Adam is indeed the *"genuine article"* and there is no evidence of *"alloy"* present in him. The American Heritage Dictionary defines *"genuine"* as *"something authentic, pure and original stock"* and goes on to define *"alloy"* as *"something debased by the addition of an inferior element"*. Adam was created genuine before being reduced to the level of an alloy, resulting from his willful act of disobedience to

God, when he ate the forbidden fruit from the *"tree of knowledge of good and evil"*.

This monumental error in Adam's judgment opened the door for the *"inferior element of sin"* to enter into his DNA, causing debilitating change and permanent alteration to the human spirit *(Matthew 5:3)*. The far reaching consequences of Adam's actions caused all that would be born of him to inherit a *"contaminated human spirit"* that existed long before their conception, causing all to be born *"in sin"*.

The inferior element of sin in man...

Jesus alludes to *"man's contaminated spirit"* in His *"Sermon on the mount"*, which focused on the eight spiritual blessing commonly referred to as the *"The Beatitudes"*. Jesus began the sermon by making reference to the *"poor in spirit"* as the first of the eight *"spiritual blessings"* that I refer to as *"kingdom blessings"*. The following is recorded in the book of Matthew chapter 5, verses 1 thru 3...

> *"And seeing the multitudes, He went up on a mountain, and when He was seated His disciples came to Him. Then He opened His mouth and taught them, saying:*
>
> *'Blessed are the poor in spirit, for theirs is the Kingdom of Heaven.'" {21st Century King James Version}*

To understand this Scripture it is important to realize that Jesus is referring to the *"human spirit"* that we inherited from Adam, which was contaminated prior to our births by sin. The spirit of man is the *"reservoir of human will"* from which springs all of one's thoughts, emotions and conscious acts of behavior. It is from within the *"spirit"* that one's nature and character is revealed. Adherence to the Word of God causes us to diminish in *"human spirit"* as we grow in the *"Spirit of the Lord"*, which is our *"Comforter"* and *"Holy Spirit"*.

Jesus born human to model man's special creation...

The fall of Adam was the catastrophic incident that rocked creation at its core and brought great displeasure to God. It is here in the book of Matthew chapter 1, verse 23 that we witness God dispatching the *"Word"* into the Earth in the *"person of baby Jesus"*, in order for the Son of God to be born a man and walk among men as *"Emmanuel"*.

> *"Behold, a virgin shall be with child, and shall bring forth a son, and they shall call his name Emmanuel, which is interpreted, God with us." {King James Version}*

God the Father birthed His Son Jesus into the world to die for the sins of man and become the *"restorative sacrifice"* for the original Adam, *"God's Master Creation"*. Jesus is the *"Last Adam"* (1st Corinthians 15:45). He was sent to restore the *"God-like character"* of the descendants of Adam, whom were made spiritual alloys through sin and were no longer fit to serve as stewards over the managerial affairs of the Earth, the Earth being the real property of God. One of the primary roles in Jesus' ministry was that He would humanly model man's special creation, *which is embodied in the* *"image"* *and* *"likeness"* *of God*. Jesus did this through living example, wherein He modeled how man is to *"think"* and *"behave"* as God's appointed representative over all the creatures and managerial affairs of the Earth.

God with us...

Jesus was not born into the world to walk as God of Heaven in "GOD'S GLORY". He was purposed to walk as man in "MAN'S GLORY", *performing physical healing, walking on water, raising the dead, etc.*. Jesus modeled the "SPIRITUAL DOMINION" that was vested in Adam prior to *"the fall of man"*. Jesus was preordained with *supernatural power* to do miraculous things during His 3½ year's ministry <u>*as a man*</u>, in order for <u>man to believe in man's special abilities and creation</u>. It was not until after Jesus' death and resurrection that He walked as God in God's glory!!! The miracles that were performed by Jesus, the *"Last Adam"* prior to His death were done under the *dominion and power* ascribed by God to the *"First Adam"* in accordance with man's *original glory* and *stewardship* prior to *the fall*. The following was recorded by the Apostle John as a testament to this fact...

> *"Most assuredly, I say to you, he who believes in Me, the*

works that I do he will do also; and greater works than these he will do, because I go to My Father." {John 14:12 - New King James Version}

*H*erein is the *"fundamental character of God"* made manifest in the restored man through Jesus Christ. It is here that we, the offsprings of the first Adam see the *"mirror image"* and *"perfect likeness"* of the original man having been birthed in Jesus… *"The Last Adam"*. <u>Jesus is man's spiritual model of the first Adam restored in Himself!!!</u>

*S*alvation is the means by which our *"conscious thoughts" (mental image)* and *"natural behavior" (spiritual likeness)* being noted in the book of Genesis chapter 1, verse 26 has been restored under the blood covenant of our Lord and Savior, Jesus Christ. I find it interesting that Jesus humbly referred to Himself as *"Son of man" (last Adam & offspring of David)*, whereas others reverently referred to Him as *"Son of God" (The Divine Christ and Lord)*. The Apostle Paul states the following in the book of Romans chapter 5, verse 19…

"For as by one man's disobedience many were made sinners, so by the obedience of One shall many be made righteous." {21st Century King James Version}

*T*hrough the death, resurrection, and ascension of Christ Jesus, man was enabled by the empowerment of the Holy Spirit to function with the *"spiritual authority"* required to *"walk with God"* as did Enoch in accordance with God's purpose. Enoch **_pleased God_**, causing him not to experience death and be translated into an immortal blessed with "ETERNAL LIFE". Moses and the Apostle Paul recorded the following in Genesis chapter 5, verses 22 thru 24 & Hebrews chapter 11, verse 5…

"And after the birth of Methuselah, <u>Enoch walked with God</u> 300 years and fathered sons and daughters. So Enoch's life lasted 365 years. <u>Enoch walked with God</u>, and he was not there, because God took him." {Holman Christian Standard version}

"By faith, Enoch was taken away so that he did not experience death, and he was not to be found because God

*took him away. <u>For prior to his transformation he was approved</u>, **having pleased God**."* {Holman Christian Standard version}

It is not coincidental that the following would be spoken by the Apostle Peter in the book of 2nd Peter chapter 1, verse 17 thru 18 concerning Jesus after He had fulfilled everything that God the Father had purposed for Him to accomplish on Earth, for He like Enoch and Noah **pleased God**.

> *"For He received from God the Father honor and glory when such a voice came to Him from the Excellent Glory "This is My beloved Son, in whom **I am well pleased**."*
>
> *And we heard this voice which came from heaven when we were with Him on the holy mountain."* {New King James Version}

The Apostle Paul recorded the following concerning God's purpose for man in the books of Romans chapter 8, verses 28 thru 30 and Ephesians chapter 1, verses 7 thru 11…

> *"And we know that in all things God works for the good of those who love him, who have been <u>called according to his purpose</u>.*
>
> *For those God foreknew he also predestined to be <u>conformed to the image of his Son</u>, that he might be the firstborn among many brothers and sisters. And those he predestined, he also called; those he called, he also justified; those he justified, he also glorified."* {New International translation}
>
> *"In him we have redemption through his blood, the forgiveness of sins, in accordance with the riches of God's grace that he lavished on us.*
>
> *With all wisdom and understanding, he made known to us the <u>mystery of his will</u> <u>according to **his good pleasure**</u>, which he <u>purposed in Christ</u>, to be put into effect when the times reach their fulfillment to bring unity to all things in*

heaven and on earth under Christ.

In him we were also chosen, having been predestined according to the plan of him who works out everything in conformity with the purpose of his will," {New International Version}

God's commandments governs our spiritual walk...

The *"Two Great Commandments"* quoted by Jesus represent a summation of the Ten Commandments, relative to how we are to *"spiritually behavior ourselves" ("walk spiritually")* in relationship to God and man. When morally comprehended and spiritually understood the Ten Commandments point to our *individual behavior* and *personal conduct*, which is our *"Corban"* or *"offering of blessing"* to God *(Mark 7:11)*, *that translates into goodwill toward our fellow man. Our behavior informs our purpose and signifies our character, and should in all cases reflect a true representation of the character of our Lord and Savior Jesus Christ, in whom we are to imitate!* The following is recorded in the book of Matthew chapter 22, verses 35 thru 40...

"One of them was an authority on the law. So he tested Jesus with a question. "Teacher," he asked, "which is the most important commandment in the Law?"

Jesus replied, "Love the Lord your God with all your heart and with all your soul. Love him with all your mind." (Deuteronomy 6:5)

This is the first and most important commandment. And the second is like it.

'Love your neighbor as you love yourself.' (Leviticus 19:18) Everything that is written in the Law and the Prophets is based on these two commandments." {New International Reader's Version}

Behavior and conduct, every creature's "offering of blessing"...

One would think that Adam would have known and understood that his individual behavior and personal conduct was his *"offering of blessing"* to God and that for him to comport himself in less than an obedient manner would have been *sorely displeasing* in the eyes of God. Adam's transgression caused man to lose sight of this very fact, which explains why Jesus taught the disciples to pray the following in the Lord's Prayer… *"Our Father who are in heaven…", "Your will be done."* Jesus was referring to God's will being done on Earth in us as it was done in Heaven and on Earth in Himself. *Our "freewill" when "aligned" with our "appointed purpose" causes us to do God's will, which brings glory and tremendous pleasure to God!*

It is interesting to note that God's will was done in all of the earthly creatures except man with *one notable exception*. The behavior that is demonstrated by the *winged creatures, sea creatures, cattle, creeping things, and beasts* was consistent with their creation model, which characterizes their behavior in conformance with their purpose. This is true with respect to all the other creatures except the serpent, which in this particular case is the notable exception *(Rev. 12:9)*.

Scripture informs us that God placed a horrible curse upon the serpent for colluding with Satan to deceive Eve and Adam into eating the forbidden fruit from the *"tree of knowledge of good and evil"*. The serpent's conduct and behavior was as *"offering of blessing"* to Satan, which violated its appointed purpose and sorely displeased God…

> *"Then the LORD God said to the woman, 'What is this that you have done?' The woman said, 'The serpent deceived me, and ate.'*
>
> *The LORD God said to the serpent, 'Because you have done this, cursed are you above all livestock and above all beasts of the field; on your belly you shall go, and dust you shall eat all the days of your life.*
>
> *I will put enmity between you and the woman, and between your offspring and her offspring; he shall bruise your head, And you shall bruise his heel.'" {Gen. 3:14-15} {English Standard Version}*

A case can be made that the serpent was a *"walking"*, *"talking"*, *"highly intelligent, appealing creature"* that was cursed by God to undergo *"amputation of its limbs" (Genesis 3:13-15) and be rendered "eternally mute"*. The serpent violated its godly appointed purpose of PLEASING GOD when it participated in the satanic scheme of deceiving the world's first humans. The serpent used its cunning and deceitful character to entice Eve and Adam into committing the "ORIGINAL SIN".

All creatures, bound by God's appointed purpose…

Jesus being "The Creator Of All Things" knew and understood that everything has a godly appointed purpose, that even the animals are bound by in the Earth *(Ecclesiastes 3:1)*. More importantly, Jesus understood that when a man's "FREE WILL" is spiritually aligned with his "APPOINTED PURPOSE" *that his vertical and horizontal relationships are spiritually balanced.* Jesus also knew that if a man's will is weak, so is his sense of godly appointed purpose. So Jesus taught His disciples the Lord's Prayer, charging them to teach it to their followers in order for *"their will"* *(freewill)* to be realigned with their *"godly appointed purpose"* of *"doing God's will"*. Man's appointed purpose is fulfilled when "OUR FREEWILL" is exercised to do "GOD'S WILL" irrespective of our personal wishes. The following is recorded in the book of Matthew chapter 6, verses 9 thru 10…

> *"In this manner, therefore, pray: Our Father in heaven, Hallowed be Your name. Your kingdom come. Your will be done. On earth as it is in heaven." {New King James Version}*

The element of freewill is unique in its execution for the simple reason that it enables man to use his mind *(Romans 8:5-7)* as a faithful servant to instruct him in all areas of human behavior. *The rational mind of man was* purposed to function as a servant to man, instead of man becoming a servant to his rational mind. Unfortunately, this is exactly what happened when man sinned by using the freewill vested in Adam and Eve to willfully disobey God's commandment.

The unadulterated freewill of humans prior to Adam's fall provided man the autonomy of thought for making conscious and prudent decisions regarding issues that were consistent with God's will, relative to man's appointed purpose in the Earth *(Ecclesiastes 12:13)*. On the other hand, the *compromised freewill of humans* after Adam's fall resulted in a *"codependent thought deliberation process"*, which linked man to a *"subordinate spirit" (Satan),* who is counter to God and destructive to man's appointed purpose in the Earth realm.

Lucifer's introduction to Eve as the serpent...

Very early in creation, we see man's introduction to a second master, *the fallen angel Lucifer.* Lucifer was cast out of Heaven into the Earth, wherein he adopted a new identity and persona. Lucifer did two things to disguise himself upon entering into the Earth realm. One, he took upon himself the new name of *"Satan"* in addition to entering into the serpent. The serpent served as a quite capable and compatible accomplice and by all accounts an agreeable bodily host.

Satan *(formally the fallen angel Lucifer)* then introduced himself to Eve as the serpent and cleverly convinces her to believe that the freewill granted her by God afforded her the "FREEDOM" and "RIGHT" to do as she pleased *"irrespective of God's commandment"* (Gen. 3:1-5) and Eve wittingly convinced Adam of the same. Satan used this opportunity to trick Eve into persuading Adam to violate the "ETERNAL LIFE COVENANT" that Adam had entered into with God prior to Eve's creation, thereby bringing destruction upon the human temple and causing death to come upon the entire human family.

Satan approaches Eve in the "image and likeness" of a serpent...

Many have asked... *why did Satan approach Eve about eating the fruit from the tree of knowledge of good and evil instead of Adam?* Satan knew that Adam had *"living proof"* that God was the *"Creator of the Universe"* and that Eve did not. Therefore, Satan used the serpent's personality and Eve's lack of faith in God's Word to carry out his plan. Eve's failure to trust in God as *"Creator"* without the need of proof to corroborate *"God's authenticity as Creator"* was similar to the Apostle Thomas' lack of faith in the Lord's resurrection following His crucifixion. The Apostle Thomas' disbelief challenged

Jesus' *authenticity as the Redeemer and "lamb slain from the foundation of the world" (Revelation 13:8)*. We have biblical record of this account in the book of John chapter 20, verses 25, 26, 27 and 29...

> *"So the other disciples told him, 'We have seen the Lord But' he said to them, 'Unless I see the nail marks in his hands and put my finger where the nails were, and put my hand into his side, I will not believe.'*
>
> *A week later his disciples were in the house again, and Thomas was with them. Though the doors were locked, Jesus came and stood among them and said, 'Peace be with you!' Then he said to Thomas, 'Put your finger here; see my hands. Reach out your hand and put it into my side. Stop doubting and believe.' {New International Version}*

The inventory...

The Apostle Thomas, one of the twelve disciples that walked with Jesus feels it necessary to perform an inventory or checklist of sorts to qualify Jesus. Thomas' checklist is similar to the inventory that was presumably performed by Adam, when he was given the assignment by God of naming the original animals. The only difference between Adam's inventory and that of the Apostle Thomas is Adam's inventory was initiated on behalf of God with emphasis being placed on "ACCOUNTABILITY" for the purpose of "PLEASING GOD". Unlike Thomas who required proof from God in order to be faithful. Unfortunately, the inventory that was initiated by the Apostle Thomas was performed for the sole purpose of fact checking Jesus' resurrection, which had been foretold by Jesus in the presence of the Apostle Thomas along with the other apostles prior to Jesus' death.

The Apostle Thomas required evidence in the form of itemized proof of Jesus' death wounds before believing that Jesus had risen from the dead. The following is recorded in the book of Mark chapter 8, verse 31...

> *"Then Jesus began to teach them that the Son of Man must suffer many things and that he would be rejected by the*

> *Jewish elders, the leading priests, and the teachers of the law. He told them that the Son of Man must be killed and then rise from the dead after three days." {New Century Version}*

As the news began to spread of Jesus' resurrection, the Apostle Thomas refused to believe that Jesus had risen from the dead, even after the other apostles told him they had spent time with Jesus. Instead, Thomas demanded proof of His resurrection, later asking Jesus to show him the spike marks in His hands and the hole in His side.

> *"Jesus said to him, 'Thomas, because you have seen Me, you have believed. Blessed are those who have not seen and yet have believed.'"*

It is here in the book of John chapter 20, verse 29 that we have record of the Apostle Thomas requiring proof to corroborate the reports given by Mary Magdalene and the other apostles of Jesus' resurrection. The same is true of Eve, who was last to be created. Eve had no proof of God as "THE CREATOR" *(Genesis 1:1)* as did Adam, so she chose to believe Satan's false accusations rather than God' Word.

Prior to Eve's creation, God brought every living creature to Adam for him to name them and Eve was not included in Adam's inventory, for Eve had not yet been created. After accounting for all of the creatures and completing his assignment, God induced Adam into a deep sleep and removed one of his ribs, which was used to create Eve. Adam awoke from his sleep only to discover a new creature in his presence that was not included in his inventory and named her "Eve". The following is recorded in the book of Genesis chapter 2, verses 21 thru 22…

> *"And the LORD God caused a deep sleep to fall upon Adam, and he slept: and he took one of his ribs, and closed up the flesh instead thereof; And the rib, which the LORD God had taken from man, made he a woman, and brought*

her unto the man." *{King James Version}*

Proof required as evidence in the absence of faith...

Eve's creation is evidentiary proof to Adam that God is Creator of all things in Heaven and Earth. Yet Eve has no proof and Satan is well aware of this fact when he decided to approach Eve. So Satan used Eve's lack of evidentiary knowledge to create ambiguity and doubt about God. Satan challenged Eve rather than Adam based upon her potential lack of faith in God as "THE CREATOR". *God having authored the original covenant, authenticated Himself as "THE CREATOR" and Eve was not included in that process!!!* Eve's *"lack of "covenant knowledge"* and *"authenticity of God as Creator"* allowed Satan to shake Eve at her foundation and he succeeded in using that *"lack of knowledge"* to coax her into sin.

In the book of 1ˢᵗ Peter chapter 3, verse 7 the Apostle Peter refers to the *"woman"* as the *"weaker vessel" (according to knowledge)*.

> *"Likewise, ye husbands, dwell with them according to knowledge, giving honour unto the wife, as unto the weaker vessel, and as being heirs together of the grace of life; that your prayers be not hindered." {King James Version}*

Sin used as a tool of spiritual subversion to bind man...

Satan's goal is to use sin as a spiritual weapon to invade the human temple of God and he used the woman as proxy to influence Adam to grant access. Adam and Eve's willful act of disobedience allowed the human temple to be invaded and defiled, resulting in man being reduced to a *"spiritual alloy"*, thus placing Satan in a strategic position to take complete control of the managerial affairs of the Earth.

The administrative headquarters of the Earth is not a physical place as one might think, but a virtual place of spiritual administration *(good and bad)* that is domiciled in the mind of man. Therefore, Satan being a spirit had to gain entry into the body with access to the mind of man to take full control of man's will. This process is referred to in

Scripture as... *"Binding up the strong man"*. The following is recorded in the book of Mark chapter 3, verses 22 thru 27 regarding the authority by which Jesus is casting demons out of the people...

> *"And the scribes who came down from Jerusalem said, 'He has Beelzebub,' and, 'By the ruler of the demons He casts out demons.' So He called them to Himself and said to them in parables: 'How can Satan cast out Satan?*
>
> *If a kingdom is divided against itself, that kingdom cannot stand. And if a house is divided against itself, that house cannot stand. And if Satan has risen up against himself, and is divided, he cannot stand, but has an end.*
>
> *No one can enter a strong man's house and plunder his goods, <u>unless he first binds the strong man</u>. And then he will plunder his house.'" {New King James Version}*

Satan's plan was ingenious; man would be introduced to an alien form of knowledge that would alter his human nature and contaminate his human spirit. The *"knowledge of good"* would cause man to be filled with vanity and self-righteousness leading to self-destruction. The *"knowledge of evil"* would expose man to the *"works of the flesh"* by which man would destroy one another. The overwhelming power of knowledge of *"good and evil"* would transform man's rational mind, laying spoil to his *"human will"* and *"natural senses"*, wherein man's <u>*"carnal nature"*</u> would overpower his spiritual nature. The following is recorded in James chapter 1, verses 14 thru 15...

> *"But each one is tempted when he is drawn away by his own desires and enticed. Then, when desire has conceived, it gives birth to sin; and sin, when it is full-grown, brings forth death." {New King James Version}*

Man was created with a rational mind that was purposed to function as a *"God-like custodian"* to his spirit nature, only for it to grow in carnality and render man captive by his own sin. Man in this weakened and vulnerable state became ineffective and spiritually incapable of behaving in the *"mental image"* and *"functional likeness"* of God that characterizes man's *"appointed purpose"* and justifies his being.

Satan knew that the *"character of God"* governed man's spiritual walk, and without it man would be precluded from doing *"God will"*, which in effect binds up the *"strong man"* (*"rational mind of Adam and his descendants"*). Satan understood the *"power of sin"* and knew that sin would render man ineffective to manage the planetary affairs of the Earth in a God-like manner *(Mark 3:27)*. More importantly, Satan knew that the revocation of man's stewardship would sabotage man's appointed purpose, ***bringing great displeasure to God!!!***

The birth of Jesus foils Satan's masterplan...

Jesus' preordained birth disrupted Satan's strategy, which had gone uninterrupted for 4,000 years and would have continued indefinitely had it not been for the blood sacrifice of Jesus, *"the lamb slain from the foundation of the world" (Rev. 13:8)*. Jesus is *"Creator"* of Heaven and Earth *(Colossians 1:15-17)*, including Satan *(aka the serpent)*, man and the *"tree of knowledge of good and evil"* from whence the forbidden fruit was taken. *Jesus Christ in His eternal Excellency and Majesty is King and Ruler over "ALL THINGS". He, the "Godhead" has the ABSOLUTE POWER to create, destroy and restore!!!*

From the good of the *"tree of knowledge of good and evil"* the redeemed of man would come to appreciate the righteousness of God that characterizes our Lord and Savior, Jesus Christ.

The Christ-like character of God is manifest in the *"fruit of the Spirit"* that is disclosed by the Apostle Paul in the book of Galatians chapter 5, verses 22 and 23...

> *"But the fruit of the Spirit is love, joy, peace, patience, kindness, goodness, faith, gentleness, self-control. Against such things there is no law." {Holman Christian Standard}*

From the *"evil"* of the *"tree of knowledge of good and evil"* fallen man would come to know and succumb to the sinful behavior that constitutes Satan's character, the one that has come to *steal, kill and destroy (John 10:10)*. The character of the devil is manifest in the *"works of the flesh" (aka "carnal nature")* that are disclosed by the Apostle Paul in the book of Galatians chapter 5, verses 19 thru 21...

> *"Now the works of the flesh are obvious: sexual immorality, moral impurity, promiscuity, idolatry, sorcery, hatreds, strife, jealousy, outbursts of anger, selfish ambitions, dissensions, factions, envy, drunkenness, carousing, and anything similar.*
>
> *I tell you about these things in advance as I told you before that those who practice such things will not inherit the kingdom of God." {Holman Christian Standard Bible}*

Jesus is the *"Good Shepherd"* and *"author of eternal life"*. When we study to understand and safeguard the *"repackaged product"* that we are in Jesus, we receive the spiritual manifestation from the Holy Spirit that empowers us to *"walk in the Father's will"* and not *"our own will"*. When man *(Satan in man... John 2:24-25)* is obeyed rather than God, the door that leads to self-destruction and death is open.

The Holy Spirit, man's Spiritual chauffeur into eternity...

THE ULTIMATE QUESTION IS... whether God's Spirit is the *"designated driver"* seated behind the steering wheel in your life; or is a spiritual entity other than God operating the levers while chauffeuring you around at your own personal expense? If you are not familiar with God's *"Manufacturer's Handbook"* that was written especially for you, chances are you are not in control of your spiritual destiny. You are undoubtedly *"spiritually intoxicated"* and *"living under the influence of Satan"*, rendering you spiritually guilty of *"LUI"*.

When living in sin, we are automatically *spiritually* and *psychologically intoxicated* by the problems of the world that we alone are powerless to resolve. In a desperate attempt to cope, many of us succumb to alcohol, drugs, and other worldly indulgences that drive us further into sin. Far too many are *"Living Under the Influence"* of Satan, versus becoming spiritually sober through adherence to the

Disclosure of the Eternal Gift | 87

commandments of God that are clearly spelled out in our *"Creator's Owner's Manual"* known to all as the *"Holy Bible"*!!!

> ⁶ *"Therefore humble yourselves under the mighty hand of God, that He may exalt you in due time, ⁷ casting all your care upon Him, for He cares for you.*
>
> ⁸ *Be sober, be vigilant; because your adversary the devil walks about like a roaring lion, seeking whom he may devour." {1 Peter 5:6-8 / New King James Version}*

THE ULTIMATE TRUTH IS… everybody needs to know God for themselves and have an intimate relationship with the *"Holy Spirit"* that is behind the steering wheel in his or her life. The Holy Bible is the only way for one to know how to choose wisely. The Apostle Paul refers to *"God's designated driver"* as the *"inner man" (2 Cor. 4:16).*

If you are not familiar with your owner's manual, you can be assured that your *"inner man"* is not present in your life. You are undoubtedly being chauffeured through life by Satan, wherein you are being picked up and dropped off at will; *"SATAN'S WILL"* and not *"GOD'S WILL"*.

It would be an awful tragedy and eternal shame to have passed by Heaven on a one-way street to *"nowhere"* and end up in hell, because you entrusted the key to your eternal life to Satan. Your entire life could be spent being chauffeured down the wrong road by the devil!!!

Jesus laid down His life to pay humanity's price, so that all might be chauffeured into eternity by the "Holy Spirit". We are "God's handcrafted products". Jehovah is our "Heavenly Manufacturer". Christ is the "Master Key" to our lives. The Holy Spirit is our "Inner Man".

"Study your owner's manual to realize your possibilities...
Heaven on Earth awaits you!!!

~Peruse the Holy Book~

Our Lord and Savior, Jesus Christ!

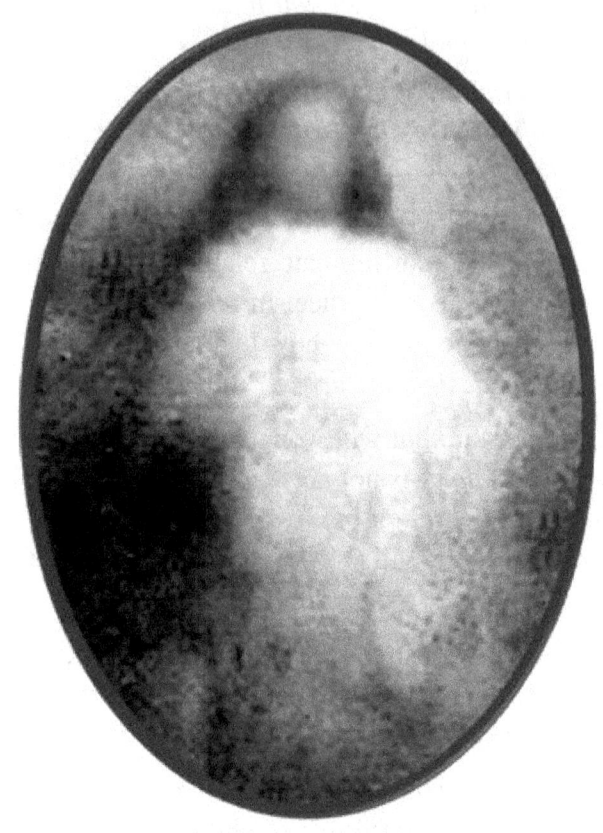

The Eternal Gift...

Revelation 17:14 {New King James Version}

"...for he is Lord of lords and King of kings; and those who are with him are called, chosen, and faithful.."

Alleluia!

First Trinity

"Glorifying Jehovah... Our Heavenly Father!"

The Shortest Poem Ever Written...

"In the beginning...
God created the heavens
and the earth!"

Genesis 1:1 {New King James Version}

Worship Him!

~ The Precious Present ~
Glorifying the "Heavenly Gift Giver"!

My life has been one of…
sheer essence without introduction…
Having come from humble beginnings…

Going back to a time when life was hard,
but living was simple.
A time when lessons were profound,
though rarely devastating.

Growing up during difficult moments, wherein history
when dauntingly pressed, birthed cultural heroes among us.

Being blessed to have parental giants always in our midst.
Many of whom we knew, some well acquainted
and others unknown.
Being influenced and sometimes mentored by those,
who would cause the courses of our lives to be permanently altered.

Big and small they walked among us.
Some with a story to tell and others with just a simple sigh
that issued from a dimly fainted whisper,
only to receive an announcement in one ear…
"You have arrived"!

Going to and fro on different stages and worldly platforms,
engaging the throws of life…
In a place where choice gives way to happenstance…
Yes, you have arrived at a place of being.

A place carved out by the notions and fears
of celebrated change and new beginnings.
Being ushered into a welcoming time of arrival,
that shouts loudly… *"You are finally here"!!!*

Here, in a place of structure where there was none.
Walking with a newly secured sense of *personal pride,*
self-confidence and *"predefined purpose"*.

A place where *"Odd"* embraces *"Even"*;
wherein the oddity of pain justifies the passions
and pleasures previously misinterpreted and misunderstood.

No longer burdened by the bonds of traditional restraints…
life takes on the challenges and beginnings of a new story.
A story to some that reads like a lullaby… that guides.

A story that changed the narrative in my life…
A story that gave me something to run from,
when I had nothing to run to.
A story that provided me with a fixed perspective,
when I had no perspective at all…

A story that granted me the gift of artful expression
and unrelenting self-persuasion…
A story that opened my heart and mind to God…
at a time when my path was twisted and dimly lit!

There's not a day goes by that I don't thank God
for my glorious and wonderful life.
A life filled with delightful pleasures without penalty.
In the Lord I've lived and experienced a colorful,
fulfilling and blessed existence.

Limitless measure and eternal thanks to…
God the Father, His Son Jesus
and the Holy Spirit, our Comforter!

I am eternally grateful for my life with all of the gifts
and treasured blessings that have been supplanted therein.
It is for this reason that I praise, honor, glorify and adore Him.

To our Heavenly Father…
be the praise, the honor and the glory!

"Scriptural Reference"
James 1:16 thru 18 & Proverbs 18:15 thru 16

Disclosure of the Eternal Gift

James 1:16 thru 18 {New King James Version}

"Do not be deceived, my beloved brethren.

Every good gift and every perfect gift is from above,
and comes down from the Father of lights,
with whom there is no variation or shadow of turning.

Of His own will He brought us forth by the word of truth,
that we might be a kind of firstfruits of His creatures."

Proverbs 18:15 thru 16 {New King James Version}

"The heart of the prudent acquires knowledge,
And the ear of the wise seeks knowledge.

A man's gift makes room for him,
And brings him before great men."

~ My Name Is Spirit ~

We shall all bear witness!

I have come only once,
but my arrivals have been many.
I have arrived in many spaces
existing behind strange and sometimes familiar faces.

For generations, centuries and millenniums…
some illusive… among others too numerous to count.
I have arrived…
many, many, times before.

My name is Spirit…

Many have witnessed My coming,
through the opening and closing of life's doors.
I have arrived…
many, many, times before.

My name is Spirit…

I have come as seasonal rain in Maine,
I have come as snow-capped mountains in Germany and Spain.
I have come as gentle breezes blowing in the Mediterranean winds.
I have arrived time and time again…

My name is Spirit…

I have come as icy lakes and frozen ponds in winter.
I have come as morning dew and fog in spring.
I have come as gamma rays and radiation in the heat of summer.
I have come as floral tree leaves transitioning in late autumn.

I have arrived… My name is Spirit!!!

"Scriptural Reference"
John 3:8, Revelation 2:7 & John 4:24

John 3:8 {American Standard Version}

"The wind bloweth where it will,
and thou hearest the voice thereof,
but knowest not whence it cometh,
and whither it goeth:
so is every one that is born of the Spirit."

Revelation 2:7 {King James Version}

"He that hath an ear, let him hear
what the Spirit saith unto the churches;

To him that overcometh will I give
to eat of the tree of life, which is
in the midst of the paradise of God."

John 4:24 {King James Version}

"God is a Spirit:
and they that worship him
must worship him in spirit and in truth."

~ Rich Little ~

A parent's resistance to a son's call to salvation!

Material is loaned
it is not to be owned
it was written, so it shall be.

Man does not own
the ground he stands on
to proudly boast how powerful is he.

When a man dies
his truths becomes lies
for the whole of the world to see.

All that man owns
is his will to go on
to witness eternity.

"Scriptural Reference"
Matthew 6:19 thru 21

Disclosure of the Eternal Gift

Matthew 6:19 thru 21 {New International Version}

"Do not store up for yourselves treasures on earth,
where moth and rust destroy
and where thieves break in and steal.

But store up for yourselves treasures in Heaven,
where moth and rust do not destroy,
and where thieves do not break in and steal.

For where your treasure is,
there your heart will be also."

~ Thou Shall Not ~

Mercy unto Adam... God's "Master Creation"!

Adam made the choice
away from God he turned,
man's *"spiritual character"* was transformed
humanity's future was ruined.

For God told them
not to eat from the forbidden tree!!!

Adam looked to heaven
they were all alone,
man's earthly dominion was lost...
Eden's *"spirit culture"* was gone.

For God told them
not to eat from the forbidden tree!!!

Our "PURPOSE" is to *"please God"*
by simply doing what we're told,
whether we've lived the years of Methuselah
or we're just a few days old.

For God told them
not to eat from the forbidden tree!!!

Remember Adam and Eve
God's first woman and man,
they were given special instructions
but they blew the plan.

For God told them
not to eat from the forbidden tree!!!

When they ate from the tree of knowledge of good and evil
and consumed the *essence of the fruit,*
the *"spiritual tie that binds"* was broken
and old Satan was loosed.

{Fruit eaten, but the "<u>forbidden knowledge of GOD</u>" consumed!}

For God told them
not to eat from the forbidden tree!!!

The serpent encouraged Eve to eat the fruit
promised they would *"be as Gods"*,
not disclosing knowledge alone
only makes one smart.

For God told them
not to eat from the forbidden tree!!!

So here we are…
prisoners of SIN,
for knowledge without power
transformed *"eternal mortals"* into fallen men.

For God told them
not to eat from the forbidden tree!!!

God's "ANOINTED POWER" is what's needed
over what we were *not suppose to know*,
without God's Holy Anointing
Satan is running the show.

For God told them
not to eat from the forbidden tree!!!

Jesus taught the multitude in parables
unlike His disciples to whom knowledge
of heavenly mysteries He revealed,
before being crucified on Calvary at Golgotha Hill.

For God told them
not to eat from the forbidden tree!!!

In the book of Mark,
Jesus instructed His disciples to go out and teach,
but not before receiving the *"Power Of Anointing"*
in order to practice what they preached.

{The Holy Spirit descends upon the people on the Day of Pentecost…}

For God told them
not to eat from the forbidden tree!!!

~~~

"Scriptural Reference"
Genesis 2:15 thru 17 & Genesis 3:12 thru 13

Genesis 2:15 thru 17 {King James Version}

"And the Lord God took the man,
and put him into the Garden of Eden
to dress it and to keep it.

And the Lord God commanded the man,
saying, Of every tree of the garden
thou mayest freely eat:

But of the tree of the knowledge of good and evil,
thou shalt not eat of it:
for in the day that thou eatest thereof
thou shalt surely die."

Genesis 3:12 thru 13 {King James Version}

"And the man said,
The woman whom thou gavest to be with me,
she gave me of the tree, and I did eat.

And the Lord God said unto the woman,
What is this that thou hast done?

And the woman said,
The serpent beguiled me,
and I did eat."

~ Daughters ~

Adam's love for Eve overshadows his obedience to God!

Adam flirted with death
when creation was innocent and young,
Eve gave birth to sorrow
for the old serpent she did not shun.

Death and Sorrow became partners
embracing one another madly,
procreating life's oldest set of surviving twins
"Happiness" and "Sadness".

Over time the daughters grew up
went about their separate ways,
romancing the corrupt hearts of men
for the fullness of their days.

Death and Sorrow became vagabonds
wandering the dreaded pathways of life,
with little concern for man's tomorrows
or his hardships and sacrifice.

Happiness and Sadness became devoted servants
in the spiritually anointed prophetic works of God,
functioning as guardians to the blessings and curses
that prosper and damn us all.

Are you peaceful?
Are you prosperous?
Are you happy?
Choose you this day!

"Scriptural Reference"
Deuteronomy 30:19

Deuteronomy 30:19 {King James Version}

"I call heaven and earth to record this day against you,
that I have set before you life and death,
blessing and cursing: therefore choose life,
that both thou and thy seed may live:"

˜ I Am That I Am ˜

Primal impact of Genesis chapter one, verse two!

When Spirit willed itself
to reign as ruler,
the *"Kingdom of Darkness"*
became illusion.

Spirit begot *light*,
Word begot *sound*,
Water begot *dust*,
creation abound.

World of worlds
cast from clones of never,
shrouded in lights
in a space called heaven.

Man stands in awe
of the macrocosm of space,
inflicting colossal fears
upon the entire human race.

The continuum is such....

Man's life is the *vineyard*,
Time is the *keeper*,
Christ is the *sower*,
Death is the *reaper*.

"I Am That I Am"!
I Am space and time.
I Am the Spirit of Creation.
I make the worlds go around.

I Am the Father of fathers,
I Am the maker of men.
I cause all things to die,
and come to life again.

I Am greenness of grass,
I Am fullness of season.
I Am soundness of mind,
I Am ration and reason.

"I Am That I Am",
God of life and life to come.
I Am the many of many,
yet I am one.

Seek ye my Spirit,
I Am balance and truth.
I Am the beginning and the end.
I Am also you!

"Scriptural Reference"
Genesis 1:1 thru 2 & 1st John 5:6 thru 8

Genesis 1:1 thru 2 {King James Version}

"In the beginning
God created the heaven and the earth.

And the earth was without form, and void;
and darkness was upon the face of the deep.

And the Spirit of God
moved upon the face of the waters."

1st John 5:6 thru 8 {King James Version}

"This is he that came by water and blood,
even Jesus Christ; not by water only,
but by water and blood.

And it is the Spirit that beareth witness,
because the Spirit is truth.

For there are three that bear record in heaven,
the Father, the Word, and the Holy Ghost:
and these three are one.

And there are three that bear witness in earth,
the Spirit, and the water, and the blood:
and these three agree in one."

~ Divine Purpose ~

Sanctification of the Christian Church!

For 6,000 blessed years
through the triumphs and the fears,
God You never left us…
You promised, we trusted, You kept us!

Beginning with the patriarch Abraham
whom You made *"Father of many nations"*,
we were blessed with Your divine deliverance
in and out of every hopeless situation.

Under Your prophetic guidance
and personalized direction,
the Children of Israel increased and survived
400 years of Egypt's enslavement and dejection.

Around the year 1491 B.C.
You forced Pharaoh to set the children of Israel free,
during a forty years sojourn in the wilderness
You said to Moses… "Prove Me"!!!

An estimated two million Hebrew children
with Pharaoh breathing down their backs,
You imparted *Your vision, plan,* and *purpose*
until today the Christian Church has not looked back.

You dedicated thirteen apostles, including Paul
dressed them in the full armor of God
charging them to proclaim liberty to the captives
wherein the faithful were divinely set apart.

Now more than thirty-six hundred years later
Christians number two billion believers strong,
boldly invading the gates of hell
emulating the praise of King David in the Psalms.

Just another chapter in an awesome story
so meticulously and eloquently told

of how God uses imperfect people
to take back what Satan stole.

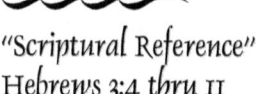

"Scriptural Reference"
Hebrews 3:4 thru 11

Hebrews 3:4 thru 11 {New King James Version}

"For every house is built by someone,
but He who built all things is God.

And Moses indeed was faithful
in all His house as a servant,
for a testimony of those things
which would be spoken afterward,

but Christ as a Son over His own house,
whose house we are if we hold fast the confidence
and the rejoicing of the hope firm to the end.

Therefore, as the Holy Spirit says:
"Today, if you will hear His voice,
Do not harden your hearts as in the rebellion,

In the day of trial in the wilderness,
Where your fathers tested Me, tried Me,
And saw My works forty years.

Therefore I was angry with that generation,
And said, 'They always go astray in their heart,
And they have not known My ways.'

So I swore in My wrath,
They shall not enter My rest."

~ Seven Seals ~

To Jesus Christ the Divine Revelator!

Passionate cries igniting static winds
here and now *"Revelation"* begins.

Crippling waves weaving woes undone
"Great Opener of Seals" Your time has come.

The prophetic events that St. John did not write
manifesting themselves in the darkness of light.

Day by day increasing agony and fear
in sea, air and earth we are dying here.

Nature is reeling from ecological harm
sounding echoes and tremors of environmental alarm.

Heavenly Host, Sweet Majesty of grace and charm,
messenger of tsunamis, quakes, fires and crop circles
freely sound Your alarms.

The Spirit of God
that once cradled the religions of man
has since glorified the Father in His *"Master Plan"*.

A symbol of sacrifice we have, crowning our partition of hope
thus striking life's pendulum in the Earth's hour of revolt.

Old *"Mother of Dust"* please absorb the shocks
until Jesus Christ's second coming You're all we've got.

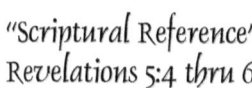

"Scriptural Reference"
Revelations 5:4 thru 6

Revelations 5:4 thru 6 {New International Version – UK}

"I wept and wept because no one was found
who was worthy to open the scroll or look inside.
Then one of the elders said to me, Do not weep!

See, the Lion of the tribe of Judah,
the Root of David, has triumphed.
He is able to open the scroll and its seven seals.

Then I saw a Lamb, looking as if it had been slain,
standing in the center of the throne, encircled
by the four living creatures and the elders.

He had seven horns and seven eyes,
which are the seven spirits of God
sent out into all the earth."

~ Babylon ~

Last days phenomenon!

Lost ties... weeping eyes,
chains of bondage in disguise.
Meek flesh melting... melting fast,
melting like hot wax on charcoal bones
avenging the wrath of the rich man's throne.

Fun, folly, drink and play
celebrating scores of yesterday.

But nobody cares to hear!!!

Eyes... brown, blue, gray and green
witnessing things they've never dreamed.
Lips thin… thick…, moving super slick,
while our lives flow like wine…
being free of purpose and free of time.

Knowingly making our children drunk for the world,
while drowning them in empty promises of yesterday.

But nobody cares to hear!!!

While living in a world filled with miseries and fears,
the fear of what was… shaping the misery of what is.

But nobody cares to hear!!!

"Scriptural Reference"
Hebrews 1:1 thru 4, Matthew 11:15 thru 17 & Matthew 13:41 thru 43

Disclosure of the Eternal Gift | 113

Hebrews 1:1 thru 4 {New King James Version}

"God, who at various times and in various ways
spoke in time past to the fathers by the prophets,
has in these last days spoken to us by His Son,

whom He has appointed heir of all things,
through whom also He made the worlds;
who being the brightness of His glory
and the express image of His person,
and upholding all things by the word of His power,

when He had by Himself purged our sins,
sat down at the right hand of the Majesty on high,
having become so much better than the angels,
as He has by inheritance obtained a more excellent name than they."

Matthew 11:15 thru 17 {New King James Version}

"He who has ears to hear, let him hear!

'But to what shall I liken this generation?
It is like children sitting in the marketplaces
and calling to their companions, and saying:

'We played the flute for you,
And you did not dance;
We mourned to you,
And you did not lament.'"

Matthew 13:41 thru 43 {New King James Version}

"The Son of Man will send out His angels,
and they will gather out of His kingdom all things that offend,

and those who practice lawlessness,
and will cast them into the furnace of fire.

There will be wailing and gnashing of teeth.
Then the righteous will shine forth as the sun
in the kingdom of their Father.
He who has ears to hear, let him hear!"

~ Mother Love ~

In search of a bride!

All the trials of wicked men
have risen to defeat,
their conscience knows of nothing
but the remnants of deceit.

Good old Mother Nature
bless peace upon the land,
You've labored long and unceasingly
since your relationship with man.

I thank You for the morning,
the wake of everyday…
the sun that lights the path of truth
that guides me along the way.

I thank You for the evening
when my duties are almost done;
I thank You for my will to live
to keep my thoughts as one.

Love… ole Mother Love…
where in the heavens can You be?
I have searched the wide world over
even beyond the seas.

Please give me strength to seek tomorrow
beneath a morning sky
to find a love as pure as Yours
to love until I die.

I want to thank You!

"Scriptural Reference"
Ecclesiastes 9:9 & Song of Solomon 8:7

Ecclesiastes 9:9 {New American Standard Bible}

"Enjoy life with the woman whom you love
all the days of your fleeting life
which He has given to you under the sun;
for this is your reward in life and in your toil
in which you have labored under the sun."

Song of Solomon 8:7 {Amplified Bible}

"Many waters cannot quench love,
neither can floods drown it.
If a man would offer all the goods of his house for love,
he would be utterly scorned and despised."

~ Cradle Of Hope ~

Blessings of a clean heart!

If a journey to the center of the human heart were possible…
after having received Jesus Christ into one's life,
upon arrival one would surely find
the province of universal love.

a place uninhabited by feelings of fear and want…
a place filled with love, joy, peace and harmony...
a place where carnal creatures die and spiritual babes are born…
a place where hurt is rendered harmless by the power of peace…
a place where confusion is blinded by the light of understanding…

a place where prejudice, pride and possession is freely surrendered…
a place where power journeys to seek compassion…
a place where coldness wanders in search of warmth…
a place where sadness awaits to bond with gladness…
a place where hatred is transformed into God's love…

A beautiful place located deep within the core of the human spirit,
where time and love when given proper space,
melts down mountains of sorrow into rivers of joy
and glimmers of hope evolves into an "Eternal Oneness".

"Scriptural Reference"
Psalm 51:10 thru 12 & 1st Peter 3:14 thru 16

Psalm 51:10 thru 12 {King James Version}

"Create in me a clean heart, O God;
and renew a right spirit within me.

Cast me not away from thy presence;
and take not thy Holy Spirit from me.

Restore unto me the joy of thy salvation;
and uphold me with thy free spirit."

1st Peter 3:14 thru 16 {New International Version – UK}

"But even if you should suffer for what is right,
you are blessed. Do not fear what they fear;
do not be frightened.

But in your hearts set apart Christ as Lord.
Always be prepared to give an answer to everyone
who asks you to give the reason
for the hope that you have.

But do this with gentleness and respect,
keeping a clear conscience,
so that those who speak maliciously
against your good behavior in Christ
may be ashamed of their slander."

~ So They Say ~

The true meaning of mission?

They're on a mission from God
or so they say,
but people are sick and dying
they've lost their way.

Blessed with an abundance of food
they carelessly throw it away,
while people are hungry and starving
without a place to stay.

They live in extravagant homes
with excesses swelling their heads,
while people sleep on the street
using rocks and cardboard for beds.

Young girls on the street
fully clothed in the nude,
daily selling their innocence
just to buy food.

Little boys in bondage
held hostage by heroine, meth and crack,
while old people eat cat and dog food
to keep warm and have clothes on their backs.

They say they're on a mission
but they've been misled,
their publicly misguided charities
have gone to their heads.

They'll put thousands of dollars in church
but won't buy a homeless person a sandwich to eat,
while proudly boasting of their Christianity
to every *"perceived sinner"* they meet.

They've lost their way!

"Scriptural Reference"
1st Corinthians 13:1 thru 2 & Matthew 5:42 thru 45

Disclosure of the Eternal Gift

1st Corinthians 13:1 thru 2 {New King James Version}

"Though I speak with the tongues of men and of angels,
but have not love, I have become sounding brass
or a clanging cymbal.

And though I have *the gift of* prophecy,
and understand all mysteries and all knowledge,
and though I have all faith,
so that I could remove mountains,
but have not love, I am nothing."

Matthew 5:42 thru 45 {New King James Version}

"For I was hungry and you gave Me no food;
I was thirsty and you gave Me no drink;
I was a stranger and you did not take Me in,
naked and you did not clothe Me,
sick and in prison and you did not visit Me.'

"Then they also will answer Him, saying,
'Lord, when did we see You hungry
or thirsty or a stranger or naked
or sick or in prison,
and did not minister to You?'

Then He will answer them, saying,
'Assuredly, I say to you,
inasmuch as you did not do it
to one of the least of these,
you did not do it to Me.'"

~ The Seer ~

Blood of the altar!

Where angels fly
mortals' feet can't tread,
for beneath God's altar
martyred saints bow their heads.

Piercing eyes of emerald,
cloven tongues of brass,
judgment being spoken
from Law and Prophecy's past.

Seen through the eyes
of the all-seeing Seer!

"Scriptural Reference"
Revelation 18:24, Revelation 16:5 thru 7 & Revelation 4: 8

Revelation 18:24 {King James Version}

"And in her was found the blood of prophets,
and of saints, and of all that were slain upon the earth."

Revelation 16:5 thru 7 {King James Version}

"And I heard the angel of the waters say,
Thou art righteous, O Lord, which art, and wast,
and shalt be, because thou hast judged thus.

For they have shed the blood of saints and prophets,
and thou hast given them blood to drink;
for they are worthy.

And I heard another out of the altar say,
Even so, Lord God Almighty,
true and righteous are thy judgments."

Revelation 4: 8 {King James Version}

"And the four beasts had each of them six wings about him;
and they were full of eyes within: and they rest not day and night,
saying, Holy, holy, holy, LORD God Almighty,
which was, and is, and is to come."

~ Thy Kingdom Come ~

Receiving the keys!

When I pause to view the world around me
what on Earth do I see?
Do I see the coming kingdom of God
with outstretched arms embracing me?

Do we live in a place where God's angels are welcome?
Were they to permanently come, could they relax and sing?
Or, do we live in a state of sinful existence
where God's angels couldn't spread their wings?

Have we come to a place in time
where it's illegal to call God's name?
When the words *"In God We Trust"*
boast America's claim to fame!

Have we approached a time in history
where dictators have no place?
When the God of the Ten Commandments
dictated His laws to Moses face to face *(figuratively)*.

Isn't it ironic... that *"demo"*
is the root word for democracy?
By *"majority rule"* was democracy born
when man authorized Satan to be his proxy
by eating the fruit from the forbidden tree!

"Prince of this world"... was Satan crowned
from man's thirst to equal God and be free
by casting the first *"majority vote"* in history
when Adam and Eve ate the forbidden fruit reserved for Thee.

Isn't it also ironic... that *"demo"*
is the root word for demon... *"devil in the flesh"*
reverse the English words *"live"* and *"lived"*
and the Lord may use you yet.

Ideologically correct it may seem
but in believing backwards we flunk the test,
in misunderstanding a great lesson of nature and history
that the *"East"* cannot be the *"West"*.

~~~

"Scriptural Reference"
Matthew 8:11 thru 12

Matthew 8:11 thru 12 {New King James Version}

"And I say to you that many will come
from east and west, and sit down with Abraham,
Isaac, and Jacob in the kingdom of heaven.

But the sons of the kingdom
will be cast out into outer darkness.
There will be weeping and gnashing of teeth."

~ You Are ~

Honoring the perpetual presence of our Creator!

Thank You Father for giving me
a face of happiness and a heart of joy,
a spirit that smiles to embrace the world.

Thank You Father for You,
for You are my blessing.
You are the air that I breathe.
You are the sun that shines.

You are infinite being, beauty, and worth... You Are!

Before light... You Are!
Before Heaven and Earth... You Are!
Before vegetation, plants and trees... You Are!

Before sun, moon, stars... You Are!
Before sea creatures, wing creatures, cattle,
creeping things, beast and man... You Are!

As stated in Revelations 3:14...
In the form of the "...*Amen, the Faithful and True Witness, the beginning of the creation of God*"... You Are!

As stated in Genesis 1:2...
Even in the mist of eternal *"Darkness"*
You were *"Spirit"* bonding with *"Water"*... You Are!

You transformed Genesis 1:2 into the *"foundation of the world"*,
by substituting the darkness with Your Word...
causing *"divinity of the Godhead"* to abound... You Are!

Before the Host of Heaven, angels, Satan, or hell,
You existed in the form of the *"Holy Spirit"*... You Are!

You are everything natural, good and life sustaining.
You are creation in its everlasting form.
That and more... You Are!

Scriptural Reference...
Colossians 1:15 thru 18 & 1 John 5:6 thru 8

Disclosure of the Eternal Gift

Colossians 1:15 thru 18 {English Standard Version}

"He is the image of the invisible God,
the firstborn of all creation.

For by Him all things were created,
in heaven and on earth, visible and invisible,

whether thrones or dominions
or rulers or authorities
all things were created
through Him and for Him.

And He is before all things,
and in Him all things hold together.

And He is the head of the body,
the church. He is the beginning,
the firstborn from the dead,
that in everything He might be preeminent."

1 John 5:6 thru 8 {New King James Version}

"This is He who came by water and blood – Jesus Christ;
not only by water, but by water and blood.
And it is the Spirit who bears witness,
because the Spirit is truth.

For there are three that bear witness in heaven:
the Father, the Word, and the Holy Spirit;
and these three are one.

And there are three that bear witness on earth:
the Spirit, the water, and the blood;
and these three agree as one."

~ God Knows ~

Honoring the omniscience of our Creator!

Father we trust You...
to direct us in the ways that we should go,
for we know not our true destinies.

For in You resides the knowledge of all things!

Father we trust You...
to grant us perfect vision to see the heavenly for we know not how,
because we are blinded by the things that are earthly.

For in You resides the knowledge of all things!

Father we trust You...
to teach us how to pray for the things that we are in need of,
for we know not what things to ask.

For in You resides the knowledge of all things!

Father we trust You...
to instruct us in the right and perfect things to do,
for we know not what choices are best for our futures.

For in You resides the knowledge of all things!

Father we trust You...
to instruct us in the right and perfect things to speak,
for we know not how to govern our tongues.

For in You resides the knowledge of all things!

Father we trust You...
to reconcile our emotions with our thought lives,
for we know not how to discern the ways of the *"Evil One"*.

For in You resides the knowledge of all things!

Father we trust You...
to balance our physical appetites with our spiritual needs,
for we know not what things are healthy and enriching for us.

Disclosure of the Eternal Gift | 131

For in You resides the knowledge of all things!

Father we trust You...
to guide our walk and order our steps until we are old,
for we know not which paths are best to reward our journeys.

For in You resides the knowledge of all things!

Father we trust You...
to guide us back into the face of Your presence,
for we know not how, because in Adam we have lost our way.

For in You resides the knowledge of all things!

Father we trust You...
to reestablish us in our rightful place of spiritual authority,
for we know not how because Satan has corrupted our minds.

For in You resides the knowledge of all things!

Father we trust You...
to continually remind us of whom we are in You,
it is through the indwelling of Your Holy Spirit
that we know You... the "I Am That I Am"

For in You resides the knowledge of all things!

Father we will forever glorify, honor and adore You.
It is through Your heavenly out-dwelling in Your Son Jesus Christ,
that we have come to know, love, trust and depend on You...
In whom "I Am" You Are!

For in You resides the knowledge of all things!

"Scriptural Reference"
Romans 8:26 thru 27, Proverbs 3:5 thru 7 & Isaiah 40:13 thru 14

Romans 8:26 thru 27 {New King James Version}

"Likewise the Spirit also helps in our weaknesses.
For we do not know what we should pray for as we ought,
but the Spirit Himself makes intercession for us
with groanings which cannot be uttered.

Now He who searches the hearts
knows what the mind of the Spirit is,
because He makes intercession for the saints
according to the will of God."

Proverbs 3:5 thru 7 {King James Version}

"Trust in the LORD with all thine heart;
and lean not unto thine own understanding.

In all thy ways acknowledge Him,
and He shall direct thy paths.

Be not wise in thine own eyes:
fear the LORD, and depart from evil."

Isaiah 40:13 thru 14 {New International Version – UK}

"Who has understood the mind of the LORD,
or instructed Him as His counsellor?

Whom did the LORD consult to enlighten Him,
and who taught Him the right way?

Who was it that taught Him knowledge or
showed him the path of understanding?"

When A Chair Is Not A Chair!

"A Tablet Moment..."

When we "sincerely" trust in God we realize that "EVERYTHING" is in God's hand and no matter what happens it comes to past in *"His Presence"* and under *"His Power"*. God's hand is SO LARGE that it is impossible for those who TRUST in Him to ever fall out of His hand. The span of God's hand is SO WIDE that *"The closer we get to the edge, the nearer we are to the center."* There are only three assumable positions in God's hand. Those of us who have accepted the Heavenly Father in the name of our Lord and Savior Jesus Christ are eternally kept in the palm of His hand in one of those positions...

- *In extraordinary times certain ones of us find ourselves standing in God's hand as "children of God" rarely do. The apostles of Christ, including the Apostle Paul, Mother Theresa, Mahatma Gandhi, Martin Luther, Abraham Lincoln, Martin Luther King Jr., Muhammad Ali, Nelson Mandela and countless others, including a host of common men and women are literally standing in God's hand.*
- *In good times each and every one of us can be found sitting in God's hand with little thought or concern for the perils that are existent around us. This is true for the average person whose been blessed, nestled, and cushioned in God's abundance of mercy, spiritual grace and daily provision.*
- *In bad or trying times we are figuratively crawling on our bellies like a serpent in God's hand, while seeking the spiritual strength to get back to our knees. Once on our knees the ordinary person prays for the opportunity to once again sit in the palm of God's hand, while the extraordinary person prays to regain his or her footing in order to stand once more in the presence of God to fight the "good fight" another day.*

I prefer to think that I like the majority of people am sitting in God's hand, in that God's hand reminds me of a chair. Everyone living in modern society should be familiar with a chair, regardless of his or her station or status in life. This is true irrespective of whether one lives in a first world country overflowing with riches, or a third world country that is ravaged with poverty. A chair is a common object in which one should be familiar. Chairs are used by the overwhelming majority throughout all the days of our lives, barring minor exceptions.

- Everybody knows that a chair is a chair, much the same as people knowing deep down inside themselves that God is God. This is very true even though many refuse to admit it until their situation becomes so dire that they need to call upon a power greater than themselves to survive and they call on God.
- Everybody knows that the purpose of a chair is to hold us up when we are unable or unwilling to stand. The same is true with God. People know that God can and will hold us up when we are emotionally stressed, spiritually burdened or physically distressed beyond our natural limits.
- Everyone exercises faith to sit in a chair without reservations, and few people if any have ever checked the legs of any chair that they have sat in regardless of the particular place or time.

This is true regardless of the places and situations that people in need find themselves. Rich people and poor people alike have sat in chairs in their *own houses, church houses, schoolhouses, firehouses, boarding houses, jailhouses, safe houses, halfway houses, dope houses, gambling houses, houses of ill repute, including the White House.* I am not knowledgeable of anyone having ever bent a knee to check the strength and stability of a chair's legs that they have chosen to sit in. *The question is why do people in times of real need place their trust in a chair more than they place their trust in God?*

The fact is that many of us are refusing to sit in God's hand without first checking His legs, as if it were necessary to execute a performance check on God in the first place. Could it be that we place our trust in the specifications of chairs, elevators and other manmade things more than we place our trust in the specifications of God *(Proverbs 30:5)*, which are clearly spelled out in His Word? I constantly witness large groups of people pressing into overcrowded elevators that have very prominent signs revealing their maximum weight capacity to be 3,000 to 4,000 pounds. I am absolutely in awe and amazed at how crowds weighing hundreds of pounds more than an elevator's stated capacity will continue to press in without apprehension or fear of danger, while at the same time will receive the truth and reliability of God's Word and steadfastly refuse to trust and believe in Him *(Psalm 20:7-7)*.

More than twenty five years ago, my wife and I purchased a three-piece French provincial living room suite that at the time was valued at nearly five thousand dollars. Interestingly enough, we've probably not sat on the loveseat more than a half dozen times in the many years that we've had it. *The question is... can a chair really and truly be considered a chair if one does not have the assurance, trust and confidence to sit in it when the need arises?* This question is incredibly profound when the scenario fits a person who is struggling to stand and refuses to sit even when in desperate need of comfort, relief and support. This is especially true when people find themselves in situations that require a hand from God and chooses not to take it.

If God's only purpose in our lives were for pure esthetics without use, then God would in affect be reduced to the status of a mere ornament. In short, an ornament's sole purpose to its possessor is to serve as a conversation piece to impress others and to cause one to feel better about oneself bases upon the intrinsic value of the ornament.

Ornaments are like idols; they serve no essential purpose in our lives and are functionally dead in times of critical need. My suggestion is to take God at His Word trusting that He *can and will* hold us up even when it appears that certain facets of our lives are similar to an elevator stressed beyond capacity. At all times God's hand is our *"Chair of Mercy" (Psalm 13:5)* that cradles us when we trust Him enough to sit in it. God's hand is also our personal *"Elevator of Grace",* which is capable of lifting us out of our worse situations and deepest despair, when we trust Him enough to sit in it *(2nd Corinthians 9:8).* Countless individuals have found this to be true when figuratively and literally crawling on their bellies while begging and pleading for mercy, when they were trusting and confident enough to submit their fate into God's hand. This is especially true when we find ourselves struggling in down-and-out times with no apparent way out.

Even when all of the signs of life are telling us not to board God's spiritual elevator that is filled beyond capacity with the presence of His love, we are to trust and have faith upon entering into His hand that the following is true. When we have faith and keep our hand in the Lord's hand, there are no *voids* that God cannot fill, *rifts* He cannot mend, *diseases* He cannot heal, *burdens* He cannot bear, *needs* He cannot supply, or *barriers* that He cannot break through!

It is interesting that few miracles occurred during Old Testament times under the Law and that the word *"faith"* is only referenced twice in the Old Testament *(Deuteronomy 32:20 and Habakkuk 2:4)*, when in the New Testament the word *"faith"* is referenced 229 times…

The Apostle John recorded the following in the New Testament book of John chapter 10, verses 27 thru 30 …

> *"My sheep hear My voice, and I know them and they follow me. And I give unto them eternal life, and <u>they shall never perish, neither shall any man pluck them out of My hand.</u>*
>
> *My Father, who gave them to Me, is greater than all; and <u>no man is able to pluck them out of My Father's hand.</u> I and My Father are one." {21st Century King James Version}*

This and more is true of God if we would only trust in His almighty hand *(1st Peter 5:6:7)*. It is in God's hand that we live and breathe; wherein we die in Christ in order that we might live for eternity.

> *"Therefore humble yourselves under the mighty hand of God, that He may exalt you in due time, casting all your care upon Him, for He cares for you." {King James Version}*

In the final analysis, our *"Christian walk"* is a spiritual journey of *spiritual transformation* and *self-actualization* that takes place on a road seldom traveled, which leads back to our place of beginning with God. When we truly trust in God, we have to lose ourselves to find Him, requiring us to go back to our place of beginning and diligently seek. In doing so, we will discover the mystery of *"Eternal Blessing"* and *"Eternal Provision"* that has been handed down to us in the "POWER" and "PRESENCE" of God's Word that is manifest in Jesus Christ.

> *All Praise, Honor and Glory to Almighty God…*
> *Blessed are the recipients of "His Eternal Gift",*
> *that is resident in the Word and Spirit of Christ!*

"But without faith it is impossible to please Him, for he who comes to God must believe that He is, and that He is a rewarder of those who diligently seek Him."
{Hebrews 11:6}

"I love those who love me,
And those who seek me diligently will find me."
{Proverbs 8:17}

~Study the Holy Book~

Second Trinity

"To Jesus, God's Only Begotten Son!"

The Greatest Name Ever Spoken...

"And behold, thou shalt conceive in your womb, and bear a son, and you shall call His name JESUS."

Luke 1:31 {New King James Version}

Praise Him!

~ The Adam Family ~

Eternal blessings to Sister Cynthia!

To our Lord and Savior Jesus Christ,
our High Priest, so anointed, so dear,
we render praise and honor to our Heavenly Father
for His mercy in dispatching You here.

For 2000 years You have strengthened our spirits,
nurturing us with Your gospel along the way,
You have prepared the souls of many
to *"bear your cross"* day-by-day.

Many false prophets are dead and gone
only You have risen from the dead to stay,
to resurrect and guide the family of Adam
into that promised Judgment Day!

"Scriptural Reference"
Genesis 5:1 thru 2 & 1st Peter 4:17 thru 18

Genesis 5:1 thru 2 {King James Version}

"This is the book of the generations of Adam.
In the day that God created man,
in the likeness of God made He him;

Male and female created He them;
and blessed them,
and called their name Adam,
in the day when they were created."

1st Peter 4:17 thru 18 {New International Version – UK}

"For it is time for judgment to begin with the family of God;
and if it begins with us, what will the outcome be
for those who do not obey the gospel of God?

And, If it is hard for the righteous to be saved,
what will become of the ungodly and the sinner?"

~ Thank You Jesus ~

I am... because You are!

I want to thank You Jesus
for all You have done for me.
I want to thank You Jesus
for setting my spirit free.

I want to thank You Jesus
for lifting me up that day.
You turned me around;
You sat me on my way.

I was lost in sin
from oh so long ago,
but You came into my life
and You told me so.

You said, listen child
There is something I'll have you do.
I have a message
I want you to take it through.

I want you to tell the world,
that I Am *"The Father's"* only child.
Tell them... God of Heaven sent Me here
to keep this old world alive.

Tell them... I died on Calvary
about two thousand years ago.
Tell them... I rose after three days
to let the whole world know.

I hold the keys to death and hell
closed in the spike marks of My hands,
I have paid the eternal price
for each and every man.

Tell them... they don't have to die no more,
oh no you don't,

for the eternal price has been paid
to satisfy your every want.

Tell them… to come on in
and dine in My Father's house.
Where the *"Bread of Life"* has been broken
to feed each and every mouth.

Tell them… they are My Father's now!
Oh yes you are…
You are the seed of Abraham,
you are My Father's shining star.

You are the staff of Moses,
you are the wine from the winepress.
You are the lily of the valley,
you are My Father's very best.

Yes you are…

"Scriptural Reference"
Philippians 4:4 thru 7 & 1st Corinthians 1:18

Philippians 4:4 thru 7 {New International Version – UK}

"Rejoice in the Lord always.
I will say it again: Rejoice!
Let your gentleness be evident to all.
The Lord is near.

Do not be anxious about anything,
but in everything, by prayer and petition,
with thanksgiving,
present your requests to God.

And the peace of God,
which transcends all understanding,
will guard your hearts
and your minds in Christ Jesus."

1st Corinthians 1:18 {New International Version}

"For the message of the cross is foolishness
to those who are perishing,
but to us who are being saved
it is the power of God."

~ In Your Name ~

The Heavenly Father's name declared in the Earth!

Lord in Your name
we give You glory.
Lord in Your name
we share Your story.

Lord in Your name
we challenge the *"poisoned seed"*.
Lord in Your name
We are created to believe.

Lord in Your name
the Holy Spirit abounds.
Lord in Your name
lost souls are found.

Lord in Your name
we receive mercy and grace.
It is in the name of Jesus
that we have no disgrace!

Thank You dear Jesus
for You alone are worthy!

~~~

"Scriptural Reference"
Philippians 2:9 thru 11 & John 17:25 thru 27

Philippians 2:9 *thru* 11 {King James Version}

"Wherefore God also
hath highly exalted Him,
and given Him a name
which is above every name:

That at the name of Jesus
every knee should bow,
of things in heaven,
and things in earth,
and things under the earth;

And that every tongue should confess
that Jesus Christ is Lord,
to the glory of God the Father."

John 17:25 *thru* 27 {King James Version}

"O righteous Father,
the world hath not known Thee:
but I have known Thee,
and these have known
that thou hast sent me.

And I have declared unto them thy name,
and will declare it: that the love
wherewith thou hast loved me
may be in them, and I in them."

~ Carpenter's Son ~

Knowledge is strength; strength leveraged is power!

Comfortable was I
supported by the LIE,
scared to death of living
and too afraid to die.

Treading life's edge
standing front and center,
walking the worldly walk
serving Satan's agenda.

Too busied by a world
wherein truth is denied,
I embraced the false realization
that in worldly knowledge we survive.

To God is the glory…
knowledge alone is not truth,
contrary to societal teachings
circumscribed in our youths.

Truth is "BALANCE"…
information and *knowledge* are keys,
tools used to transport us into a space
where we all can believe.

Jesus came not to the Earth to destroy
but lived and died to fulfill,
when he drank the deathly cup of Adam
atop of Golgotha Hill.

One April's day I awoke
from the sin of spiritual death unto life,
to the teachings of *"spiritual truth"*
that only the Holy Spirit can provide.

God's "Word" is *"Truth"*…
Peace and Love is *"Balance"*.

The Holy Spirit sheds *"Light"*…
Jesus Christ is our example.

~~~

"Scriptural Reference"
2nd Peter 1:2 thru 4 & Matthew 13:55 thru 56

2nd Peter 1:2 thru 4 {King James Version}

"Grace and peace be multiplied unto you
through the knowledge of God,
and of Jesus our Lord,

According as his divine power hath given unto us
all things that pertain unto life and godliness,
through the knowledge of him
that hath called us to glory and virtue:

Whereby are given unto us
exceeding great and precious promises:
that by these ye might be partakers of the divine nature,
having escaped the corruption that is in the world through lust."

Matthew 13:55 thru 56 {New King James Version}

"Is this not the carpenter's son?
Is not His mother called Mary?
And His brothers James, Joses, Simon, and Judas?

And His sisters, are they not all with us?
Where then did this *Man* get all these things?"

~ Cry Of The Poet ~

The anointing of the gift received!

The perfect poem
that I never wrote,
until in You Lord Jesus
I found my yoke.

Not in words
but in spiritual deeds,
the *"I Am That I Am"*
You are all I need.

Outside of sin
I have found the *"TRUTH"*,
without Your precious love
what would I do?

Would I make a case?
Perhaps run a race?
Would I trample the kind
or embattle the human race?

O' Lord, from deep within us…
Your Spirit cries out…
"Abba" Father, "Abba" Father,
there is no doubt.

"Scriptural Reference"
Colossians 3:17, Galatians 4:4 thru 6 & Psalm 45:1

Psalm 45:1 {New International Reader's Version}

"My heart is full of beautiful words
as I say my poem for the king.
My tongue is like the pen of a skillful writer."

Colossians 3:17 {King James Version}

"And whatsoever ye do in word or deed,
do all in the name of the Lord Jesus,
giving thanks to God and the Father by Him."

Galatians 4:4 thru 6 {New American Standard Bible}

"But when the fullness of the time came,
God sent forth His Son, born of a woman,
born under the Law,
so that He might redeem those
who were under the Law,
that we might receive the adoption as sons.

Because you are sons,
God has sent forth the Spirit of His Son into our hearts,
crying, "Abba! Father!""

~ Your Holiness ~

The eternal light of man!

O' Holy magnet
You are my heart's desire,
You ignite my spirit
You set my soul on fire.

You magnify my thoughts
You make me see,
the abundance of life
long buried in me.

From the days of my yearning
You heard and saw my plight,
You pricked my heart
You brought forth the *"LIGHT"*.

Out of a sea of darkness
from whence I had come,
by Your almighty hand
a miraculous work was done.

You cleansed my soul
You established my sight,
You are the *"Messenger of Love"*
You are the Father's delight.

You are an endless breath of scripture
the everlasting illumination of men,
You shine in our hearts
and we are made to live again.

You are our power of redemption;
You surrendered Your precious life for us.
You died to redeem our souls
from Satan's wanton touch.

"Scriptural Reference"
John 1:1 thru 5 & John 1:11 thru 13

John 1:1 thru 5 {New King James Version}

"In the beginning was the Word,
and the Word was with God,
and the Word was God.

He was in the beginning with God.
All things were made through Him,
and without Him nothing was made that was made.

In Him was life, and the life was the light of men.
And the light shines in the darkness,
and the darkness did not comprehend it."

John 1:11 thru 13 {New King James Version}

"He came to His own,
and His own did not receive Him.

But as many as received Him,
to them He gave the right
to become children of God,

to those who believe in His name:
who were born, not of blood,
nor of the will of the flesh,
nor of the will of man, but of God."

~ The Messiah ~

Promise of the coming Savior fulfilled!

Jesus is a mortal's way of dying,
He is a human's way of trying.
Jesus is man's best friend,
He is a lover of our lives
from beginning to end.

Jesus is man's extension of time.
Jesus sacrificed His life for all mankind.

Through Jesus, the Father expresses
His innermost harmonious feelings
of His love for the world.

The Spirit of Jesus is that silent force
that causes life to confess all truth.

So, let us pause and ask ourselves,
just as Pontius Pilate once asked Jesus…
What is truth?

Jesus is *"THE TRUTH"* of all creation!
Jesus is the *"ETERNAL LIGHT"* of man's salvation!
Jesus is that *"GOOD SHEPHERD"* that guides us…

When the brighter side of darkness
resonates like a sparkle in the sunset!

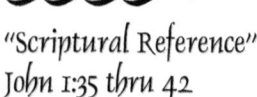

"Scriptural Reference"
John 1:35 thru 42

John 1:35 thru 42 {New American Standard Version}

"Again the next day
John was standing with two of His disciples,
and he looked at Jesus as He walked,
and said, "Behold, the Lamb of God!"

The two disciples heard Him speak,
and they followed Jesus.
And Jesus turned and saw them following,
and said to them, "What do you seek?"

They said to Him, "Rabbi, where are you staying?"
He said to them, "Come, and you will see."

So they came and saw where He was staying;
and they stayed with Him that day,
for it was about the tenth hour.
One of the two who heard John speak
and followed Him, was Andrew,
Simon Peter's brother.

He found first his own brother
Simon and said to him,

"We have found the Messiah"."

~ Christ Risen... ~

Beyond the breach!

Fear, hate, and schism
Jesus Christ has surely risen,
from the manger to the grave
resurrected to redeem the human race.

Three days swallowed up by the Earth
destined to fulfill the Savior's immaculate birth.
Swallowed up like Jonah in the belly of a whale
Jesus descended into the fiery depths of hell.

The *"cup of sin and death"* that Adam filled
Jesus drank to do His Father's will,
to save a bunch of sinners lives
that squandered dominion in paradise.

Rejected by His very own
Jesus walked the road to death alone,
undeterred by the religious schism
Jesus fulfilled His Father's business.

Although Lord… He calls us friends
a love hard for unredeemed sinners to comprehend,
One from whom the disciples fearfully scattered,
One in whom the Jews chose to free *"Barabbas"*.

Jesus promised a triumphant return
from Whom the mountains will flee and run,
at which time the Earth will soon discover
"there will not be one stone left upon another".

Jesus is coming back!
Every knee shall bow!
Every tongue shall confess…
that Jesus Christ is Lord!

Thus saith the Lord of Hosts!!!

"Scriptural Reference"
Mark 8:31, Matthew 28:2 thru 5 & Luke 24:6 thru 7

Mark 8:31 {New Century Version}

"Then Jesus began to teach them that the
Son of Man must suffer many things and that
he would be rejected by the Jewish elders,
the leading priests, and the teachers of the law.

He told them that the Son of Man must be killed
and then rise from the dead after three days."

Matthew 28:2 thru 5 {21st Century King James Version}

"And behold, there was a great earthquake;
for an angel of the Lord descended from heaven,
and came and rolled back the stone from the door, and sat on it.

His countenance was like lightning,
and his clothing as white as snow.
And the guards shook for fear of him,
and became like dead *men*.

And the angel answered and said unto the women,
'Fear ye not, for I know that ye seek Jesus,
who was crucified.'"

Luke 24:6 thru 7 {New Century Version}

"He is not here; he has risen from the dead.
Do you remember what he told you in Galilee?

He said the Son of Man must be handed over to sinful people,
be crucified, and rise from the dead on the third day."

~ P. E. S. ~

Miracles performed to the glory of God, not Satan!

Satan's triple threat is targeting me,
it's called *"P. E. S."* ...oooh can't you see?
God's latest manifestation
of an ages old mystery.

P̲rovocation, E̲nticement, S̲ubmission...
the Tempter's tools of the game,
but don't be surprised...
Satan is his name.

Satan appeals to our carnal nature...
this is crucial... check it out!
Jesus overcame three models of human weaknesses,
so there would be no doubt.

"Then Jesus was led up by the Spirit
into the wilderness to be tempted by the devil."
Examine the Holy Scriptures
to understand Satan's cleverness.

Satan Said... "If thou be the Son of God
command that these stones be made bread."
Provocation.... Provocation.... Provocation....
Don't be misled!

Satan Said... "If thou be the Son of God
cast thyself down and the angels shall bear thee up."
Enticement... Enticement... Enticement...
Same old stuff!

Satan Said... "If thou be the Son of God things will I give thee,
if thou wilt fall down and worship me."
Submission... Submission... Submission...
Don't be deceived!

Miracles are performed to the glory of God,
for God does not glorify the devil.

Had Jesus been provoked to perform a miracle…
He would have elevated Satan to God in Heaven.

Satan hasn't power to destroy,
he can only spiritually disrupt.
Had Jesus been enticed to cast Himself down,
He would have violated prophesy and self-destructed.

The Holy Spirit is our *"Comforter";*
His mission is to spiritually guide and instruct.
We are to submit ourselves to God only,
for in our Heavenly Father we trust.

All glory be to God,
God and God alone…
the Universe is God's house,
and Heaven is His throne.

"Scriptural Reference"
Hebrews 4: 15, Ephesians 3:16 & 1st John 4:4

Disclosure of the Eternal Gift | 165

Hebrews 4:15 {New King James Version}

"For we do not have a high priest
who cannot sympathize with our weaknesses,
but was in all points tempted as we are,
yet without sin."

Ephesians 3:16 {King James Version}

"That he would grant you,
according to the riches of his glory,
to be strengthened with might
by his Spirit in the inner man;"

1st John 4:4 {King James Version}

"Ye are of God, little children,
and have overcome them:
because greater is he that is in you,
than he that is in the world."

~ Convicted ~

Personal sacrifice... the true measure of service!

Spiritual addiction...
enduring worldly affliction,
I heard *"by His stripes we are healed"*.
Remember...

There is no conviction... without suffering!

From within the Lamb's Book of Life,
Jesus is our eternal sacrifice.
Hear Him...

There is no conviction... without suffering!

The prison of life poses no earthly escape,
for this reason Jesus became a death row inmate.
"Choose ye this day..."

There is no conviction... without suffering!

To receive *"abundant life"*
we must deny ourselves.
In God we survive and are spiritually kept...

There is no conviction, without suffering!

Jesus and His apostles endured the tests,
by surrendering their lives.
We must never forget...

There is no conviction... without suffering!

"Scriptural Reference"
1st Peter 4:12 thru 14 & Colossians 1:23 thru 24

Disclosure of the Eternal Gift

1st Peter 4:12 thru 14 {American Standard Version}

"Beloved, think it not strange
concerning the fiery trial among you,
which cometh upon you to prove you,
as though a strange thing happened unto you:

but insomuch as ye are partakers of Christ's sufferings,
rejoice; that at the revelation of His glory
also ye may rejoice with exceeding joy.

If ye are reproached for the name of Christ,
blessed are ye; because the Spirit of glory
and the Spirit of God resteth upon you."

Colossians 1:23 thru 24 {New King James Version}

"…if indeed you continue in the faith,
grounded and steadfast, and are not moved
away from the hope of the gospel which you heard,
which was preached to every creature under heaven,
of which I, Paul, became a minister.

I now rejoice in my sufferings for you,
and fill up in my flesh what is lacking
in the afflictions of Christ,
for the sake of His body,
which is the church…"

~ Resurrected ~

God of the eternal awakening!

You are the reason why
I did not die,
You called me out
I cannot deny.

You brought me back
You made me see,
those spiritual truths
born dead in me.

Like biblical Lazarus
from sleep I awoke,
stepped out of my sin
cast down my yoke.

I heard Your knock,
the "WORD" transformed my life,
You revealed *"The Truth"*
in You I survive.

You are justified dear Lord
to hold the key,
You pleased our Heavenly Father
when You died for me.

A worthless sinner was I
before You saved my soul,
You are my *"Living Testimony"*
a story worthy to behold.

"Scriptural Reference"
Romans 8:10 thru 11 & Romans 6:4

Romans 8:10 thru 11 {New International Version}

"But if Christ is in you,
your body is dead because of sin,
yet your spirit is alive because of righteousness.

And if the Spirit of Him who raised Jesus
from the dead is living in you,

He who raised Christ from the dead
will also give life to your
mortal bodies through His Spirit,
who lives in you."

Romans 6:4 {New International Version}

"We were therefore buried with him
through baptism into death in order that,
just as Christ was raised from the dead
through the glory of the Father,
we too may live a new life."

~ All Come ~

Accepting redemption!

Everlasting life, abundant and free
surrender your heart and soul and freely eat,
Christ's Word when eaten
is spiritual food for meat.

By the shedding of the Lamb's blood
unto the Heavenly Father we are called,
every race, sex, creed and color
come one, come all!

The door to redemption,
salvation and eternal life
is open…
All come!

"Scriptural Reference"
Revelation 22:14 thru 17 & Matthew 11:28 thru 30

Revelation 22:14 thru 17 {21st Century King James Version}

"Blessed are they that do His commandments,
that they may have right to the Tree of Life,
and may enter in through the gates into the city.

For outside are dogs and sorcerers,
and whoremongers and murderers and idolaters,
and whosoever loveth and maketh a lie.

I, Jesus, have sent Mine angel to testify unto
you these things in the churches.
I am the Root and the Offspring of David,
and the Bright and Morning Star."

And the Spirit and the bride say, "Come."
And let him that heareth say, "Come."
And let him that is athirst come;
and whosoever will,
let him take the Water of Life freely."

Matthew 11:28 thru 30 {New International Version – UK}

"Come unto me,
all you who are weary and burdened,
and I will give you rest.

Take my yoke upon you and learn from me,
for I am gentle and humble in heart,
and you shall find rest for your souls.
For My yoke is easy, and my burden is light."

~ Wismatic Gesture ~

Finding our inner path!

People that continuously walk
forever watching their feet,
blindly trip over the mistakes of others
that contributes to their defeat.

Rough roads are seldom traveled
discouraging bumps they do possess,
the *"chosen"* and *"faithful"* are servants
unto sacrifice, wherein Christ we find our rest.

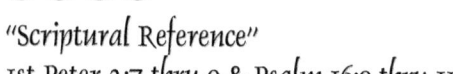

"Scriptural Reference"
1st Peter 2:7 thru 9 & Psalm 16:9 thru 11

1st Peter 2:7 thru 9 {21st Century King James Version}

"Unto you therefore who believe,
He is precious; but unto those who are disobedient,

"The stone that the builders disallowed,
the same is made the head of the corner,"

and, "A stone of stumbling and a rock of offense,"
even to those who stumble at the Word,
being disobedient, unto which also they were appointed.

But ye are a chosen generation,
a royal priesthood, a holy nation, a peculiar people,
that ye should show forth the praises of Him
who hath called you out of darkness
into His marvelous light."

Psalm 16:9 thru 11 {21st Century King James Version}

"Therefore my heart is glad and my spirit rejoiceth;
my flesh also shall rest in hope.

For Thou wilt not leave my soul in hell;
neither wilt Thou suffer Thine Holy One to see corruption.

Thou wilt show me the path of life;
in Thy presence is fullness of joy;
at Thy right hand there are pleasures for evermore."

~ The Good Fight ~

On the right side of Right!

Although some are rich
and many are poor,
there is one simple truth
that all should know.

When it comes to life
be it wrong or right,
we are commanded to stay the course
and fight the *"good fight"*.

Be we weak or strong
against thick or thin,
trust in the power of God
and not in the traditions of men.

The righteous were chosen
even before time began,
keep your faith and hope in Jesus
until the very end.

"Fight the good fight"

"Scriptural Reference"
1st Timothy 6:11 thru 12 & Colossians 2:8

Disclosure of the Eternal Gift | 175

1st Timothy 6:11 thru 12 {New International Version – UK}

"But you, man of God,
flee from all this,
and pursue righteousness, godliness,
faith, love, endurance and gentleness.

Fight the good fight of the faith.

Take hold of the eternal life
to which you were called
when you made your good confession
in the presence of many witnesses."

Colossians 2:8 {New Century Version}

"Be sure that no one leads you away
with false and empty teaching that is only human,
which comes from the ruling spirits of this world,
and not from Christ."

~~~

~ The Apostle Paul ~

The apostle of the Gentiles!

The Holy Scriptures record
that during the days of old,
Jesus anointed a persecutor of Christians
to preach the gospel of Christ
who was exceedingly bold.

He was Saul of Tarsus
a very zealous and learneth man,
a devout disciple of the law of Moses
before taking a righteous stand.

God struck a zealous murderer blind
to allow the renowned Apostle Paul to see,
how the crucifixion of the *"Lamb of God"*
would set the whole of humanity free.

"Scriptural Reference"
Acts 8:1 thru 3 & Romans 1:1

Disclosure of the Eternal Gift

Acts 8:1 thru 3 {New King James Version}

"Now Saul was consenting to His death.

At that time a great persecution arose
against the church which was at Jerusalem;

and they were all scattered throughout
the regions of Judea and Samaria,
except the apostles.

And devout men carried Stephen to His burial,
and made great lamentation over him.

As for Saul, he made havoc of the church,
entering every house,
and dragging off men and women,
committing them to prison."

Romans 1:1 {New International Version}

"Paul, a servant of Christ Jesus,
called to be an apostle
and set apart for the gospel of God."

~ No Questions Asked ~

Jack Eugene Walker... My guiding light to Christ!

When I look to my past,
and think of my life;
I am reminded of the perfect love of Jesus,
and *"His ultimate sacrifice"*.

Born into a cash driven world,
moving much too fast;
I was not surprised to find...
that I was wearing a mask.

From beyond the veil,
I was permitted a glimpse...
of *"the Lamb"* appointed to die,
One in Whom the world would deny.

Before my relationship with Christ,
my life was simply a token...
superficially camouflaged,
mis-managed and severely broken.

Completely void beyond measure,
I had forfeited every treasure,
until with a peaceful voice I clashed,
hearing... *"There are no questions asked"*

Get up and speak!!!

"Scriptural Reference"
John 10:27 thru 28 & 2nd Peter 1:17 thru 18

John 10:27 thru 28 {King James Version}

"My sheep hear my voice,
and I know them,
and they follow me.

And I give unto them eternal life;
and they will never perish,
neither shall any man
pluck them out of my hand."

~~~~~

2nd Peter 1:17 thru 18 {New International Version}

"He received honor and glory from God the Father
when the voice came to him from the Majestic Glory, saying,
"This is my Son, whom I love; with him I am well pleased."

We ourselves heard this voice that came from heaven
when we were with him on the sacred mountain."

~~~~~

~ Hands Of Praise ~

Blessed be Havaughnia!

From You Holy Father
I received believing hands of praise,
that emulates Your power and glory
in a myriad of ways.

Not stagnant hands
that do not fashion or build,
but resourceful hands
empowered with creativity and skill.

Hands that when pressed
meet the Heavenly Father's mark,
adorned to bless
and touch the broken hearted.

Hands that heal
to mend shattered lives,
hands that have endured suffering
and have been deprived.

Hands that are worthy…
in Your Son they are blessed,
hands that are highly favored
to withstand every test.

Father it is with these hands
that I give You honor and glory;
Father it is with these hands
that I inscribe Your story.

Father it is from within the hollow of Your hands
that I have received spiritual touch.
By Your hands was my life made eternal
and granted spiritual worth.

Father, it is with these hands
that I give You the highest praise;

Disclosure of the Eternal Gift | 181

For by the works of Your mighty hands
were all things created that are made.

You are worthy!

~~~

"Scriptural Reference"
Isaiah 40:10 thru 12

Isaiah 40:10 *thru* 12 {New King James Version}

"Behold, the Lord GOD will come
with a strong hand,
and His arm shall rule for Him;

Behold, His reward is with Him,
and His work before Him.

He will feed His flock like a shepherd:
He will gather the lambs with His arm,
and carry them in His bosom,
and gently lead those who are with young.

Who hath measured the waters in the hollow of His hand,
and meted out heaven with the span,
and calculated the dust of the earth in a measure,
and weighed the mountains in scales,
and the hills in a balance?"

~ Kingdom Keepers ~

Doing what Christians do!

We were born to be believers,
We are here to take a stand,
talking about God's mercy
and His grace toward every man.

Speaking to all nations,
living witnesses of God's truth,
rendering praise, honor and glory
as we do what born again Christians do.

Lord we adore, honor and love You
because You are God all alone.
We humble ourselves in Your presence
and commit our lives to Your heavenly throne!

"Scriptural Reference"
Psalm 47:7 thru 8 & Matthew 24:14

Psalm 47:7 thru 8 {New King James Version}

"For God *is* the King of all the earth;
Sing praises with understanding.

God reigns over the nations;
God sits on His holy throne."

Matthew 24:14 {New King James Version}

"And this gospel of the kingdom
shall be preached in all the world
for a witness unto all nations,
and then shall the end come."

~ In His Image ~

God is man's mirror!

The mirrors of life
are the windows of the soul
through which all great truths are seen.

How can we
being blind of God and ourselves
witness what we've not dreamed?

Dreams manifest life's possibilities
unimaginably small and great,
issuing from the Creator of all visible and invisible things,
whose blessings we cannot predate.

Man is a reflection of God's image
illuminating spiritual gifts within ourselves,
a human copy of our heavenly Creator
fashioned in the image and likeness of God Himself.

Ask what you will in the name of Jesus
and let God the Father prove you this day,
we receive not because we ask not...
Jesus Christ is our heavenly Advocate!

Know your purpose...
Live your dreams...

"Scriptural Reference"
Genesis 1:27, Mark 11:24, John 16:24 thru 25 & 1st Corinthians 2:9

Genesis 1: 27 {New International Version}

"So God created man in His own image,
in the image of God He created him;
male and female He created them."

Mark 11:24 {King James Version}

"Therefore I say unto you,
what things so ever ye desire,
when ye pray,
believe that ye receive them,
and ye shall have them."

John 16:24 thru 25 {New King James Version}

"Until now you have asked nothing in My name.
Ask, and you will receive, that your joy may be full."

"These things I have spoken to you in figurative language;
but the time is coming when I will no longer
speak to you in figurative language,
but I will tell you plainly about the Father."

1st Corinthians 2:9 {21st Century King James Version}

"But as it is written: "Eye hath not seen, nor ear heard,
neither have entered into the heart of man the things
which God hath prepared for them that love Him.""

~ Damascus Road ~

The road seldom traveled!

As I walk the roads of life,
projecting an image for all to see,
do they see a lantern of God,
that Jesus established in me?

Or do they see a gaping black hole,
all dressed and decked in stone;
Or do they see an aging body
constructed of dead dry bones?

Or do they see a Christ-like victor?
An overcomer in the trials of life,
having faithfully run the race against Satan,
while enduring life's challenges with a smile.

In the light of my eternal eye,
the Lord has made me be…
what He desires in each of us
a blinding light for all to see.

"Scriptural Reference"
Acts 22:6 thru 11 & Acts 13:9

Acts 22:6 thru 11 {New Century Version}

"About noon when I came near Damascus,
a bright light from heaven suddenly flashed all around me.
I fell to the ground and heard a voice saying,
'Saul, Saul, why are you persecuting me?'

I asked, 'Who are you, Lord?'
The voice said,
'I am Jesus from Nazareth whom you are persecuting.'
Those who were with me did not understand the voice,
but they saw the light.

I said, 'What shall I do, Lord?'
The Lord answered, 'Get up and go to Damascus.
There you will be told about all the things
I have planned for you to do.'

I could not see,
because the bright light had made me blind.
So my companions led me into Damascus."

Acts 13:9 {New King James Version}

"Then Saul, who also *is called* Paul,
filled with the Holy Spirit,
looked intently at him…"

~ Prodigal Son ~

Welcome home...!

Don't be shocked or disturbed
by what you see...
Jesus wasn't just beaten, stabbed and wounded,
please hear my plea!

He was hated and rejected by a world
that has turned its back on you and me.
Thank You Heavenly Father
for having mercy upon me!

Many are enraged by the horrible thoughts
of Jesus' bloody, tattered stains,
not realizing that humanity is the *"Prodigal Son"*
and old Satan is the blame.

I took the treasures of God's goodness
that were abundantly bestowed upon me,
and carelessly sowed them to the wind
for the entire world to see.

After having fallen down spiritually,
totally broken in despair,
Satan whispered in my ear...
"Eat the slop, nobody cares!"

I knew that he was lying,
for in my heart of hearts I could spiritually see,
Jesus standing wounded on life's road,
with outstretched arms awaiting me.

I tearfully looked into the eyes of my Lord...
His head pricked and punctured by a crown of thorns!
His hands spiked and dripping with blood!
His garment blooded, tattered, and torn!

His ribs pierced by the sword of a Roman soldier!
Abandoned by His disciples to die alone,

Jesus unselfishly rushed down from Calvary's cross
to personally welcome me home.

Jesus, the human manifestation of the Father
and I the spiritual *"prodigal son"*,
one who threw away his purchased inheritance
by turning away from God's only begotten Son.

Thank you dear Jesus for understanding,
You promised You would never forget my name;
You are the... *"lamb slain from the foundation of the world"*
and resurrected from the grave to bare my shame.

I know for years that I have been slack,
There is nothing justified I can possibly say,
but thank You my Holy Jesus
for receiving me back into Your kingdom to stay.

Welcome home my child... welcome home!

"Scriptural Reference"
Luke 15:11 thru 19

Disclosure of the Eternal Gift

Luke 15:11 thru 19 {New American Standard Version}

"And He said, "A man had two sons.
The younger of them said to his father,
'Father, give me the share of the estate that falls to me.'
So he divided his wealth between them.

And not many days later,
the younger son gathered everything together
and went on a journey into a distant country,
and there he squandered his estate with loose living.

Now when he had spent everything,
a severe famine occurred in that country,
and he began to be impoverished.

So he went and hired himself out
to one of the citizens of that country,
and he sent him into his fields to feed swine.

And he would have gladly filled his stomach
with the pods that the swine were eating,
and no one was giving *anything* to him.

But when he came to his senses, he said,
'How many of my father's hired men
have more than enough bread,
but I am dying here with hunger!

I will get up and go to my father,
and will say to him, "Father,
I have sinned against heaven, and in your sight;
I am no longer worthy to be called your son;
make me as one of your hired men."

~ Perfect Fruit ~

The "Alpha and Omega"!

Dear Jesus…

You are the Father's perfect fruit
from life's spiritual family tree,
from within the Garden of Eden
You were reserved for all to eat.

In crucifixion You were planted
a tree of eternal life to be,
in salvation and communion
You are eaten to be free.

There is nothing more majestic
beneath heaven, earth, nor sea,
than You my Holy Jesus
You lived and died for me.

Long generations ago
in an era long gone past,
You fulfilled the sacred *"Laws of Moses"*
that seeded our sinful past.

You are the blessed *"Ten Commandments"*
the anatomy of the unborn Christ,
You are the vows of the Christian Church
Your consecrated *"Holy Bride"*.

Born in a manger
You became living Scriptures of flesh,
You are the key to the *"Holy Mystery"*
in Your name we all are blessed.

From the works of Your Father's hands
we were shaped of earthen clay,
in Your divine *"Image and Likeness"*
we live justified day-by-day.

Perfect Fruit…

"Scriptural Reference"
John 15:1 thru 8

John 15:1 thru 8 {New International Version — UK}

"I am the true vine,
and my Father is the gardener.

He cuts off every branch in me that bears no fruit,
while every branch that does bear fruit He prunes
so that it will be even more fruitful.

You are already clean
because of the word I have spoken to you.
Remain in me,
and I will remain in you.

No branch can bear fruit by itself;
it must remain in the vine.
Neither can you bear fruit unless you remain in me.
I am the vine; you are the branches.

If a man remains in me and I in Him,
he will bear much fruit;
apart from me you can do nothing.

If anyone does not remain in me,
he is like a branch that is thrown away and withers;
such branches are picked up,
thrown into the fire and burned.

If you remain in me and my words remain in you,
ask whatever you wish, and it will be given you.
This is to my Father's glory, that you bear much fruit,
showing yourselves to be my disciples."

~ Reason For The Season ~

A Holy Child is born!

When I pause to celebrate Christmas,
realizing what Jesus means to me,
I am reminded of our resurrected Lord and Savior,
innocently crucified and left dying on a tree.

With limp body idly suspended…
pierced arms spiked and nailed outstretched;
Jesus Christ surrendered His glorious life,
to expunge humanity's every debt.

When I look to the hills of Calvary,
I am reminded of an image of a bloodied cross;
assembled vertically and horizontally,
crisscrossed and fashioned for us all.

Christ is the essence of the *"Holy Season"*,
celebrating the immaculate birth of *"baby Jesus"*,
for without the life, death and resurrection of our Lord,
December 25th would be a day without cause.

Satan's double-cross for the world today…
is tailored for those who have lost their way;
Every Christian should take a bold stand and say…
No Christ… No Christmas…No Holy Day!

From 2000 years ago in Bethlehem,
to Calvary throughout the world today…
Jesus is the one and only Lord and Savior,
and Christmas is here to stay!!!

No Christ, No Christmas, No Holy Day!

"Scriptural Reference"
Matthew 1:19 thru 21, Matthew 2:1 thru 4 & Proverbs 9:10

Matthew 1:19 thru 21 {Contemporary English Version}

"Joseph was a good man and did not want to
embarrass Mary in front of everyone.
So he decided to quietly call off the wedding.

While Joseph was thinking about this,
an angel from the Lord came to him in a dream.
The angel said, "Joseph, the baby that Mary will have
is from the Holy Spirit.
Go ahead and marry her. Then after her baby is born,
name him Jesus, because he will save his people from their sins."

Matthew 2:1 thru 4 {New King James Version}

"Now after Jesus was born in Bethlehem of Judea
in the days of Herod the king, behold, wise men from
the East came to Jerusalem, saying,

"Where is He who has been born King of the Jews?
For we have seen His star in the East and have come to worship Him."

When Herod the king heard this,
he was troubled, and all Jerusalem with him.

And when he had gathered all the chief priests
and scribes of the people together,
he inquired of them where the Christ was to be born."

Proverbs 9:10 {New King James Version}

"The fear of the Lord *is* the beginning of wisdom,
And the knowledge of the Holy One *is* understanding."

"The Eternal Gift"

"A Tablet Moment..."

Reflections of the small child...

As a small child, I simply could not wait until Christmas morning to race to the Christmas tree to see what *gifts* Santa Claus had brought me, not realizing that Jesus had died an agonizing death by hanging on a tree *(Acts 5:29-31)* to become the Heavenly Father's *"Anointed Gift of Eternal Blessing"* for me. All of my birthdays, Easters and Halloweens were great as holidays go, but nothing could compare to the sheer anticipation, excitement and exhilarating joy of Christmas. The true meaning and purpose of Christmas became clear to me many years later upon realizing that *"Calvary's cross of crucifixion"* is the authentic Christmas tree of Christ. Wherein, Jesus stated... *"And I, if I be lifted up from the earth, will draw all men unto Me." (John 12:32)*

As I reflect on my experiences as a very small child, I realize that my most memorable holidays were those established on a spiritual foundation revolving around celebrated icons and benevolent sponsors, whom all came bearing gifts. Christmas had Santa Claus, Easter had the Easter Bunny, Halloween with all of its ghostly characters had a host of charitable neighbors, but most importantly my birthdays had family and friends whom would shower me with unsolicited cards and gifts. I could not have imagined that the Holy Father's *"Anointed Gift of Blessing in Christ"* would translate into a second birth that would be far greater than the first. No one had bothered to tell me that "JESUS" was the "AUTHENTIC CHRISTMAS PRESENT" sent down from Heaven.

Santa Claus, my childhood philanthropic hero...

At this point in my life Santa Claus was the most benevolent and caring provider out of everyone included in my *"gifting oriented experience"*. Santa Claus was the unrivaled *"icon of gifting"* during my childhood for every happy and joyous Christmas past. Like the majority of American kids, I was *systematically taught, institutionally trained* and *socialized* into believing that *Santa Claus* provided the toys of Christmas without mention of "God's TOTAL PROVISION" in my life. I was also taught and encouraged to believe that the *Easter Bunny* provided the eggs of Easter without mention of God's total provision. It was impressed upon me that our *immediate and distant neighbors* provided the candy on Halloween irrespective of *God's total provision*. It was also impressed upon me that *family and friends* provided the birthday cards and gifts that honored my blessed arrival on Earth, while lacking the vital acknowledgement of *God's total provision* for all things received in my life regardless of the source.

I am joyfully reminded of being taken to countless toy stores and shopping malls by my parents during the start of every Christmas season to visit Santa and give him my cherished list of gifts. When Christmas morning finally arrived, I yearned to look into Santa's eyes and hug his neck for loving me enough to leave North Pole and travel around the world just to bring the toys that he had faithfully promised. Unfortunately, there were billions of other kids on Santa's roster whom were just like me and Santa only had the one day to travel the world over to deliver gifts to them also. There was nobody in the whole wide-world that loved and cared for me as much as my best friend and good buddy, Santa Claus. Santa was nearest to my heart and there was no one in the world that meant more to me on Christmas.

Holiday favorites...

In terms of holiday favorites, Easter was pretty neat considering I would normally receive a new Easter outfit in addition to the countless Easter eggs that were generous gifts of the *Easter Bunny*. Birthdays were special also; the birthday cake and presents received from *loved ones* would stir my emotions and make me feel that my life was unique and especially important, if only for the one day. Last but not least on my list was Halloween, which is remembered for its dark masquerading and devilish pranks. The Halloweens of old truly exemplified the saying that... *"It takes a village to raise a child"*. Neighbors and strangers from far and near would supply large stockpiles of candy among other treats, which could only be eaten over several weeks and sometimes months at a time. The candy, fruit, nuts, cookies and loose change was all complimentary of the *immediate and distant neighbors in the community*, whom reinforced the belief that the world is a compassionate and extremely wonderful place overflowing with *unconditional love*, which is evidenced by *affectual*

Disclosure of the Eternal Gift | 201

gifts. The term *"affectual"* was coined to lend special meaning to the customary gifts that crown the special occasions in our lives, stemming from the gifting celebration surrounding Christmas.

Early childhood development, the seat of understanding…

When I think back to my childhood and reminisce about Santa Claus and Christmas when I was only four or five years of age, I am soberly reminded of how it all began. It was here at this particular stage in my early childhood development that I started to *connect and formulate my ideas, beliefs, thoughts* and *experiences* into a series of psychological patterns that would establish the linear path that lead to and became the foundation for my *"seat of understanding"*. So, it was here that my *"foundational values"* arose and were etched into the cornerstone of my *"psyche"* and *"core system of beliefs"*. Only now do I realize the underlying affects that *"affectual gifting"* had on my social perception, traditional values, sense of being and self-worth.

The "preeminent Gift" of Christ, undermined…

In hindsight, the gifts and showing of affection was wonderful, but herein lie the problem… Santa arrives in the wee hours of December 25th (…*the night before Christmas*) bearing *"affectual gifts"* that by design preempts and undermines the *"celebration of the birth of Jesus Christ"* that takes place within a matter of hours later on *"Christmas morning"*. The gifts of Santa are meant to swat the long awaited celebrated birth of Jesus, which is the *"preeminent Gift"* of Christ to the world embodied in man. Christ is the *"Universally Divine Spirit"* that *creates, animates and binds* all things in existence. The gift of Christ was purposed by the Heavenly Father to spiritually transform man back into the *"image and likeness of God"* in which man was fashioned at the time of his creation *(Genesis 1:26). This universal solitary act restored man's common purpose, reestablished man's spiritual authority and recreated the divine character of God in man*.

The spiritual significance of the Christmas celebration is to commemorate the fact that *"Jesus Christ"* is the most precious gift that the world could ever receive *(John 3:16)*. Christmas would not be holy and complete without the conscious acknowledgment of this very important and celebratory fact. Every person born on Earth should be familiar with the following verse of scripture...

> "*For GOD so loved the world that he gave His only begotten Son, that whosoever believeth in Him should not perish, but have everlasting life.*" {21st Century King James Translation}

Jesus, the good and perfect "Spiritual Gift"...

"*For GOD so loved the world that He gave...*". Undoubtedly, the gift that God gave was Jesus. Jesus is the "IMMACULATELY CONCEIVED GOODNESS" in humanity. The birth of Jesus is the good and perfect "SPIRITUAL GIFT" that was given to the world in order for man's "*appointed purpose*" to be illuminated in humanity. Jesus is the Heavenly Father's gift of spiritual restoration to the world, being given for man to learn how to "*walk with God*" again. Jesus is the heavenly perfected embodiment of Christ in man, believed by many to have been sent from Heaven in the years ranging from 3 B.C. to 2 B.C..

The birth of Jesus provides Holy witness that is acknowledged in the spirit and title of "*CHRISTMAS*", which commemorates the "*Spiritual Gift*" that the world received in the form of "*Jesus Christ*", the long awaited and promised Messiah. Christmas is celebrated on December 25th and is not to be confused with the "*affectual gifting*" of material things that has been perpetuated by Satan through the acceptance of the mythical Santa Claus, whom stirs our spirits and emotions on the eve of the celebration of the Messiah's birth. The following is recorded in the book of James chapter 1, verse 17...

> "*Every good gift and every perfect gift is from above, and cometh down from the Father of lights, with whom is no variableness, neither shadow of turning.*" {King James Translation}

This I believe is the best example of acknowledging that every tangible gift is not necessarily a "*good gift*", which brings to mind the saying that... "*Things aren't always what they seem.*" In hindsight, I now realize that the material gifts that I received before accepting Jesus Christ as my Lord and Savior were not necessarily bad gifts, but were not the <u>good and perfect gifts</u> that can only come down from above from our Heavenly Father. I can only imagine how my early life before accepting Christ would have been had I been taught during my *"formative stage of early childhood development"* that <u>ALL PROVISIONS COME FROM GOD</u> irrespective of the hands and sources from whence they are received. Unfortunately, the media hype and exhilaration surrounding the celebration of Christmas tend to stimulate the hearts and minds of millions into overlooking the *"authentic Christ"* by the highly anticipated and misguided arrival of Santa Claus. Thus when fused with the increasing commercialization of material gifting, there leaves very little room for the conscious acknowledgment of "God's TOTAL PROVISION" or the acceptance of God's "HEAVENLY ANOINTED GIFT" that is given in the personage of Jesus Christ.

Mythical Santa, believed to be real...

Santa was my *"legendary wish-master"* and *"all-time gift-giver"* and without fail Santa would always come through for me. Christmas after Christmas I would awake with the thought of material gifts swirling around in my head, while having celebrated thoughts of Santa bumping me on his knee. I truly believed in my heart of hearts as a little child that Santa Claus was a *"real person"* and that he alone was the sole provider of all my gifts and Christmas joy. My socialization into a world of *"affectual gifting"* precluded me from realizing that every gift came from our Father in heaven, whom I had only heard about and not seen.

So upon turning on the water each morning to wash my face as one being baptized in the blood of Christ, I would imagine myself being the faucet that is attached to the basin, thus prompting the question...

> *"To whom does the water belong?"* And I imagined the faucet saying... <u>*"The water belongs to me, because the water flows out of me!"*</u> As the water flowed out of the faucet into the basin, I imagined myself being the basin, thus prompting the question...

"*To whom does the water belong?*" And I imagined the basin saying… "*The water belongs to me, because I possess the water that has flowed into me!*" I next imagined hearing a solemn and commanding voice speaking out of the ether, saying… "*The water belongs not to the faucet from which it flows, nor to the basin into which it was received, but the water belongs to Me. For I AM the Fountain of Life; the "I AM THAT I AM" from whence all waters flow, including the "Water of Everlasting Life"*! (John 4:9-11 & John 7:37-38)

Every gift, not necessarily a "good gift"…

*U*nfortunately, we live in a world where the emotions, desires and sentiments of the majority are influenced and fueled by the receipt of gifts. Gifts in and of themselves are very powerful tools of expression that serve the underlying purpose of shaping and formulating ones appraisal of one's self and sense of self-worth in relationship to the giver of the gift. With this in mind, it is extremely important for us to acknowledge that every gift is not necessarily a good gift… for the "*perfect gift*" comes from God in Heaven.

*A*s a small child, I was not taught to give thanks to our Heavenly Father for gifts received on *Easter, Halloween, birthdays and Christmas*. I was taught to thank those who cared enough to give; this was considered polite and proper in keeping with good manners. I was trained and expected to honor the hands of my appointed worldly "*gift-givers*" from whom the gifts of material were received. I was ignorant of the fact that God is the "PROVISIONAL FOUNTAIN" for all of our gifts, regardless of the hands and sources from whence they are received. The following is recorded in John chapter 4, verses 9 thru 10…

> "*The Samaritan woman said to Him, How is it that You, being a Jew, ask me, a Samaritan [and a] woman, for a drink? For the Jews have nothing to do with the Samaritans.*
>
> *Jesus answered her, If you had only known and had recognized God's gift and Who this is that is saying to you,*

Give Me a drink, you would have asked Him [instead] and He would have given you living water." {Amplified Version}

Jesus… God's gift of "Spiritual Redemption" to the world!!!

The good and perfect gift of Christmas is the birth of God's only begotten Son, Jesus Christ; *"Jesus is God's gift to the world!"* The gift of Jesus is unlike any other gift that one can receive. The gift of Jesus is *"The Key to the Kingdom of Heaven"* and *"The Door to Eternal Life"* for those whom receive Him. Not until past Christmas did I *"the elder"* look back upon the omissions of all the Christmases past, wherein the small child that grew into the adult lacked the realization of thanking our Heavenly Father for the "GIFT of Christ" and wished Jesus a happy birthday for being my celebrated "GIFT of Salvation"!!!

Upon reminiscing over the experiences of my youth, I now realize that the cap pistols, GI Joe's, tonka trucks and the like have all perished and long been forgotten. *The only nonperishable gift that I have ever received during the many years of my lifetime is the "Anointed Gift of Jesus Christ"*. All of the other gifts from the countless sources are gone, but the precious gift of Jesus Christ remains perfectly preserved, being securely wrapped in the *"Jesus heart of Christ"* that it came in. The following is recorded in 1st John chapter 4, verses 7 thru 10…

> *"Dear friends, let us love one another, for love comes from God. Everyone who loves has been born of God and knows God. Whoever does not love does not know God, because God is love. This is how God showed his love among us. He sent his one and only Son into the world that we might live through him. This is love: not that we loved God, but that he loved us and sent his Son as an atoning sacrifice for our sins." {New International Version}*

The authenticity of Jesus Christ…

When we consider the *"authenticity of Jesus"* as the only living God, relative to all the idol gods of other religions that no longer exist, Jesus' best earthly comparison is likely to be the Great Pyramid of

Giza *(also known as The Great Pyramid of King Khufu aka King Cheops)* that has existed for more than 4,500 years. The Great Pyramid of Giza is the lone survivor of the Seven Wonders of the Ancient World, which were the praise and admiration of millions during their existence, only for the other six wonders to have long passed away.

When the Seven Wonders of the Ancient World were all in existence, they consisted of the Great Pyramid of Giza in Egypt, Hanging Gardens of Babylon, Temple of Artemis at Ephesus, Statue of Zeus at Olympia, Mausoleum at Halicarnassus, Colossus of Rhodes and Lighthouse of Alexandria. During the highlight of their time, they each received the praise and adoration of millions. They were celebrated throughout the world and were thought to last forever.

Although, history has proven that only the Great Pyramid of Giza, which bears a hole in its side *similar to that of the crucified Jesus* has lasted for more than 4,500 years and continues to defy time and mystifies all that witness its continued existence.

The resurrection of Jesus following His crucifixion goes back nearly 2,000 years and He continues to be revered and praised throughout the world today. History has proven that Jesus alone continues to live as the eternal God of the Universe from among the myriad of idol gods of other religions that were praised and revered to last forever, but unfortunate for the believers their idol gods are no longer here *(Jeremiah 10:10-11 & 1st Thessalonians 1:9-10).*

Jesus was immaculately conceived of God, the Heavenly Father and was born into the Earth of a virgin mother over 2,000 years ago in the form of the *"humanly manifested Christ" ("The Messiah")* for the purpose of restoring man's spiritual character and establishing His heavenly kingdom on Earth. The birth, death and resurrection of Jesus consolidated His eternal reign of Lordship as King and *"Universally Divine Spirit"* over the provincial estates of the heavens and the Earth, which constitutes the entire Universe.

Unfortunately, our social traditions have placed more emphasis on exchanging material gifts that in-part has more to do with our desires to imitate the *"spirit of giving"* that was modeled by the wise men, which was <u>incorrectly interpreted</u>. Instead, we should be exchanging the *"authentic gift of unconditional love"*, which is the *"agape love"* given to us by God the Father in the personage and character of our Lord Jesus Christ, our heavenly model in bodily form *(Luke 3:22)*.

Gifts of the wise men imitated, but totally misunderstood...

The gifts that were given to baby Jesus by the wise men were not *"affectual gifts"* or *"feel good gifts"* as one would think. They were actually corporate-styled *"business gifts"* *(to be discussed in greater detail later...)* that were intended for a missionary purpose that would take place later in the life of the adult Jesus, the *"long awaited Messiah"*. Far too many people are unaware of the fact that their charitable practices of *"affectual gifting"* as it relates to the celebration of Christmas is actually misguided and intentionally so. If we were to examine our social tradition of affectual gift-giving that evolved from the <u>*inappropriately revered benevolent acts*</u> of the wise men, we would find a mysterious figure by the name of *"Satan"* posing as the mythical *"Santa Claus"* at the very heart of the tradition.

Satan and mythical Santa, one and the same...

Santa Claus is so mysterious that neither he nor Satan, his creator has a *"birth record"* that can authenticate and legitimize either of their existences on planet Earth, <u>*but Jesus does (Luke 2:1-7)*</u>*!!!* What I find absolutely ironic is that neither Santa nor Satan were born of a woman, which would make them legal citizens of the Earth, yet their combined existences exceeds the lifespan of any person recorded in human history, including Methuselah who lived 965 years.

Jesus, the "Good Shepherd"...

In the book of Psalms, King David identifies Jesus as his *"Lord and Shepherd"* when he states... *"<u>The Lord is my Shepherd; I shall not want...</u>" (Psalm 23, verse 1)*. Therefore, when Jesus is speaking in the Gospel of John chapter 10, verse 11; He identified Himself as the *"<u>Good Shepherd</u>"*, while referring to the world as a *"sheepfold"* metaphorically. *{John 10:1-11 New King James Version}*

¹ "Most assuredly, I say to you, he who does not <u>enter the sheepfold by the door</u>, but climbs up some other way, the same is a thief and a robber. ² But he who enters by the door is the shepherd of the sheep. ³ To him the doorkeeper opens, and the sheep hear his voice; and he calls his own sheep by name and leads them out. ⁴ And when he brings out his own sheep, he goes before them; and the sheep follow him, for they know his voice. ⁵ Yet they will by no means follow a stranger, but will flee from him, for they do not know the voice of strangers." ⁶ Jesus used this illustration, but they did not understand the things which He spoke to them.

⁷ Then Jesus said to them again, "Most assuredly, I say to you, <u>I am the door of the sheep</u>. ⁸ All who ever came before Me are thieves and robbers, but the sheep did not hear them. ⁹ <u>I am the door. If anyone enters by Me, he will be saved, and will go in and out and find pasture</u>. ¹⁰ The thief does not come except to steal, and to kill, and to destroy. I have come that they may have life, and that they may have it more abundantly. ¹¹ "<u>I am the good shepherd. The good shepherd gives His life for the sheep</u>."

The Merriam Webster's Dictionary defines *"sheepfold"* as a *"<u>pen or shelter for sheep</u>"*. Therefore, when sheepfold is applied to humans, *"sheep"* is being used as a *metaphor* in the biblical sense with Jesus being the *"shepherd"*. When this passage of scripture is viewed in proper context with Jesus being our *"Lord and Shepherd"* it becomes clear that Jesus is using the word *"sheepfold"* in the *shepherd's vernacular* to identify *"<u>Planet Earth or the world in which we live</u>"*.

Likewise, Jesus is using *"<u>door of the sheepfold</u>"* to represent the *"<u>womb of a woman</u>"* (Matthew 11:11). Undoubtedly the *"<u>first door</u>"* referenced by Jesus is the *"<u>gateway of physical birth</u>"* into the Earth. Jesus goes on to state that the *"<u>thief and robber</u>"* entered into the *"<u>sheepfold</u>"* another way. Unlike Jesus, Satan's entry into the Earth was not by the womb of a woman. <u>Satan is a "bodiless spirit" that uses humans as "bodily host", in the same way that he used the serpent!!!</u>

Jesus is unmistakably identifying *"Satan" aka "Lucifer"* as the *"thief and robber"* whom God kicked out of Heaven into the Earth, wherein he did not receive a physical body as did Jesus and the rest of us. Jesus' reference to a *"second door"* represents *"spiritual rebirth"*, which brings us to the baffling question posed to Jesus by Nicodemus...

> *"How can someone be born when they are old?"* Nicodemus asked. *"Surely they cannot enter a second time into their mother's womb to be born!"* {John 3:4}

Jesus Christ... "Our Lord and Shepherd"... Voice of the Church...

There is an increasing acceptance among many of today's Church congregations that their pastor is their *"shepherd"*, wherein many pastors regard their congregation as *"their flock"*. This belief, although false, is rapidly becoming a "PASTORAL TRADITION" that is gaining global acceptance among Christian congregations around the world. This belief although common is in direct contradiction to Scripture, therefore the following verse of Scripture has been broken down to provide clarity and understanding for the Christian Church of today...

> *"My sheep hear my voice, and I know them, and they follow me:"* {John 10: 27} {King James Version}

This seemingly simple verse is critical to our understanding the preordained role of the preacher in relationship to the dispensation of the Voice of God among His people. When simplified, it reads... *"My sheep hear my voice, and I know who they are, and the voice of another they will not follow"*. Upon translating this verse of Scripture based upon "REVELATION", this is what Jesus is really saying... *"My disciples hear my commandments, and I know who they are and they know who I Am, and the commandments of another they will not follow."*

To fully comprehend what Jesus is saying based upon *"revelation and Scriptural interpretation"*, we must know and understand the significance of the *"three voices"* of the *"speaker"* and the *"three ears"* of the *"listener"*.

The *"three voices"* of the speaker are, the *"voice of silence"* which is known as *"thought"*, and when one thinks out loud the voice of silence becomes the *"speaking voice"*, and the speaking voice once spoken becomes the *"spoken voice"*.

The *"three ears"* of the listener are the *"deaf ear"*, the *"listening ear"* and the *"hearing ear"*. All are born with a spiritual deaf ear that causes us not to hear God, due to being born in sin *(Psalm 51:5, James 2:26)* with contaminated spirits. God has therefore appointed preachers to study His Word in silence, with the *"voice of silence"*, until His *"Spoken Word"* is revealed to the pastors that He has divinely anointed *(Jeremiah 3:15)* to speak to the congregations in *"His Churches"*.

> *"He that hath an ear, let him hear what the Spirit saith unto the churches; To him that overcometh will I give to eat of the hidden manna, and will give him a white stone, and in the stone a new name written, which no man knoweth saving he that receiveth it." {Revelation 2:17}*

Upon receiving revelation from God, the preacher uses the *"speaking voice"* to fine tune the *"deaf ear"* of the nonbelievers and those that are lacking in the fullness of faith to hear the *"Spoken Voice"* of the Lord. Once the deaf ear is activated by the preacher, he uses the *"speaking voice"* to transform the *"listening ear"* into the *"hearing ear"*, in order for the Church to hear the commandments spoken over 2,000 years ago by Jesus Christ, our Lord and Shepherd.

Now clearly understood, let's take a look at what Jesus really meant. Jesus <u>was not</u> talking about the *"present"* or *"speaking voice"*, He was talking about the *"Spoken Voice"*. Jesus is referencing things that He spoke to His apostles and disciples that were recorded as *"The Gospel"* and passed down to us as *"His commandments"*.

Unfortunately, the counterfeit preachers are elevating themselves to the level of God by passing their *"speaking voice"* off to their congregations as the *"Spoken Voice"* of God. This is a growing tradition that is demonically inspired with the goal of weakening the Church at the highest level, by circumventing the *"Voice of God"* by the workers of Satan that are passing themselves off as *"ministers of Light"*. This tradition had its birth during the Old Testament period with the Pharisees and was made known to the people by Jesus during the

Disclosure of the Eternal Gift | 211

establishment of the Early Christian Church. The Apostle Paul recorded the following in 2nd Corinthians chapter 11, verses 12 thru 15...

> *"But what I do, I will also continue to do, <u>that I may cut off the opportunity from those who desire an opportunity to be regarded just as we are</u> in the things of which they boast.*
>
> *<u>For such are false apostles, deceitful workers, transforming themselves into apostles of Christ.</u>*
>
> *And no wonder! <u>For Satan himself transforms himself into an angel of light.</u>*
>
> *<u>Therefore it is no great thing if his ministers also transform themselves into ministers of righteousness</u>, whose end will be according to their works." {New King James Version}*

Tradition, an enemy to the Christian Church and man...

The role of tradition in all societies establishes the communal guidelines for our faith and beliefs as individuals and without it secular societies would fail to coalesce in an orderly manner. <u>Tradition creates the cultural continuity in social attitudes, customs, and institutions</u>. The Merriam Webster Dictionary defines tradition in this way...

> *"an inherited, established, or customary pattern of thought, action, or behavior (as a religious practice or a social custom)"*

Secular tradition is without doubt an enemy to Christian doctrine, for it *socially coerces and influences* the majority of people to obey man rather than God pointing to the counterfeit preachers. There is a marvelous religious example of this that is demonstrated by Jesus in the book of Mark chapter 7, verses 5 thru 13...

> *"So the Pharisees and teachers of religious law asked him,*
> *'Why don't your disciples follow our age-old tradition?*
> *They eat without first performing*
> *the hand-washing ceremony.'*
>
> *Jesus replied, "You hypocrites!*

Isaiah was right when he prophesied about you, for he wrote,
'These people honor me with their lips,
but their hearts are far from me.
Their worship is a farce,
for they teach man-made ideas as commands from God.'

For you ignore God's law
and substitute your own tradition."

Then he said, "You skillfully sidestep God's
law in order to hold on to your own tradition.

For instance, Moses gave you this law from God:
'Honor your father and mother,'
and 'Anyone who speaks
Disrespectfully of father or mother must be put to death.'

But you say it is all right for people to say to their parents,
'Sorry, I can't help you. For I have vowed to give to God
what I would have given to you.' In this way,
you let them disregard their needy parents.

And so you cancel the word of God
in order to hand down your own tradition.

And this is only one example among many others."
{New Living Translation}

Secular tradition instructs us to do as our fathers did even when history and wisdom dictates a more reasonable and prudent course of action. We see very clear examples of this during the transition from the Old Testament order of Levitical Priesthood under the Law of Moses to that of the New Testament order of Apostolic Priesthood under Grace through Jesus Christ.

One of the most notable examples involved the *Jerusalem High Council of high priest*, whom thought it best to have Jesus crucified in order to preserve the established tradition of religious Law that was given by Moses, rather than accepting Jesus in whom the scriptural had prophetically pointed to as being the long awaited Messiah *(Son of the living God)*. <u>The following is recorded in the book of Acts...</u>

> *"Then they brought the apostles before the high council, where the high priest confronted them. "Didn't we tell you never again to teach in this man's name?" he demanded. "Instead, you have filled all Jerusalem with your teaching about him, and you want to make us responsible for his death!" But Peter and the apostles replied, "<u>We must obey God rather than any human authority</u>." {Acts 5:27-29} {New Living Translation}*

Of course, the following translation of this key passage, which is recorded in the New King James Version probably best articulates the tenor and tone that was voiced by the apostles at that particular place and time…

> *"But Peter and the other apostles answered and said: '<u>We ought to obey God rather than men.</u>'"*

Will you obey God, or will you continue to obey Satan and man?

The question is… <u>Are we to obey the worldly traditions of our forefathers that were taught to them by Satan? The same traditions that influences us to accept Santa Claus over Jesus, or are we to obey the commandments of God? Better yet, are we to respond to the affectual and material gifts of man that have clouded and pervaded the true meaning behind our holidays?</u> Or, should we avoid the similar pitfalls of the high priest of the Jerusalem High Council by responding to the "PERFECT GIFT OF GOD" in the personage of our Lord and Savior, Jesus Christ? The following is recorded in John chapter 8, verse 44…

> *"<u>You are of your father the devil, and your will is to do your father's desires.</u> He was a murderer from the beginning, and does not stand in the truth, because there is no truth in him. When he lies, he speaks out of his own character, for he is a liar and the father of lies." {English Standard Version}*

Tradition compels us to render a higher appraisal than what is deserving of the material gifts that are provided by <u>Santa Claus</u>. The truth is that we have been so conditioned to respond to the affectual gifts that can be held in our hands and are tangible to the touch that we have failed to seek out the truth about the "HEAVENLY ANOINTED GIFT" that was given to us in the person of Jesus Christ. Unfortunately, few are cognizant of the nontraditional types of gifts that influence our life-long decisions and experiences on a *business, social, spiritual and communal level*, which have aided in shaping our personal and social values as individuals and collective values as a Christian society.

Santa Claus and Satan, "participating partners of illusion"...

On today we can trace every bit and piece of evidence that acquaints us with the traditional practices of *"affectual gift-giving"* back to our mythical friend and spiritual foe, *Santa Claus and Satan*. Santa Claus and Satan are the *"participating partners of illusion"* that have gone about the business of perpetrating deceit and deception upon non-suspecting, would-be believers under the banner of peace, love and goodwill for centuries. Christian society has actually been duped into believing that the gifts that were presented to the baby Jesus by the wise men were in fact *"affectual gifts"* or *"feel good gifts"* that are representative of the *"material gifts given to us by Santa Claus"*. The following is recorded in the book of Matthew chapter 2, verse 11...

> *"And when they had come into the house, they saw the young Child with Mary His mother, and fell down and worshiped Him. And when they had opened their treasures, they presented unto Him gifts: gold and frankincense and myrrh." {21st Century King James Translation}*

The acceptance of this myth has become the traditional model for *"social gift-giving"* that has spawned the crazed and insane *commercial gifting exchange* between God's people, which has increased exponentially over the many centuries.

Gifts of the wise men... Business gifts thought to be affectual...

If we simply accept the status quo and not examine the scriptures further, it would appear that the *gold, frankincense and myrrh* were indeed *"affectual gifts"* that were purposed to demonstrate love and adoration toward our Lord and Majesty, baby Jesus and nothing more.

However, what we fail to acknowledge is that the gifts that were presented to baby Jesus by the wise men were not affectual gifts at all. The gifts were not purposed to stimulate the emotions and rouse the sentiments and affections of Joseph, Mary on behalf of baby Jesus, but were actually intended for the missionary work of the adult Jesus during His 3½ years of earthly ministry, some 30 years later. The *gold, frankincense and myrrh* were representative of a great deal more than what the traditions of our forefathers have led us to believe. The gifts of the wise men were in fact corporate-styled *"business gifts"* that were purposed by God the Father for carrying out the *"business"* that Jesus spoke of to Joseph and Mary when he was twelve years of age...

"Did you not know that I must be about my Father's business?"

The gifts that were received from the wise men were in fact *"Messianic Tools"* purposed for the *"Missionary Toolbox"* of the Anointed Christ that were to be used in carrying out *"His assignment"*. The gifts of the wise men were corporate styled *"business gifts"* supplied by God the Father to His Son for the preordained purpose of symbolizing the three distinct and equally important roles of sovereign authority that were to be fulfilled during Jesus' brief stay on Earth.

Threefold ministry of Jesus...

Jesus was born into the world as the long awaited Messiah to the Jewish people and Savior of the world at large. Jesus' timely birth was purposed to fulfill the prophetic roles of *"King"*, *"Redeemer"* and *"Sacrificial Lamb"*. The fore-stated roles were prophetically preordained and divinely established based upon the tri-fold ministry of Jesus as *preacher, teacher and healer* during the 3½ years ministry that would take place beginning at age 30 *(Luke 3:23)* nearing the end of Jesus' lifetime.

The heavenly commission of the young Messiah misunderstood...

The use of the wise men's gifts as *"Messianic Tools"* by the Messiah culminated into the fulfillment of the *"Law"* and the *"Prophets"*, thus setting up the New Testament Age of the *"new heavens"* and *"new Earth"*. This fact will become clearer as we continue to explore Jesus' role as the Messiah on Earth in relationship to the statement spoken by Him to His parents when He was only 12 years of age. The following account is recorded in the book of Luke chapter 2, verses 41 thru 50...

> *"His parents went to Jerusalem every year at the Feast of the Passover. And when He was twelve years old, they went up to Jerusalem according to the custom of the feast. When they had finished the days, as they returned, the Boy Jesus lingered behind in Jerusalem. And Joseph and His mother did not know it; but supposing Him to have been in the company, they went a day's journey, and sought Him among their relatives and acquaintances. So when they did not find Him, they returned to Jerusalem, seeking Him.*
>
> *Now so it was that after three days they found Him in the temple, sitting in the midst of the teachers, both listening to them and asking them questions. And all who heard Him were astonished at His understanding and answers. So when they saw Him, they were amazed; and His mother said to Him, "Son, why have You done this to us? Look, Your father and I have sought You anxiously."*
>
> *And He said to them, "Why did you seek Me? <u>Did you not know that I must be about My Father's business?</u>" <u>But they did not understand the statement which He spoke to them.</u>" {New King James Translation}*

Satan transforms himself into the mythical Santa Claus...

This <u>seemingly minuscule misunderstanding</u> surrounding the wise men's gifts would pave the way for Satan's development of the "TRADITIONAL SYSTEM OF AFFECTUAL GIFTING" that disguises him as the *"mythical Santa Claus"*. One who took *"manmade material gifts"* and developed a "CELEBRATORY SYSTEM OF GIFTING" around himself, which was purposely designed to preempt the celebratory birth of the long awaited Messiah. Material gifting is purposed by design to make one feel good about one's self and rouse human affection toward the giver, who in this particular case is none other than Satan, the fallen angel *"who deceives the whole world"* {Revelation 12:9} in mythical disguise. If Satan has the ability to transform himself into an *"angel of light"* {2^{nd} Corinthians 11:13 15}, we should not be surprised to learn that Satan is wise and shrewd enough to transform himself into little ole *"Santa Claus"*.

> *"For such are false apostles, deceitful workers, transforming themselves into the apostles of Christ. And no marvel; for Satan himself is transformed into an angel of light.*
>
> *Therefore it is no great thing if his ministers also be transformed as the ministers of righteousness; whose end shall be according to their works."* {King James Version}

Satan, Santa Claus and the Early Christian Church...

There were two events of major historical significance that occurred in the 4th century A.D. that would position and brand Satan as a "MASQUERADING PERPETRATOR OF GOODWILL" and "RELIGIOUS IMPOSTER OF GOD".

The first event was the nationalization of the early Christian Church under Roman authority, whereby Emperor Constantine's conversion to Christianity brought an end to Christian persecution throughout the Roman Empire. In the year 313 A.D. the Edict of Milan was established by the Roman Emperor Constantine *(Ruler of the West)* and the Roman Emperor Licinius *(Ruler of the East)*. The edict was a proclamation that permanently established religious tolerance for Christian worship within the Roman Empire after decades of Christian persecution by many ruling Roman authorities.

The Christian Church would later emerge as the official religion of the Roman Empire, thereby opening the door for a myriad of pagan practices to enter into the Christian Church. The unorthodox beliefs and practices, which were later embraced, were introduced by-way of pagan traditions and customs that over a period of time became integrated into the larger body of Christian thought and ultimately exceeded the scope of previously established Jewish teachings. The unavoidable deviation served as a historical marker that would signal a gradual shift away from the strict and regimented teachings of Jewish tradition that had been so rigidly structured and deeply engrained in the rule of Law under the auspices of the Leviticus Priest hood.

Sunday worship, Satan's counterfeit to Sabbath observance...

The introduction of pagan practices into the post Apostolic Church, which was foundered by Jesus and established by the apostles, would upon acceptance become traditional norms in the Christian Orthodox Church of Rome. The acceptance of such practices fostered liberal tolerances on behalf of Christian converts and would-be believers that were characteristic of pagan culture and traditions. Probably the most far reaching pagan practice that would enter into the Christian Church was the adoption and acceptance of *"Sunday worship"* on the first day of the week, versus worshiping God on the seventh day as recorded in the Ten Commandments. The Roman Emperor Constantine changed the day of the biblically recognized Sabbath from Friday-Saturday to Sunday *(in concealed acknowledgment of Sun Worship)* through the adherence to the Sunday Law that was passed on March 7, 321 A.D..

This was by far the most notable and flagrant deviation that served as an opening to allow sorted elements of pagan tradition to be adopted into the Christian Church, only for the practices to become so pervasive and widespread that the mythical characters of Satan began to creep into the minds, hearts and practices of the believers unaware. There is evidence of early Christians' acceptance of Santa Claus, the Easter Bunny and Halloween characters that would come bearing gifts.

Mythical Santa emerges as a fictitious imposter of Saint Nicholas...

In addition to Sunday worship, Santa Claus emerges as a fictitious imposter to Saint Nicholas. Saint Nicholas was a very popular and famous Greek bishop whose Christian legacy and noble character was admired, honored and accepted in both the religious and secular realms. It is here that the *"legacy of goodwill"* that legitimately popularized Saint Nicholas, led to the mythical birth and worldly acceptance of Santa Claus. These two historic events placed Satan in the unique position of sabotaging man's willingness to receive the *"good and perfect Spiritual Gift of God"* in the person of Jesus Christ. Satan's plan was simple; he would introduce himself as one who had come bearing gifts in the spirit of Saint Nicholas of the 4th Century A.D., only to alter the recognized date of annual celebration from *December 6th* and rededicate it to Santa Claus on *December 25th*.

This seemingly noble approach appealed to church leaders, parents, civic leaders and the like only to become a widely established, religious tradition. The Merriam-Webster Encyclopedia records Saint Nicholas as being an authentic historical figure that flourished in the 4th century. He was a Greek bishop of the biblical and historical city of Myra, Lycia that was located in Asia Minor. Myra is identified in Scripture as the city where Saint Paul changed ships at its port on his way to trial in Rome. This event occurred in approximately 60 A.D. *("Acts chapter 27, verses 1 thru 5")*, after Paul had been arrested in Jerusalem and charged with inciting a riot.

> *"Saint Nicholas is a minor saint associated with Christmas. Probably bishop of Myra, he is reputed to have provided dowries for three poor girls to save them from prostitution and to have restored to life three children who had been chopped up by a butcher. He became the patron saint of Russia and Greece, of charitable fraternities and guilds, and of children, sailors, unmarried girls, merchants, and pawnbrokers.*
>
> *After the Reformation his cult disappeared in all the Protestant countries of Europe except Holland, where he was known as Sinterklaas. Dutch colonists brought the tradition to New Amsterdam (now New York City), and English-speaking Americans adopted him as Santa Claus, who is believed to live at the North Pole and to bring gifts to children at Christmas." {"Encyclopedia Britannica"}*

Satan's mission of world-wide deception fulfilled in Santa Claus...

Satan being one who knew the hearts of men and the weaknesses of the flesh was well aware of how material gifts would appeal to the

the time of their births, infant babies have been aroused and mesmerized by material objects that are present in their environment, even to the point of clinging passionately to them and placing them in their mouths, wherein they experience an oral sensation similar to that of a pacifier. The material gifts received from Santa Claus have purposely rendered their small minds helpless of responsibly choosing between the *"intangible gift of Jesus Christ"* our *"Savior", One* in whom they could not see, conceive, nor touch, versus the *"material gifts of Santa Claus"* that were deeply cherished, affectionately embraced, often shared, repeatedly handled, while being passionately and extensively used over very long periods of time.

So the acceptance of *"mythical Santa"* by little children was central to the plan of Satan in the secular realm and the spiritual positioning of the Pontiff was central to Satan in the religious realm. The following is recorded in Daniel chapter 7, verses 19 thru 25, and is interpreted by many to apply to the Pontiff... *"He will intend to change religious festivals and laws..."*. Once implemented, the twofold plan provided perfect cover and positioning for Satan as he went about the business of successfully preempting God's *"Heavenly Anointed Gift of everlasting life"*, which is acknowledged on Christmas Day with the birth of the divine Christ as *"God of man, in man"* (John 12:34).

Damaging effects of "affectual gifting" on little children...

The preordained package of lies that are told to little children regarding the legitimacy of Santa Claus and his fictitious counterparts begins with our parents and filters down through every tier of society until the list of savory untruths affect everyone. The insidious effect of *"affectual gifting"* is vested in the belief that material gifts can be substituted for the *"Spiritual Gift"* of God. The seed once planted does permanent damage to children during their premature stages of early childhood development during their *"period of innocence"* before he or she becomes fully aware of trespass and sin. The fabricated truth of Santa's existence is then affirmed and reinforced in the subconscious mind of the child by *cultural institutions, mass media, family, friends and loved ones* to the detriment of the acceptance of Jesus as *"God's Eternal Gift"* to man.

By the time little children grow into adults, they have already been caught-off and bought-off by Satan, whose been masquerading out in the open as *Santa Claus, the Easter Bunny, the goodwill merchants of Halloween,* and the like. These mythical figures and their worldly accomplices share a long historical past, which serves to endorse their legitimacy as permanent fixtures in our lives and social traditions. They become *"legendary providers"* of the *"fictitious social trappings"* that are instilled in our lives even before our journeys of life begin.

"Effectual gifting" and *"EARLY CHILDHOOD DEVELOPMENT"*...

When reminded of the seemingly empty and rather barren space in my life formally known as "EARLY CHILDHOOD DEVELOPMENT", I can vividly remember two familiar and believable characters that standout from the teachings of my earliest memories. The first and foremost is *Santa Claus;* the second and more subtle is *Jesus Christ.* Santa was a permanent mental fixture to me, due in large measure to the tangible nature of the gifts and Jesus was but a vague memory that I related to in song... *"Yes, Jesus loves me..."*. More importantly, the Christmas carols about Jesus struggled to resonate due to the skewed backdrop and mixture of religious and secular Christmas carols that further complicated the real celebration and true meaning of Christmas.

Christ, subliminally upstaged by Christmas carols of Santa Claus...

I am reminded of the songs about Santa that really rocked my world as a small child; songs like... *"Jingle Bell Rock"*, *"Santa Clause Is Coming To Town"* and many others like them. I now realize that I was confused by the secular Christmas carols, which further complicated matters for me in ways that I could not begin to understand until now. There was an undeniable high stakes competetion taking place between Santa Claus and Jesus Christ that had been going on for centuries, but Santa's public relations campaign was so smooth and subtlety inviting that it all blended in to everyone's consciousness without notice. In retrospect, it has become clear to me that Satan is the perpetrator in this brazen crime against humanity and little children are the victims. If forensics were possible, evidence would reveal the presence of Satan's fingerprints on each of the *"affectual gifts"* that littered the young hearts and minds of those whom were present at all of the celebrated crime scenes of Christmas past!

In hindsight, the joy that I experienced as a young child had little to do with the carols about Jesus who was born to save the world, but was more a result of the abundant gifts of Santa. I can still hear the lyrics from the litany of carols that filled the Christmas air when I was a child, but when examined through the ears of a <u>spiritually awakened grownup</u>. I am acutely aware of the heated rivalries that ensued between the *secular carols of Santa* and the *spiritual carols of Christ*, very similar to hotly contested boxing matches and NBA slam-dunk contests.

Where are the gifts?

As an adult, I love and adore Jesus, but as a little child I was still left with the lingering question of… "<u>*If Jesus really loves me like the song says, where are the gifts?*</u>" The only gifts that I knew of that were connected with Jesus were the fabled *gold, frankincense and myrrh*. These were the gifts given to Jesus by the wise men of the Bible, but yet there were no gifts that flowed from Jesus to me. So the mere notion of the *"celebrated, but less appreciated Jesus"* being esteemed above Santa and his celebrated host of idols that filled my infinitely small and very fragile world with bountiful gifts was without merit. This could not be truer when viewed based upon the sheer evidence of believing in and choosing Jesus over Santa Claus, whom showered me with the affectual gifts of my wishes, year after year. The same was true for the Easter Bunny, whom I was told had laid the colorful and tasty Easter eggs that I can remember counting and recounting before eating to my heart's desire for days at a time. At least the neighboring strangers had given me candy on Halloween, but what about Jesus from whom I had not received, the lingering question still remained...

"If Jesus really loves me like the song says, where are the gifts?"

The irony in all of this is that my parents, loved ones, and civic leaders whom I loved, respected, celebrated and admired, all endorsed the practices of those whom were the *"bearers of the affectual gifts"* that touched my heart and conditioned my mind to accept and embrace Santa Claus. Interestingly enough, the affectual gifts continued to flow and there was never a shadow of a doubt that they would cease to arouse my affections toward those who were doing the giving. Sadly, I was ignorant of the fact that the sole purpose and intent of the affectual gifting was to *promote loyalty and favor on behalf of the gift-givers*.

So, I grew from the tender age of a little child into a fully grown adult, and the affectual gifts continued to be an integral part of my psychological and social conditioning. This fact alone would account for my having difficulty in accepting Jesus over the myriad of mythical icons that had become permanent fixtures in my life. They were my official role models of *"worldly care and affection"*, based upon the affectual gifts that preceded and complimented their presence.

Choosing Christ over Santa Claus and his host...

The mere thought of choosing Jesus over the mythical icons was irrational and absolutely absurd, for the simple reason that I had received and entertained the gifts of all the celebrated idols of my youth and embraced their presence. I was left with the impression that receiving *"feel-good gifts"* represented the truest expression and highest form of love. Only to learn much later that the tangible affectual gifts are not worthy of consideration alongside the spiritual expressions of *"Agape Love that is found in Jesus Christ"*, which is the unconditional love that can only come from God! *The true measure of agape love is the tested ability to indiscriminately love everybody and everything that "God loves" without forethought or precondition.*

The tangible proof that served as sheer evidence for the convictions that I would come to socially embrace were simple, I had sat in Santa's lap and talked with him in person on numerous occasions, before playing with the toys that he promised and faithfully supplied for my pleasure on December 25th of every year. I had held and petted the Easter Bunny before eating the eggs that I had been told were laid by the bunny rabbit. I had visited the homes and played in the yards with the children of those whom had given me candy on Halloween. I had lived, slept and ate with my parents, family members and friends whom were responsible for the birthday cards and gifts. In addition, I had been taught and mentored by the noblest of community leaders who sponsored and endorsed the *"social tradition of affectual gift-giving"*. This factor alone provided the infallible proof that the giving and receiving of affectual gifts was the greatest expression of true and sincere love for one at any age. So, I repeatedly asked the question that I the small child had grown accustomed to asking over the many years…

"If Jesus really loves me like the song says, where are the gifts?"

Who was I the little child to trust?

So, at the very foundation of my thinking and seat of understanding lies the "BIG QUESTION"! Who was I to trust, when it came down to making a conscious choice about who loved me the most? Was I to choose Jesus, whom I had only heard about and not seen? Or was I to choose Santa Claus and my worldly host of celebrated icons with whom I had met and entertained; those who had adorned the most memorable and celebrated moments on my relatively short life with their *presence* and *presents,* which came in the form of material gifts?

Well, for a little child that was only four or five years of age or even for a fully grown adult, this was the "ULTIMATE QUESTION"! The answer is very problematic at any age, especially for those who have not accepted Jesus Christ as their personal Lord and Savior. This is true for the very simple reason that the affectual gifts when viewed based upon our social orientation, represent the body of evidence that points to the common belief that the practice of *"affectual gifting"* is the greatest expression and highest form of *"true and sincere love"*.

The worldly cornerstones of commercialized Christmas…

Furthermore, when we look to Christmas as the mega model for *"affectual gifting"* in western societies, we find two common practices upon which the model is established. Unfortunately, <u>substitution and usurpation</u> have become the worldly corner stones of Christmas, rather than our Lord and Savior, Jesus Christ. When we take the mythical characters surrounding Santa Claus at Christmas and compare them to the central characters of the Bible that surrounded Jesus at birth and during His missionary ministry, a very interesting picture and pattern emerges. All of the hype and pomp surrounding the celebration of Christmas serves to distract by taking away the focus of the true mission and identity of Jesus as Christ and Savior, *wherein we are confused by the nature of the affectual gifts.* Secondly, the tradition of exchanging affectual gifts as an expression of love for one day, rather than practicing the *"Agape love"* that is recorded in the book of Matthew chapter 22, verse 39 each and every day. Agape love causes us to love our neighbor in spirit and truth every day. *"...Love your neighbor as you love yourself." {New Century Version}*

Affectual Gifting, the life blood of the Christmas economy...

Many of us exhaust ourselves emotionally and financially by spending far too much money and time on gifts that many do not want or use just to satisfy a misguided tradition that makes the merchants richer and the poor even poorer. The following was stated to the Children of Israel by Moses regarding the *"<u>blessing of prosperity</u>"* for those who obey God versus the *"<u>curse of lack and insufficiency</u>"* for those who disobey God. The Amplified Translation records the following in Deuteronomy chapter 28, verse 13 and verses 43 thru 44...

{The blessing...}

"And the Lord shall make you the head, and not the tail; and you shall be above only, and you shall not be beneath, if you heed the commandments of the Lord your God which I command you this day and are watchful to do them."

{The curse...}

"The transient (stranger) among you shall mount up higher and higher above you, and you shall come down lower and

lower. He shall lend to you, but you shall not lend to him; he shall be the head, and you shall be the tail."

The "GREATEST WORLDLY ILLUSION"...

This is not meant as an indictment of Christmas, which is celebrated in commemoration of the birth of the promised Messiah. None the less, this is an indictment of the "GREAT WORLDLY ILLUSION" that has been perpetrated upon humanity under the fraudulent practice of substituting the North Pole for Heaven *("source of Christmas gifts")*, the Christmas Tree for the Cross *("source of our redemption")*, Christmas lights for the Light of Christ *("bright and morning Star")*, elks for angels *("workers")*, our parents for the wise men *("deliverers of the gifts")*, reindeer for the apostles *("disciples of Jesus")*, ourselves for baby Jesus *("recipients of the gifts")* and worst of all we have agreed in the "SPIRIT OF WORLDLY CELEBRATION" to substitute Santa Claus *(Satan's impersonation of Saint Nicholas)* in place of our Heavenly Father *("Creator and Gift-giver of all heavenly and earthly things")*.

We have been socialized as little children and conditioned from birth to do all of these things in mock celebration of Jesus Christ under the banner of *"Christmas"* without consciously realizing that Satan is masquerading out in the open as Santa Claus, while perpetrating the celebratory spirit of Christ in God the Father, our *"Heavenly Gift-giver"* and Creator of the Universe!

We need only look to the name *"Santa"*, which is a slightly disguised variation of the name *"Satan"*. Both names are spelled with the identical set of alphabets, which are arranged in a slightly different order. If one were to take the letter *"n"*, which is in the third lettering position in the name Santa and move it into the fifth lettering position, the name *"Sa*n*ta"* becomes *"Sata*n*"*. One might consider this a mere coincidence, but upon careful review of *"Lucifer's declaration"* to God after being cast out of Heaven into the Earth, the reckoning of the name *"Satan"* to *"Santa"* is clear. The Book of Revelation chapter 12, verses 7 thru 9 and Isaiah chapter 14, verses 12 thru 14 states...

> [7] *"And there was war in Heaven: Michael and his angels fought against the dragon; and the dragon fought and his*

⁸ *and prevailed not; neither was their place found any more in Heaven.*

⁹ *And the great dragon was cast out that serpent of old called the Devil and Satan, who deceiveth the whole world. He was cast out onto the earth, and his angels were cast out with him." {21st Century King James Translation}*

¹² *"How art thou fallen from heaven, O Lucifer, son of the morning! How art thou cut down to the ground, who didst weaken the nations!*

Note: *I find it extremely interesting that the following vows that were made by Lucifer aka Satan in his declaration to God upon being kicked out of Heaven onto the Earth are identical to the modus operandi of Santa Claus!!! (Intentional... or a mere coincidence?)*

¹³ *"For thou hast said in thine heart, 'I will ascend into heaven,"* {Santa Claus ascends into the first heaven with his reindeer and sled: ¹ˢᵗ ʰᵉᵃᵛᵉⁿ Earth's atmosphere, ²ⁿᵈ ʰᵉᵃᵛᵉⁿ The Cosmos, ³ʳᵈ ʰᵉᵃᵛᵉⁿ City of God}. {2 Corinthians 12:2}*

"I will exalt my throne above the stars of God;"
{Satan via the aid of Santa Claus exalts his principality and power above the saints and the Church of Our Lord leading up to the second coming of Jesus Christ.}{Rev. 11:15}

"I will sit also upon the mount, in the sides of the north."
{Santa Claus establishes his Headquarters at North Pole.}

¹⁴ *"I will ascend above the heights of the clouds;"*
{Santa Claus ascends above the clouds in his sled, while delivering Christmas toys to children around the world.}

"I will be like the Most High."
{Santa Claus usurps the worldly prestige of the Heavenly Father when he assumes the role of "Affectual gift-giver" at Christmas. He overshadows the Heavenly Father's "Anointed Gift" of Jesus Christ with "material gifts" that are purposed to distract and indoctrinate little children.}
{21st Century King James Translation}

Lucifer, the world's greatest deceiver...

The aforementioned scriptures provide a record of the events that transpired in heaven that led to the archangel Lucifer being cast into the Earth realm to become the "DECEIVER OF THE WHOLE WORLD" in the name of Satan. Lucifer's agenda has not changed; the only things that changed were *his address* and *his name*, which are central to his plan of deception in the Earth. The fallen angel Lucifer, known to the world as Satan, has used Christmas, which is the celebration of Jesus' birth as diversionary cover to disguise himself as Santa Claus in order to deceive the small children of the world. Satan has unscrupulously used the *"celebratory act of gifting"* that was portrayed by the wise men to divert humanity from the true doctrine of Christ's birth through the use of *usurpation* and *gifts*. We the believers have allowed the little children of the world to be brainwashed and indoctrinated into a *"system of false belief"* that portrays *Satan* as *Saint Nicholas*, while substituting the *affectual gifts of Santa Claus* for the *missionary gifts of Jesus Christ* that were received by-way of the wise men. The following is recorded in Matthew chapter 19, verses 13 thru 14...

> "Then people brought little children to Jesus for him to place his hands on them and pray for them. But the disciples rebuked them. Jesus said, 'Let the little children come to me, and do not hinder them, for the kingdom of heaven belongs to such as these.'" {New International Version}

Gifting, the granddaddy of roots for commercial marketing...

Satan has used the *"system of affectual gifting"* as the first and foremost effective marketing and promotions campaign ever aimed at children in the entire history of the world. "GIFTING" is the granddaddy of roots for many of the commercial marketing campaigns that we see in today's western culture. Satan has employed gifting as a *"branding strategy"* for shaping and molding our social and human behaviors. The branding is born out of a traditional system of gifting that employs subtle techniques that serve to entice, allure and orient children when they are small to surrender their souls for material goodies that are later replaced by *"subtle vices of seemingly enjoyable consequences"* once they become grownups. The marketing strategy that Satan engineered centers around the effectual gifts of Christmas, which is no different than that of McDonalds with Ronald MacDonald, the tobacco industry with its candy cigarettes or the gun industry with its cap pistols and BB guns that millions of baby boomers played with when they were kids.

If we were to honestly reflect on those intimate moments of effectual gifting during our childhoods and remember the joy and adulation that we felt when holding the Ronald MacDonald's toy in our small and fragile hands, or the grownup feeling that we experienced when posing with our candy cigarettes wedged between our tiny little fingers, I think we would view things a lot differently. In doing so we would be reminded of the innocent joy and jubilation that we felt as little kids when pointing and shooting our cap pistols and bb guns at one another that in many ways were the models of experience for the horrors of today. If we were to do this with open minds toward the future, we would better understand the tremendous damage that is being done to our children and the problem that this long overdue tradition poses for our nuclear families and the Christian Church.

Residual effects of toys in later life...

Toys engender *"real-time animation"* in the minds of little kids creating a psychological void that craves to be filled with *"identical real-life activity"*, but on a much larger and grander scale as we grow into our adolescent and adult years. It is here in the late adolescence and early adult stages of life that the effects of having played with *"grown-up styled toys"* during the early stages of EARLY CHILDHOOD DEVELOPMENT began to manifest, pointing to the fact that toys are the *youth oriented shapers and molders of future human behavior.*

For example, the baby dolls, dollhouses, and the like are responsible for seeding the developing minds of little girls, thereby causing them to assume the social roles of *"caretakers"*, *"nurturers"* and in many instances *"adolescent mothers"* as they grew older. The same is true for little boys with their cap pistols, bb guns, and Tonka trucks that men of my age played with as little boys, which causes them to assume the social roles of *"adventurers", "conquerors"* and even *"murderers"* as they grew older. The little girl's baby doll becomes her real-life baby and her playhouse becomes her real house. The little boy's cap pistol becomes his real pistol, his BB gun becomes his shotgun, his cowboy boots become his real western boots, his Tonka truck becomes his pickup truck and worst of all his video games of animated violence become the real-life experiences of many little boys as they grow older and become gang members and violent criminals.

In retrospect, those gleeful experiences appear on the surface to be harmless, but upon rolling the tape forward to today we find ourselves drowning in a worldly culture that is embroiled with material lifestyles of violence, entrapment, sickness, death and total psychological distraction. The fast-foods have led to out-of-control obesity and rampant hypertension, the candied cigarettes have led to costly smoking addiction and lung cancer, in addition to the toy guns and the like that have led to rampant gun violence and mass murders that are played out in settings that defy comprehension like *"Columbine"*.

All of these things are happening to adults today, because when we were children our parents and their encampment of social accomplices endorsed the seemingly innocent tradition of *"affectual gifting"* issuing from Santa Claus and the commercialization of Christmas, which led to our believing many things that promoted and mimicked behaviors that were not conducive for healthy, well-adjusted, adult lifestyles.

*The formative years of "*EARLY CHILDHOOD DEVELOPMENT*"...*

We were and still are being subjugated to damaging experiences resulting from toys received from Santa Claus during the formative years of our early childhood development, at a time when we have no control over the consequences. Research has shown that 90% of human brain development and behavioral knowledge is acquired between birth and eight years of age. It has been stated that the remaining 10% of behavioral knowledge received during our lifetimes is acquired in the process of validating the things that were learned during our formative years of "EARLY CHILDHOOD DEVELOPMENT".

*I*nterestingly, our formulation of social attachments occur between the ages of 1 and 3, when our minds are open to receive and embrace the things taught and exampled to us by the authoritative figures that are present in our lives. The list includes, but is not limited to *Church pastors, scoutmasters, Sunday schoolteachers, public schoolteachers, Grandparents* and the like. These are just a few of the well-respected icons that I as a little child honored, emulated, respected and trusted, while welcoming their time-honored teachings and traditions. Traditions that in some ways would in the long-term serve to indoctrinate me into an *"accepted way of thinking"* as the social gravity weighing upon those traditions began to take root in my life.

*S*urprisingly, all of the aforementioned icons tended to fit into this wide ranging *"gifting scenario"* in one way or another. All of the icons of my world were all complicit through *"direct or indirect gifting"* by-way of association, resulting from overt or silent endorsement. This *"seemingly innocent cadre of well-intentioned liars",* whom themselves were programmed and duped as little children into becoming willing agents of Satan appear to be unaware of the affect that their teachings of Santa Claus and the Easter Bunny, among others is having on little children, relative to their Christian faith. The following is recorded in Proverbs chapter 22, verse 6…

> *"Train up a child in the way he should go: and when he is old, he will not depart from it." {King James Version}*

Breaking the traditional cycle…

*U*ntil now, Christians have been rendered powerless by our "IGNORANCE OF THE TRUTH" concerning the socially sanctioned, celebratory practice of *"affectual gifting behavior"*. Now that we know the truth we have a responsibility to Christ, the Church and our children of discontinuing the telling of traditional lies that were fostered by those whom came before us in the name of tradition. Prior to the revelation of Satan posing as Santa Claus we could not do better, because we did not know better. <u>BUT NOW WE KNOW!!!</u> Therefore, we have a responsibility as *parents* and *born-again Christians* of telling Satan and his establishment that we no longer serve his demonic agenda. The following is recorded in Romans chapter 10, verse 3…

> *"For they being ignorant of God's righteousness, and seeking to establish their own righteousness, have not submitted to the righteousness of God."*

As born-again Christians, we must reeducate our children about the *"true celebration of Jesus' birth"*, which is our one and only *"Good and Perfect gift"* and began to celebrate the *real meaning of Christmas*. When we take a stand as *"born-again Christians"*, we will weaken *"Satan's power of seduction over our children"*. We are no longer to obey the flawed traditions of man, while allowing Satan to trample on the *"Anointed Gift of Christ"* in the name of Santa Claus. The Apostle Paul tells us in the Ephesians chapter 6, verse 12…

> *"For we wrestle not against flesh and blood, but against principalities, against powers, against the rulers of the darkness of this world, against spiritual wickedness in high places." {Authorized King James Version}*

I interpret this to mean that we wrestle with the "ESTABLISHMENT", which is the *business structure, power brokers* and *false religions* of this world. As Christians, we need to do away with pagan celebrations, myths and practices that when passed down without examination of truth or validation of origin erodes our Christian faith and destroys our children. These supposedly harmless lies support the continued existence of Santa Claus, the Bunny Rabbit and the ghost and goblins of Halloween, which appear on the surface to be developmentally helpful to kids, while working in tandem in very insidious ways to nullify the core belief by children that the *"immaculate birth of Christ"* is the most precious and *"Anointed Gift"* that one can receive.

I believe it relevant and important to note that the most prominent and publicized nickname for the night before Halloween is *"Devils Night"*. Devils Night is infamous for acts of vandalism and destruction of physical property that began in the 1940s and escalated to more devastating acts, such as arson in the 1970s. I also believe there to be a direct correlation between the vandalism and destruction of physical property on the night before Halloween, which points to vandalism and desecration of the "HEAVENLY FATHER'S SPIRITUAL PROPERTY" that begins on the night before Christmas and climaxes the day of with *"physical gifts"* overshadowing the *"Heavenly Gift"* of our *"Savior"*. The *"vandalism" and "desecration"* is Satan's use of Santa Claus to overshadow the celebratory birth of our Lord and Savior, Jesus Christ.

One might ask… <u>how the giving of physical gifts to little children on Christmas Eve by Santa Claus is an act of vandalism and desecration?</u> Well it is rather simple, I believe there to be a direct correlation between the *"vandalism and desecration of physical property"* that takes place on the night of *Halloween aka "Devil's night"* and the *"preemptive acts of affectual gift-giving"* that is employed on *Christmas Eve aka "The night before Christmas"*.

It stands to reason that the celebration of Santa Claus' arrival should coincide with the *"Saint Nicholas feast day"* that takes place on the date of December 6th from which it is derived, rather than the eve of the celebrated birth of Christ. To clone the centuries old *"Saint Nicholas feast day"* that has occurred annually on the same date for hundreds of years and then arbitrarily move the celebration to December 25th in acknowledgment of *"Santa Claus"* is very revealing.

"Saint Nicholas"
Greek bishop _ 4th Century A.D.

If the celebration of Santa Claus is intended to imitate the spirit and *"celebratory gift-giving deeds of Saint Nicholas"*… why then change the date that embraces the legacy of *"Saint Nicholas"* to a different date, which celebrates the prophetic birth of Jesus Christ *(Matt. 1:20-23)?* This is especially relevant in consideration of the fact that Jesus Christ was born into the world to save it from none other than *Lucifer aka Satan and the devil himself,* one who parades around openly disguised in the fictitious image and mythical persona of Santa Claus.

Age old motive for deception…

The date change for the celebration of Saint Nicholas provides motive and intent for a mythical figure being invented to mimic the character and persona of a charitable saint, Saint Nicholas by declaring a day of annual celebration that falls on the Messiah's birth. Why not choose the historical date that coincides with the traditional celebration of the saint, which is the *"Saint Nicholas' feast day"* that falls on December 6th? The mere fact that the *"gifting celebration"* surrounding Santa Claus does not coincide with the celebration of *"Saint Nicholas"* raises the question of whether the date was intentionally changed for the purpose of distracting humanity from the true meaning of Christmas, which is the *"Eternal Gift of blessing"* in our Savior, Jesus Christ. There is no doubt that the date was changed for the sole purpose of sabotaging man's receipt of the *"Gift of Salvation",* which is man's celebrated gift of spiritual redemption!!!

The mere thought of this having occurred would suggest premeditation and willful intent on behalf of Satan in the century's old plot of overthrowing the *"coming Kingdom"* by overshadowing the "KING" with the "AFFECTUAL GIFTS of Santa Claus". Most importantly, the event is initiated only hours prior to the celebration of our Savior's birth that was purposed as a *"Gift of blessing"* for the healing of the world. Baby Jesus is our long-awaited *"Redeemer", "promised Messiah"* and *"King",* Who was immaculately conceived before being gift wrapped in *"swaddling clothes"* for presentation to the world.

Interestingly enough, *"affectual gifts"* are traditionally *"swaddled"* or *"wrapped".* Jesus is "THEE DIVINE GIFT OF OUR HEAVENLY

FATHER'S AFFECTION" that was swaddled in the flesh for us. The following is recorded in the book of John chapter 3, verses 16 thru 17...

> *"For God so loved the world that <u>He gave His only begotten Son</u>, that whoever believes in Him should not perish but have everlasting life.*
>
> *For God did not send His Son into the world to condemn the world, but that the world through Him might be saved."*
> *{New King James Translation}*

Loyal disciples of Satan, unaware...

The fallen angel, Lucifer *(also known as Satan)* has effectively used the world's system of *"affectual gifting"* that was formed around the celebration of the holy days for the purpose of transforming our *"innocent youth"* and *"future leaders of the Christian world"* into loyal disciples of Satan unaware. This incredibly clever and shrewd maneuver was introduced through the insane commercialization and usurpation that surrounds the *"Holy Day"* of our Lord, Jesus Christ.

To better understand the demonic roots of *"affectual gifting"* and the Satanic sway and influence that this misguided traditional practice has over us, we only need to read the coming account of *"worldwide rejoicing"* and *"frantic gift-giving celebration"* that takes place when two prophets of God are murdered and left lying dead in the street for 3½ days for prophesying on behalf of God. <u>Pay special attention to verse 10, there is a *"gift-giving frenzy"* that ensues, which is an identical reenactment of the *"affectual gifting"* that surrounds the celebration of Christmas!!!</u> This is a prophetic snapshot of what is yet to come, thus demonstrating that *"affectual gift-giving"* is a product of Satan. The following is recorded in Revelation chapter 11, verses 7 thru 10...

> *⁷"When they finish their testimony, the beast that ascends out of the bottomless pit will make war against them, overcome them, and kill them. ⁸And their dead bodies will lie in the street of the great city which spiritually is called Sodom and Egypt, where also our Lord was crucified.*
>
> *⁹Then those from the peoples, tribes, tongues, and nations*

will see their dead bodies three-and-a-half days, and not allow their dead bodies to be put into graves. <u>¹⁰And those who dwell on the earth will rejoice over them, make merry, and send gifts to one another</u>, because these two prophets tormented those who dwell on the earth." {New King James Translation}

Beware of those who come bearing gifts!

I am reminded of an adage that says... *"Beware of those who come taken from the "original Greek"* wherein it was properly stated... *"Beware of Greeks bearing gifts"*. The literal meaning originated from the people of the city of Troy whom would say... *"I fear the Greeks, even those bearing gifts"*. The saying arose from the preliminary outcome of the Trojan War, which resulted in a stalemate after 10 years of indecisive battle. The war is believed to have begun around 1194 B.C. and ended in or around 1184 B.C. when the Greeks placed a large wooden horse filled with soldiers at the gate of the city of Troy.

As the story goes, the Trojans shielded themselves from their tenacious Greek attackers by fortifying themselves within the walls of the City of Troy. So Odysseus, the legendary commander of the Greek Army and King of the Island of Ithaca devised the idea of constructing a large hollowed-bellied wooden horse that could be presented as a *"supposed gift"*.

The horse came to be known as *"The Trojan Horse"* after being left outside the gated walls of Troy as a parting gift that signaled a truce. The Trojans accepted the horse as a conciliatory gesture of peace and brought it inside their city walls, only for the City of Troy to be overtaken by the armed soldiers that filled the belly of the wooden beast. From which the old sayings... *"In the belly of the beast..."* and *"Never look a gift horse in the mouth"* are believed to have originated.

How many categories of gifts are there?

The historical account of the Trojan War provides the perfect segue-way into the heart of the subject and subtitle of this book. Not until I began exploring the subject of *"Gifts"*, which is at the core of this book, did I realize what few of us do. My research exposed me to four categories of gifts, versus the *"affectual gifts"* that we are accustomed to giving and receiving. In addition to the *affectual gifts,* there are *natural gifts, spiritual gifts* and *corporate gifts a/k/a business gifts:*

Affectual gifts are definitely the most common of all. These gifts are customarily given to express affection and are generally linked to special occasions, such as… Christmas, birthdays, anniversaries, etc..

- **_Biblical example:_** Jonathan, the son of King Saul gave his heir apparent rights to the *"throne of Israel"* to David, whom would later become King and inherit the throne of Israel upon the death of King Saul *(1st Samuel chapter 18, verses 1 thru 4).*
- **_Secular example:_** The gift of the *"Cullinan stone"* to Britain's King Edward the VII for his 66th birthday on November 9, 1907. The Cullinan stone is the largest diamond ever found. The stone was a near flawless, perfectly clear and colourless diamond that weighed 1.37 pounds (3,106 carats) at the time of its discovery. Prior to being cut into smaller stones the Cullinan stone measured more than 3 feet long, more than 2 feet high and was 2.8 inches short of being 2 feet wide.

Natural gifts are celebrated and acknowledged on a daily basis in all societies as a matter of course. The bearers of such gifts are the social icons in our lives whom become *celebrities, entertainers, athletes and movie stars* based upon their varying degrees of talent. Others are oftentimes *business and community leaders, scholars, scientist, and famous entrepreneurs, among others notable personalities* in our mist.

- **_Biblical example:_** The dreams and dream interpretations of Israel's youngest son Joseph was a natural gift that caused him to be sold into slavery by his brothers. He would eventually become the Governor of Egypt, leading to the Israelites being saved from famine and living in Egypt before becoming enslaved *(Genesis chapter 40 & Acts chapter 7, verses 9 thru 10).*
- **_Secular example:_** The naturally gifted cultural icons like Michelangelo, Leonardo da Vinci, Steven Spielberg, Mozart,

Amedeo Modigliani, Picasso, Muhammad Ali, Michael Jackson, Jimi Hendrix, Michael Jordan and intellectual geniuses like Albert Einstein.

Spiritual gifts are those referenced by the Apostle Paul in the New Testament book of 1st Corinthians, they are: *word of wisdom; word of knowledge, gifts of healing, working of miracles, prophecy, discerning of spirits; various kinds of tongues, interpretation of tongues.* Each of the noted gifts are recorded in the book of 1st Corinthians chapter 12, verses 1 thru 31…

- <u>**Biblical example**</u>*:* King Solomon prayed to God and received wisdom, which exceeded the wisdom of all the kings of the Earth *(2nd Chronicles chapter 1, verses 10 thru 12 and 1st Kings chapter 10, verse 23)*
- <u>**Secular example**</u>*:* There are no secular examples to note. The Spiritual gifts spoken of by the Apostle Paul are supernatural in nature; they are manifested via the Holy Spirit to chosen ones of God to be used in matters of Church administration for the edification of the body of Christ.

Business gifts come in a variety of forms and are probably the least talked about of all gifts outside of the corporate circle. Business gifts are oftentimes given as compensation and bonuses, but in certain rare and unusual cases *"business gifts"* are given as *"tools of special purpose"* for carrying out a particular service or assignment on behalf of its benefactor. In these particular instances, the given task or project could not be performed if the laborer were not in receipt of the gift.

During the recent *"housing market crash"*, I listened to God and made a <u>spiritually driven decision</u> *of hiring an out-of-work, non-professional to paint my house,* whom did not have the *"résumé"* or *"needed equipment"* to perform the job. The equipment was donated to the individual as a gift <u>*and the end result was literally a masterpiece.*</u>

Our home was purchased by the first of two potential homebuyers that viewed the property. A contract was entered into within 5 days of the property being placed on the market and it sold for approximately *$40,000.00 above the rapidly declining market values.*

- **_Biblical example:_** The *"rod"* that was given to Moses by God to aid in carrying out the assignment of bringing the children of Israel out of Egypt, wherein they were enslaved. *(Exodus chapter 4, verses 1 thru 5)*
- **_Secular example:_** The most common example would be the staggering amount of foreign aid and military hardware that is provided to one government by another for the purpose of ensuring military success. The United States is just one of many countries that gifts millions of dollars in military aid and hardware to satisfy America's national interest and strategic objectives abroad.

This brings us to the *gold, frankincense and myrrh* that was given to baby Jesus by the wise men to serve as "BUSINESS GIFTS" instead of "AFFECTUAL GIFTS" as we have been deliberately taught by Satan.

Gold represented the royalty of Jesus as Son of the most-high God; Jesus in His heavenly majesty is the *"King of kings and Lord of lords"*. The Apostle John states the following in the book of John chapter 18, verse 37 and the book of Revelation chapter 19, verse 16...

"*'Pilate therefore said to Him, 'Are You a king then?'*

Jesus answered, 'You say rightly that I am a king. For this cause I was born, and for this cause I have come into the world, that I should bear witness to the truth. Everyone who is of the truth hears My voice.'" {New King James Translation}

"On his robe and on his thigh he has a name written, King Of kings and Lord of lords." {New International Translation}

Frankincense is defined as *"incense"* in the Hebrew language. Frankincense was used on the *"Day of Atonement"* in the administration of the annual sin offering that was performed in the *"holy place"* by the High Priest. Frankincense was applied to the burn offering, which served as a substitute for the "CRUCIFIED CHRIST" prior to the birth, death and ascension of Jesus, Who is identified in Scripture as the *"Lamb slain from the foundation of the world"*.

Once applied to the burnt offering, the burning of the incense symbolized the sins of man rising up to the throne of Heaven on the smoke of the altar to be forgiven by God the Father for the atonement of man's sin. The following is recorded in the book of Leviticus chapter 6, verses 14 & 15...

> *"And this is the law of the meat offering: the sons of Aaron shall offer it before the LORD, before the altar. And he shall take of it his handful, of the flour of the meat offering and of the oil thereof, and all the frankincense which is upon the meat offering, and shall burn it upon the altar for a sweet savour, even the memorial of it, unto the Lord."*
> *{King James Translation}*

Myrrh is defined as *"oil"* in the Hebrew language. Myrrh was representative of the oil that Mary Magdalene would use to anoint Jesus' body during the last supper, which was symbolic of Jesus' prophetic death and embalmment. Mary Magdalene's use of the oil, which was valued at 300 pence according to Scripture became a contested issue by the Apostle Judas Iscariot, leading up to his betrayal of Jesus to the high priest of Jerusalem for thirty pieces of silver. The following is recorded in the book of John chapter 12, verses 1 thru 8...

> *"Six days before Passover Jesus went back to Bethany, where he had raised Lazarus from death. A meal had been prepared for Jesus. Martha was doing the serving, and Lazarus himself was there.*
>
> *Mary took a very expensive bottle of perfume and poured it on Jesus' feet. She wiped them with her hair, and the sweet smell of the perfume filled the house. "A disciple named Judas Iscariot was there. He was the one who was going to betray Jesus, and he asked, "Why wasn't this perfume sold for three hundred silver coins and the money given to the poor?"*
>
> *Judas did not really care about the poor. He asked this because he carried the moneybag and sometimes would steal from it. Jesus replied, "Leave her alone! She has kept*

this perfume for the day of my burial. You will always have the poor with you, but you won't always have me." {Contemporary English Version}

The greatest business gifts ever given!

The THREE CORPORATE GIFTS *described herein as business gifts (gold, frankincense* and *myrrh)* were in fact *"Messianic Tools"* to be used by Jesus in carrying out "HIS FATHER'S BUSINESS" of laying down His life on Calvary and picking it up again for the world to be saved.

The Scriptures provide record in John chapter 19, verses 28 thru 30 of Jesus accomplishing *"the business"* that He referred to at *"age 12"*, when He drank the dreaded *"CUP OF SIN AND DEATH"* that Adam filled by eating the *"FORBIDDEN FRUIT"*. Jesus symbolizes this prophetic event by drinking the jar of sour wine before surrendering His spirit.

> *"After this, Jesus, knowing that all things had already been accomplished, to fulfill the Scripture, *said, "I am thirsty."*
>
> *A jar full of sour wine was standing there; so they put a sponge full of the sour wine upon a branch of hyssop and brought it up to His mouth.*
>
> *Therefore when Jesus had received the sour wine, He said, "It is finished!" And He bowed His head and gave up His spirit."* {New American Standard Bible}

This event was symbolized in the Old Testament with Abraham's interrupted death sacrifice of his only son Isaac *(Gen. 22:1-13)* with the *"ram in the bush"*. It was fulfilled in the New Testament by Jesus!!!

JESUS' death on the cross is our *"Eternal Gift of Salvation"* that was manifested from the foundation of the world in the form of Jesus being crucified by hanging on a tree *(Acts 5:30 & Acts 10:39)*. Jesus' death fulfills what is written in the book of Revelation chapter 13, verse 8 concerning *"...the lamb slain from the foundation of the world"*.

The DEATH OF JESUS provides remission for humanity's sins through the shedding of JESUS' BLOOD *(Matthew 26:28)*. The RESURRECTION OF JESUS provides the power of restoration of *"God's spiritual character"* within man, which is expressed in and through the divine "IMAGE AND LIKENESS OF GOD" in those who receive Jesus as their Lord, Savior, and Redeemer.

*U*pon receiving Jesus into our lives, we regain our "SPIRITUAL DOMINION" and "MORAL AUTHORITY" as children of the most-high God and are thereby reinstated into our rightful place of "SPIRITUAL AUTHORITY" as the *"spiritual seeds of Abraham"* and *"Christ-like stewards"* of the "NEW HEAVEN AND NEW EARTH" that is yet to come.

"Study to show thyself approved unto God, a workman who needeth not to be ashamed, rightly dividing the word of truth."

2nd Timothy 2:15

~Devour the Holy Book~

Third Trinity

"In Honor Of Our Comforter... The Holy Spirit!"

The Greatest Temple Ever Created...

"Do you not know that your body is
a temple of the Holy Spirit, who is in you,
whom you have received from God?
You are not your own;"

1st Corinthians 6:19 {New International Version — UK}

Follow Him!

~ Little Bittie Seed ~

Remembering Paul Daniels... an eternal friend!

From within the shadow of a thought
i was only a seed, simply living to be sown,
but by and by my life corrupted
i was stranded all alone.

The other seeds all scattered about
to be sown wherever they lay,
there i was trapped alone... denied,
ensnared by deeds of yesterday.

But all of a sudden my life sprang open
i was moved by words on high,
i was carried away to a beautiful place
and left not to die.

By what fate could it be
that i grow so tall and strong,
when all the seeds ahead of me
grew so infinitely wrong.

Could it be that a gracious God
is so resourceful and so rich,
that He causes a seed to bloom and blossom
that was gathered from a ditch.

"Scriptural Reference"
Matthew 13:3 thru 8 & Matthew 17:20

Disclosure of the Eternal Gift

Matthew 13:3 thru 8 {New King James Version}

"Then he spoke many things
to them in parables, saying:
Behold, a sower went forth to sow.

And as he sowed, some seed fell by the way side;
and the birds came and devoured them.

Some fell on stony places,
where they did not have much earth;
and they immediately sprang up,
because they had no depth of earth.

But when the sun was up they were scorched,
and because they had no root they withered away.

And some fell among thorns;
and the thorns sprang up and choked them.

But others fell on good ground
and yielded a crop: some a hundredfold,
some sixty, some thirty."

Matthew 17:20 {New King James Version}

"So Jesus said to them, "Because of your unbelief;
for assuredly, I say to you, if you have faith as a mustard seed,
you will say to this mountain, 'Move from here to there,'
and it will move; and nothing will be impossible for you."

~ He Lives In Me ~

The spiritual abode?

Inside me He speaks!
Inside me He weeps!
He whispers
a midmorning prayer.

As I gaze out upon the world
I see through His eyes,
as I witness human suffering
inside me He dies...

He lives in me!

Inside me He screams
as He chases the money changers out,
those who bring filth to the human temple
our Lord's flesh and blood house.

More silent than a rose
He came like a thief,
more passionate than a priest
He made peace within me.

He lives in me!

Like the feel of hot lava
tracing upon earthen clay,
He flowed into my life
He reshaped me that way.

An old dust bag was I
right from the start,
until the love of Jesus Christ
invaded my heart.

He lives in me!

I am in Him...
He is in me...

He is in the Father...
we all agree...

He lives in me!

~~~~~

"Scriptural Reference"
1st John 4:12 thru 13 & 1st Corinthians 6:19 thru 20

1st John 4:12 thru 13 {King James Version}

"No man hath seen God at any time.
If we love one another, God dwelleth in us,
and His love is perfected in us.

Hereby know we that we dwell in Him,
and he in us, because he hath given us of His Spirit."

1st Corinthians 6:19 thru 20 {New King James Version}

"Or do you not know that your body is
a temple of the Holy Spirit who is in you,
whom you have from God?

You are not your own,
for you were bought at a price;
therefore glorify God in your body
and in your spirit which are God's."

~ A Man ~

An island not unto itself!

I was taught my lessons as a child
only to learn them as a man.

When shall I ever learn?

A man is a grain...
he is just like sand...
he is moved by the weight of the world.

He could be a boulder if he would,
he would be a mountain if he could,
but after all... he is only a grain!

A man!

"Scriptural Reference"
1st Corinthians 13:11 & Psalm 1:1 thru 3

1st Corinthians 13:11 {New King James Version}

"When I was a child,
I spoke as a child,
understood as a child,
I thought as a child;

but when I became a man,
I put away childish things."

Psalm 1:1 thru 3 {New King James Version}

"Blessed is the man
Who walks not in the counsel of the ungodly,
Nor stands in the path of sinners,
Nor sits in the seat of the scornful;

But his delight is in the law of the LORD,
And in His law he meditates day and night.

He shall be like a tree
Planted by the rivers of water,
That brings forth its fruit in its season,
Whose leaf also shall not wither;
And whatever he does shall prosper."

~ Expediency ~

Disclosing destiny's key!

In a mood of expediency
we rush to live our lives,
only to become so involved in living
that we merely learn to survive.

We take the wildest chances
seeking fun and fortune in our youth,
by repeating the errors of the fallen
we fail to know "THE TRUTH".

We focus our views of yesterday
through a lens with frozen eyes,
embellishing shattered visions…
of success unrealized.

From the depths of our decisions
we create our space,
by exercising spiritual execution,
we secure our place.

Success is an unwritten formula
that the Holy Spirit within us creates,
when God is granted control of our schedules
we become *"Masters"* of our fate.

"Scriptural Reference"
Psalm 25:7 thru 10

Psalm 25:7 thru 10 {New American Standard Bible}

"Do not remember the sins of my youth
or my transgressions;
According to Your lovingkindness remember me,
For Your goodness' sake, O LORD.

Good and upright is the LORD;
Therefore He instructs sinners in the way.
He leads the humble in justice,
And He teaches the humble His way.

All the paths of the LORD
are lovingkindness and truth
To those who keep His covenant
and His testimonies."

~ Lessons ~

The world is our classroom... the Lord is our teacher!

Not long ago when parents were parents
and kids were kids...
We earned what we learned!
We believed in what we did!

Unlike today
when few really care,
Heaven help us all
we have lost ourselves.

Mistakes are poor choices
resulting in valuable lessons learned,
we must revisit our life's errors
from whence our futures are exhumed.

From our trials come the testimonies
about which I solemnly speak,
witnessed in the presence of the Holy Spirit
which are never to be repeated.

Recounting the trials and tests
that we have experienced and overcome,
empowers our resolve for spiritual healing
until the race for salvation is run.

"Scriptural Reference"
Ephesians 5:15 thru 18

Ephesians 5:15 thru 18 {New International Version — UK}

"Be very careful, then, how you live
not as unwise but as wise,
making the most of every opportunity,
because the days are evil.

Therefore do not be foolish,
but understand what the Lord's will is.

Do not get drunk on wine,
which leads to debauchery.

Instead, be filled with the Spirit."

~ My Dad ~

A gift from my Heavenly Father!

"Sixty Eight"... that's great!
Thank God, Oh what a break,
it is through you that I live today.
Thanks dad... you're special!

Now that I am older
remembering all you told me;
you taught me quite a lot,
I owe you all I've got.

You are truly a remarkable man,
having done the best you can;
assuming a positive stand,
you left me the *"Master Plan"*.

For all the days I live,
in your precious shadow
I'll plan, I'll build.
Oh what a life worth living!

I thank God for your giving,
I am truly blessed among the living.
Unlike many I have a lot,
You have granted me the *"Master Slot"*.

You are more than great.
You are better than wonderful.
It is in you...
That I found my God-like example!

Departed December 1, 1990

"Scriptural Reference"
Proverbs 1:7 thru 8 & Proverbs 23:24

Proverbs 1:7 thru 8 {King James Version}

"The fear of the LORD is the beginning of knowledge: but fools despise wisdom and instruction.

My son, hear the instruction of thy father, and forsake not the law of thy mother:"

Proverbs 23:24 {Holman Christian Standard Version}

"The father of a righteous son will rejoice greatly, and one who fathers a wise son will delight in him."

˜ Ma`at ˜

A message from Margarita!

I speak with conviction
knowing life is a song,
all God's children
hum along, hum along.

Life is a symphony
composed of spiritual truths,
vibrating rhythmic expressions
and earthly harmonies to you.

Lift your voices
shout blessings of praise,
sing melodies of love
Heaven's chorus will play.

Be a trumpeter like the angel Gabriel
proclaim life's blessings with a shout,
sound crescendos of love
until the *"Good News"* comes out.

There is a universal principle
bridging God and man,
it is a spiritual investment
upon which Heaven depends.

We all get back
what we ourselves put in,
the measure has been the same
since time began.

We pay once going
or twice coming back,
like repetitive beats in timing
it's a natural fact.

I speak with conviction
knowing life is a song,

all God's children
hum along, hum along.

"Scriptural Reference"
Ephesians 5:19 thru 20 & Colossians 3:15 thru 16

Disclosure of the Eternal Gift

Ephesians 5:19 thru 20 {New International Version}

"Speak to one another with psalms,
hymns and spiritual songs.
Sing and make music
in your heart to the Lord,

always giving thanks to God
the Father for everything,
in the name of our Lord Jesus Christ."

Colossians 3:15 thru 16 {New International Version – UK}

"Let the peace of Christ rule in your hearts,
since as members of one body you were called to peace.
And be thankful.

Let the word of Christ dwell in you richly as you teach
and admonish one another with all wisdom,
and as you sing psalms,
hymns and spiritual songs with gratitude in your hearts to God."

~ Flashback ~

Divine principle of stewardship!

The aftermath of life's
most critical instructions,
becomes the consequences
of duties… completed,
or simply left undone.

Discover your purpose!
Finish your assignments!
Live your dreams!
Do it now!

"Scriptural Reference"
John 9:4

John 9:4 {21st Century King James Version}

"I must work the works of Him that sent me,
while it is day; the night cometh,
when no man can work."

~ Backslider ~

A house built on sand!

I am, I want,
I might, I should.
If I would, I could, so I'd be.

But since I can't,
I aint… in all my trials.
I'll tell you just what I'll be.

I am what I am,
that's all I am.
What else can I possibly be?

At times I will…
At times I won't…
After all I'm only me!

~~~

"Scriptural Reference"
Proverbs 14:14, Jeremiah 3:14 & Revelation 3:16

Disclosure of the Eternal Gift

Proverbs 14:14 {New King James Version}

"The backslider in heart
will be filled with his own ways,
But a good man will be satisfied from above."

Revelation 3:16 {English Standard Version}

"So, because you are lukewarm,
and neither hot nor cold,
I will spit you out of my mouth."

Jeremiah 3:14 {21st Century King James Version}

"Turn, O backsliding children, saith the Lord;
For I am married unto you…"

~ God's "Do" Diligence ~

A work in progress!

Thank You Father
for loving me enough
to do all that You have done…
for me!

Thank You Jesus
for being patient enough
to do what You continue to do…
for me!

Thank You Holy Spirit
for being devoted enough
to do what You are doing…
for me!

"Scriptural Reference"
Colossians 2:8 thru 14

Colossians 2:8 thru 14 {King James Version}

"Beware lest any man spoil you
through philosophy and vain deceit,
after the tradition of men,
after the rudiments of the world,
and not after Christ.

For in Him dwelleth all the fullness
of the Godhead bodily.
And ye are complete in Him,
which is the head of all principality and power:"

~ Under Pens ~

Life's mimicry of worldly illusion!

What poor people regard as homes
rich people view as pens,
domestic confinements for preparation
before being sent forth to work again.

While common people live like swine
in a society casting pearls at the wealthy's feet,
the poor are consuming culinary slop
while boasting of the delicacies they eat.

Do you ever sit alone and wonder
will I ever get out of this mess,
while the well-off live like royalty
and you're always struggling to be blessed.

We are children of the most-high God,
the Father of blessings from on high,
He promised to prosper all the days our lives
if in His commandments we trust and abide.

Embrace the teachings of Jesus,
the *"Holy Bible"* is your companion guide,
acknowledge the Holy Spirit as your eternal witness,
and all of your needs will be satisfied!

"Scriptural Reference"
Luke 18:18, Luke 18:24 thru 25 & Matthew 7:6

Luke 18:18 {New International Reader's Version}

"A certain ruler asked Jesus a question.
"Good teacher," he said,
"what must I do to receive eternal life?"

Luke 18:24 thru 25 {New Century Version}

"Jesus looked at him and said,
"It is very hard for rich people to enter the kingdom of God.
It is easier for a camel to go through the eye of a needle
than for a rich person to enter the kingdom of God."

Matthew 7:6 {New King James Version}

"Do not give what is holy to the dogs;
nor cast your pearls before swine,
lest they trample them under their feet,
and turn and tear you in pieces."

~ Ring Your Own Bell ~

It begins with God and ends with you!

Ain't gonna get out of bed
nor comb my hair;
Ain't gonna look my best
cause nobody cares!

Ain't gonna wash my face
nor brush my teeth;
Ain't gonna offer up praise
cause I ain't got expensive food to eat!

Ain't gonna read my Bible
nor say my prayers;
Ain't gonna go to church
cause nobody cares!

Ain't gonna clean my house
nor wash my sheets;
Ain't gonna worship the Lord
cause I ain't got new shoes on my feet!

I have searched life's mirror
surviving from day to day;
until I saw the face of a stranger
who had lost his way!

Today I have vowed in my heart
to look beyond pride and despair;
I now praise and worship the Lord
for giving me the reason to care.

Ring-A-Ding... Ding...
Jesus Christ is my bell!

"Scriptural Reference"
Psalms 23:1 thru 6

Psalms 23:1 thru 6 {New King James Version}

"The LORD is my shepherd;
I shall not want.
He makes me to lie down in green pastures;
He leads me beside the still waters.

He restores my soul;
He leads me in the paths of righteousness
for His name's sake.

Yea, though I walk through the valley
of the shadow of death,
I will fear no evil;
For You are with me;
Your rod and Your staff,
they comfort me.

You prepare a table before me
in the presence of my enemies;
You anoint my head with oil;
My cup runs over.

Surely goodness and mercy shall follow me
all the days of my life;
And I will dwell in the house of the LORD Forever."

~ Orphan ~

Fannie Mae... Mother-in-law & friend!

As an unredeemed sinner
I lived life on Earth alone,
akin to a wandering gypsy
without the comforts of a home.

Dwelling deep-down without cover
or the Lord's promised daily bread,
unaware of God's everlasting *"MERCY"*
and His wondrous *"GRACE"* ahead.

I know now with total assurance
that my *"Heavenly Father"* truly lives,
in a house filled with heavenly mansions
currently existing... but not yet revealed.

I once lived unbelievably small
because I had not yet been told,
of an eternal city gated with pearls
with streets paved with gold.

Heaven is my future home
and I am yearning to go there,
to live forever in total peace
without concern, worry or care.

I long to dwell for eternity
with my long-awaited spiritual kin,
in a place free of disease...
poverty, hate and sin.

Heaven doesn't have embalmers
there aren't any doctors or nurses there,
because people live forever
and there's no need for medical care.

The Church is my spiritual family
and I'm no longer alone or ashamed,
for I am now a child of *"The Master"*
and I live in Jesus' name.

Jesus... Jesus... Jesus...

"Scriptural Reference"
Ephesians 1:3 thru 5, John 14:2 thru 3 & Revelation 2:17

Ephesians 1:3 thru 5 {New King James Version}

"Blessed be the God and
Father of our Lord Jesus Christ,
who has blessed us with every spiritual
blessing in the Heavenly places in Christ,

just as He chose us in Him
before the foundation of the world,
that we should be holy and without
blame before Him in love,

having predestined us to adoption
as sons by Jesus Christ to Himself,
according to the good pleasure of His will, "

John 14:2 thru 3 {King James Version}

"In my Father's house are many mansions:
if it were not so, I would have told you.

I go to prepare a place for you.
And if I go and prepare a place for you,
I will come again, and receive you unto myself;
that where I am, there ye may be also."

Revelation 2:17 {New American Standard Bible}

"He who has an ear, let him hear what the Spirit says
to the churches. To him who overcomes, to him I
will give *some* of the hidden manna, and I will give
him a white stone, and a new name written on the
stone which no one knows but he who receives it."

~ Sanctuary ~

The promised abode!

For years in sin I freely lived
praying to God for peace revealed,
a solitary place deep inside my head
trusting in God for what lie ahead.

Blessed with mercy and grace unknown
I sensed the presence of redemption and life reborn,
until my brush with Christ I could not see
the treasure of eternal life residing in me.

Cherished sins once engaged I could not do
telling actions now clear in final review,
a hedge surrounded my life by God was placed
guaranteeing the heavenly sanctum that would await.

Amazing enough,
all of life's roads led here…
paved in the blood of Jesus Christ
in whom I honor and revere.

"Scriptural Reference"
St. John 14:21 thru 23

St. John 14:21 thru 23 {Holman Christian Standard Version}

"The one who has My commands
and keeps them
is the one who loves Me.

And the one who loves Me
will be loved by My Father.
I also will love him
and will reveal Myself to him."

Judas (not Iscariot) said to Him,
"Lord, how is it
You're going to reveal Yourself to us
and not to the world?"

Jesus answered,
"If anyone loves Me,
he will keep My word.

My Father will love him,
and We will come to him
and make Our home with him."

~ Brother's Keeper ~

Brother to brother!

Why should I grope in darkness
continuing to bare my soul?
While surrendering my blessings,
guaranteeing you total control.

I am sick and tired of sweating tears
bleeding anguish, blood, and guts;
while living in a world of plenty,
where enough… is not enough.

We are all God's children,
or don't you solemnly agree?
The character and intellect embodied in you
was created abundantly in me.

So, I ask the brotherly question…
Who on Earth do you think you are?
Are you truly my spiritual brother?
Or is your Christianity… simply a farce?

Receive this truth as a warning,
be not culturally or spiritually deceived.
You cannot be in *"right relationship"* with God
when you are in *"wrong relationship"* with me.

In the image and likeness of the Creator am I,
exceeding every creature in the earth, air and sea,
be it known that God's character and image is abused
when you knowingly mistreat me.

I am a beloved child of the Creator,
the one and only "I Am That I Am";
to those who disobey this commandment…
you are spiritually and eternally damned!

"Scriptural Reference"
1st John 4:18 thru 21 & Mark 12:28 thru 31

1st John 4:18 thru 21 {New American Standard Version}

"There is no fear in love; but perfect love casts out fear,
because fear involves punishment,
and the one who fears is not perfected in love.

We love, because He first loved us. If someone says,
"I love God," and hates his brother, he is a liar;
for the one who does not love his brother
whom he has seen, cannot love God whom he has not seen.

And this commandment we have from Him,
that the one who loves God should love his brother also."

Mark 12:28 thru 31 {New International Version}

"One of the teachers of the law came and heard them debating.
Noticing that Jesus had given them a good answer,
he asked Him, Of all the commandments,
which is the most important?

The most important one, answered Jesus, is this:
'Hear, O Israel, the Lord our God, the Lord is one.

Love the Lord your God with all your heart
and with all your soul and with all your mind
and with all your strength.

The second is this:
'Love your neighbour as yourself.
There is no commandment greater than these."

~ Touched By An Angels ~

An awakening from Jangel!

Even the most loyal of angels,
having ever come my way;
were creatures fashioned for elevation,
predestined to eloquently fly away.

They ascend to the greatest pinnacles,
transcending the loftiest and highest of heights;
as they gracefully spread their wings,
in wondrous and sheer delight.

You are certainly akin to those creatures,
the world knows it without doubt to be true;
the strength of GOD'S HEAVENLY CHARACTER,
is His "IMAGE" and "LIKENESS" in you.

May you always trust and believe...
in what the Lord has commanded for you;
Christ Jesus paid the price on Calvary,
for the wings that are especially fitted for you!

Satan would have us believe as caterpillars...
that we can only grope, quiver and crawl...
when in the Holy Spirit we are "BUTTERFLIES"
blessed and spiritually anointed to rise above it all.

"Scriptural Reference"
Hebrews 13:2 & 1st Corinthians 6:2 thru 3

Hebrews 13:2 {New King James Version}

"Do not forget
to entertain strangers,
for by so *doing*
some have unwittingly
entertained angels."

1ˢᵗ Corinthians 6:2 thru 3 {Holman Christian Standard Version}

"Or don't you know that the saints will judge the world?
And if the world is judged by you,
are you unworthy to judge the smallest cases?

Don't you know that we will judge angels
not to mention ordinary matters?"

~ More Than An Idol ~

Shattered vision... broken pieces!

As sinners we present ourselves,
humbled by Your holiness...
sacrificing our vanity...
surrendering our personal pride.

We stand unafraid...
trusting as little children...
agreeing to deny ourselves in order to grow,
unashamed to proudly say...

"Heavenly Father, in You I know".

When it comes to perpetrators...
there are many of whom we have known,
that have presented themselves as Christians,
whom were less than disciples or saints.

Ones who have shared...
a corrupt and vile brand of theology.
Therefore, we examine the Holy Scriptures...
and we tremble in the face of "Your WORD".

Father... it was in April of 1974,
that You drew me to a small,
white steeple church on Zaragoza Street
in the downtown area of Pensacola, Florida.
It was here at this peaceful place,
that You whispered in my ear three times...

"Get up and speak!!!"

It was here that I unveiled my shame
and exposed my wretchedness for all to see.
On that day my soul was saved,
You forgave my sins and set me free.

If it had not been for You...
I would have self-destructed long ago...

and died a miserable death in sin,
but you were faithful toward me.

Thank You Jesus, You saved me!

Dear Heavenly Father I thank You,
if it were not for Your Son Jesus being on my side,
I would have been in jail or dead decades ago
awaiting the slam of the prison door
or the fiery flames of hell's fire.

Thanks to the divine knowledge magnified in Your Word,
tribulation and hardship has become a motivation;
I now understand that there is no conviction without suffering,
and I yearn to see Your face!

Christ Jesus has taught me how to
physically bend and not spiritually break.
While having the resolve to love my adversaries,
even when faced with the greatest of trials and adversity!

Therefore, I stand tall supported by
the promised assurance of Your love.
When things look doubtful
I have learned to pray and not fear...
because I know that I am a blessed child of *"The Master"*.

Lord, it is Your kingdom that I seek,
and Your Word that I struggle to obey...
realizing daily that yielding is not easy,
I release and submit myself to You.

I need Thee O' Father!
It is within thy Spirit that I have belonging...
and in thy presence that I know no waste,
You are my rock and my tower.

A carnal babe was I,
born into a world preordained by Satan
to become a human idol prone to self-worship.

This was me before being spiritually broken,
prior to my being blessed to become a disciple of Your Word.
Thank You Heavenly Father for being the potter,
and letting *"Your Almighty Hand"* to be the wheel.

You have continuously turned me
around, and around, and around...
in the hollow of Your hand
that I might live.

Unto You almighty God I give the honor,
realizing that Your *"Might"* is the presence of Your *"Power"*.
Unto You dear Father I give the glory
knowing that Your *"Glory"* is the power of Your *"Presence"*.

Dear Father in the name of Your Son Jesus,
our Redeemer, Lord and Savior...

I thank You for life and divine citizenship
in Your glorious heavenly kingdom
that is destined to reign on Earth
for ever and ever more!

Honor and blessing to You for Eternity!!!

"Scriptural Reference"
2nd Colossians 6:16 & Luke 20:17 thru 18

2nd Corinthians 6:16 {New International Reader's Version}

"How can the temple of the true God
and the statues of other gods agree?
We are the temple of the living God.

God has said, "I will live with them.
I will walk among them.
I will be their God.
And they will be my people."

Luke 20:17 thru 18 {King James Version}

"And he beheld them, and said,
What is this then that is written,

The stone which the builders rejected,
the same is become the head of the corner?

Whosoever shall fall upon that stone shall be broken;
but on whomsoever it shall fall, it will grind him to powder."

~ God's Best Friend ~

The greatest love affair!

They say I'm dying...
but I say they are lying,
because I know...

I am God's best friend!

They say I only have months to live,
but I know that time is not theirs to give,
because I know...

I am God's best friend!

When I heard the news,
I fell on my knees and prayed...
not believing a word they had to say,
because I know...

I am God's best friend!

They told me that my end was finally here,
but my mind and heart was very clear.
because I know...

I am God's best friend!

I just could not see myself dying there,
sitting in that old hollow chair,
because I know...

I am God's best friend!

Today I embrace a life filled with cheer,
my life is in God's hand... I have no fear,
because I know...

I am God's best friend!

So on this day I say to you,
believe every word that God says is true.
We all should know...

We are God's best friend!

In God there is no death there is only life,
to this end Jesus became our human sacrifice.
For this we know…

We are God's best friend!

To believe Him…
Is to receive Him…

I am God's best friend!

"Scriptural Reference"
John 15:12 thru 16

John 15:12 thru 16 {New King James Version}

"This is My commandment,
that you love one another as I have loved you.
Greater love has no one than this,
than to lay down one's life for his friends.

You are My friends if you do whatever I command you.
No longer do I call you servants,
for a servant does not know what his master is doing;
but I have called you friends,
for all things that I heard from My Father
I have made known to you.

You did not choose Me,
but I chose you and appointed you
that you should go and bear fruit,
and that your fruit should remain,
that whatever you ask the Father in My name
He may give you."

~ What Does It Mean? ~

In search of the eternal answer!

Rose pedicels, rainbows,
mixed feelings of a dream,
purple passion lollipops
just what does it mean?

Shades of aqua, purple, lavender and gold
draping the emotional walls of ambivalent souls.
Blue, red, yellow, orange and green,
ambient solace, just what does it mean?

Sullen smiles on beautiful faces
feelings of sadness, so out of place.
For Christ did die, shall GOD deny?
Jesus resurrected from the dead; is the WORD a lie?

In a manner of speaking
the race has been run.
No more... cap pistols,
Barbie Dolls and bubble gum.

Counting the hours
while chasing the dream,
life is a vapor
just what does it mean?

"Scriptural Reference"
James 4:13 thru 15 & 1st John 5:11 thru 13

James 4:13 thru 15 {New International Version – UK}

"Now listen, you who say,
Today or tomorrow we will go
to this or that city, spend a year there,
carry on business or make money.

Why, you do not even know
what will happen tomorrow.
What is your life?

You are a mist that appears
for a little while and then vanishes.

Instead, you ought to say,
If it is the Lord's will,
we will live and do this or that."

1st John 5:11 thru 13 {New King James Version}

"And this is the record,
that God hath given to us eternal life,
and this life is in his Son.

He that hath the Son hath life;
and he that hath not the Son of God hath not life.

These things have I written unto you
that believe on the name of the Son of God;
that ye may know that ye have eternal life,
and that ye may believe on the name of the Son of God."

~ Metamorphosis ~

Mystery of mysteries!

As a soul I live
as a body I die,
I spread my wings
like a butterfly.

As a cocoon I come
into life this way,
much like larva
not here to stay.

The cocoon is body,
the larva is soul,
the butterfly is life
in its spiritual mode.

Man was created mortal
formed from dust of the earth,
given the breath of life
in measured reserve.

Much like larva
given hidden wings to fly,
a creature of destiny
bound to die.

It is in deed God's purpose
that all should understand
that in life lie the mystery
not in the death of man.

Man is not to confuse
"life's package" with the *"gift"*,
in joy the package should be opened,
the gift a treasure to be missed.

The Spirit is the gift
wrapped within the body of man,

being explained in the Holy Scriptures
for all to understand.

Once the physical package is opened
the soul sprouts wings and flies,
soaring back into the kingdom
where it becomes immortalized.

Fly hard and long my beautiful
as you always flew for me,
as you spread your wings of love
may your shadow smile on me.

"Scriptural Reference"
1st Corinthians 15:50 thru 57

Disclosure of the Eternal Gift

1st Corinthians 15:50 thru 57 {New King James Version}

"Now this I say, brethren,
that flesh and blood cannot inherit the kingdom of God;
nor does corruption inherit incorruption.

Behold, I shew you a mystery;
We shall not all sleep, but we shall all be changed,
In a moment, in the twinkling of an eye, at the last trump:
for the trumpet shall sound, and the dead shall be raised incorruptible,
and we shall be changed.

For this corruptible must put on incorruption,
and this mortal must put on immortality.

So when this corruptible shall have put on incorruption,
and this mortal shall have put on immortality,
then shall be brought to pass the saying that is written,
Death is swallowed up in victory.

O death, where is thy sting? O grave, where is thy victory?
The sting of death is sin; and the strength of sin is the law.
But thanks be to God, which giveth us the victory
through our Lord Jesus Christ."

~ A Time To Be Born And A Time To Die ~

My mom... she sleepeth!

Weepeth not...
O' gentle one!
The last trump has sounded...
the hour has come!

The heavenly hosts have been summoned,
the honored guests are here.
The earthly hourglass has emptied,
but have no fear.

The bridesmaids have entered,
even the dead and resurrected have arrived.
Christ, the Bridegroom has appeared
to receive the Church, His Holy Bride.

The table of eternity has been set...
God's heavenly throne is revealed.
The judgment seat has descended
to weigh the deeds of our years.

Make no amends or excuses now,
for the time has past gone to sort it out.
Sleep peaceful and gently in thy day of rest,
lay thy weary head upon God's eternal breast.

Birth is an appointment made!
Death an appointment kept!
Jesus drank *"Adam's cup of sin and death"*
after He prayed and wept!

The morning star that once shined
has finally dimmed its light,
far beyond the celestial horizon
one sleeps tonight.

God's angels are smiling...
hoping you have done your best.

Jesus Christ is our Teacher…
did you pass the test?

The light of day is gone
the sun is permanently at rest,
no more time to labor,
life's wages are eternally set.

Awake and see God's face!

"Scriptural Reference"
Ecclesiastes 3:1 thru 2, Revelation 22:10 thru 12 & Isaiah 38:18

Ecclesiastes 3:1 thru 2 {King James Version}

"To every thing there is a season,
and a time to every purpose under the heaven:

A time to be born, and a time to die; a time to plant,
and a time to pluck up that which is planted;"

Revelation 22:10 thru 12 {New King James Version}

"And he said to me, "Do not seal
the words of the prophecy of this book,
for the time is at hand.

He who is unjust, let him be unjust still;
he who is filthy, let him be filthy still;
he who is righteous, let him be righteous still;
he who is holy, let him be holy still."

"And behold, I am coming quickly,
and My reward *is* with Me,
to give to every one according to his work."

Isaiah 38:18 {21st Century King James Version}

"For the grave cannot praise Thee,
death can not celebrate Thee;
they that go down into the pit
cannot hope for Thy truth."

~ The Wall ~

The greatest of life's mysteries decoded!

From out of the womb
into a crowded tunnel I came,
brandishing the thought
of becoming a man.

From among the talented and gifted
I was given a call,
being counted truly blessed
to touch the wall.

For all can see…
though only the gifted can touch,
God's earthly mural that is prepared,
to speak to us.

Out of the darkness…
from water and Spirit I have come,
traveling life's tunnel
until God's work is done.

A *"Great Mystery"* of life
embraces and eludes us all,
why does God only allow
the *"spiritually gifted"* to touch the wall?

The wall of humanity
written upon for all to see,
yet only God's personal elect
are permitted to write upon it.

A glimpse, touch, or feel
is but a morsel to the taste,
of what the writing will reveal
to the entire human race.

There is one whom has come
to *steal, kill, and destroy,*

he paints the wall with blasphemous graffiti
after he has taken away our joy.

There is another Whom spiritually dares us
to diligently look upon the wall,
to search out and understand the *"Great Mystery"*
that confounds to save us all.

Life is the tunnel
communicating an awesome story told,
decipher the meaning of the wall
let the writing save your soul.

At life's end there is a *"LUMINARY SPIRIT"*
that exists to translate and separate all of us,
interpret the meaning of the wall
and be translated from the dust.

Christ Jesus is the *"Great Mystery"*…
once hidden…, now revealed!!!

"Scriptural Reference"
Daniel 5:5 thru 7 & Romans 16:25 thru 26

Disclosure of the Eternal Gift | 299

Daniel 5:5 thru 7 {New King James Version}

"In the same hour the fingers of a man's hand
appeared and wrote opposite the lampstand
on the plaster of the wall of the king's palace;
and the king saw the part of the hand that wrote.

Then the king's countenance changed,
and his thoughts troubled him,
so that the joints of his hips were loosened
and his knees knocked against each other.

The king cried aloud to bring in the astrologers,
the Chaldeans, and the soothsayers.
The king spoke, saying to the wise men of Babylon,

"Whoever reads this writing, and tells me its interpretation,
shall be clothed with purple and have a chain of gold around
his neck; and he shall be the third ruler in the kingdom."

Romans 16:25 thru 26 {New King James Version}

"Now to him that is able to establish you
according to my gospel, and the preaching of Jesus Christ,
according to the revelation of the mystery
kept secret since the world began,

but now is made manifest, and by the prophetic Scriptures
made known to all nations, according to the commandment
of the everlasting God, for obedience to the faith:"

A "Maze" In "Grace"!

"A Tablet Moment..."

Have you ever considered the importance of just one 24-hour period in the fulfillment of God's plan for your life? The Bible states that God allotted the Children of Israel three scores and ten years of life while in the wilderness. Psalms chapter 90, verse 10 states…

> *"The days of our years are threescore years and ten; and if by reason of strength they be fourscore years, yet is their strength labour and sorrow; for it is soon cut off, and we fly away." {King James Version}*

Life is like a vapor…

This scripture serves as *"the official hourglass of man's earthly longevity"*, especially in view of the most recent *"World Health Organization Report"*. According to an April 16, 2014 news article posted on the TheHuffingtonPost.com website, the World Health Organization made the following announcement concerning the global life expectancy for women and men: *"Global life expectancy at birth was 72 years for women and 68 years for men in 2011."* Interestingly enough, the 3 scores and 10 years life span applied to the Children of Israel during their 40 years sojourn in the wilderness was equivalent to the 70 years average lifespan of humans living today. Unfortunately, when broken down into twenty-four hour increments this seemingly large block of time is only 25,568 days, which equates to 365.25 days per year multiplied times 70 years.

It is common knowledge that the average life span of one individual can exceed or be considerably less than another living under very similar conditions in a shared environment. There are those among us whose lives will exceed the number of years recorded in this scripture, while others will live far fewer years in many nations and countries around the world, as noted in the *"World Health Organization Report"*. It is readily apparent upon doing a simple comparison based upon *"days lived"* rather than *"years counted"* that 70 years is considered by most to be a very long time. However, when observed from God's perspective it becomes clear that an average life span of 70 years more often than not translates into a *"perceivably long, but very short life"*. The Apostle James states the following in the book of

Disclosure of the Eternal Gift | 303

James chapter 4, verse 14...

> "Yet you do not know what your life will be like tomorrow. You are just a vapor that appears for a little while and then vanishes away". {New American Standard Version}

The Amplified version of the Bible translates this scripture with a bit more clarity, by going on to state...

> "Yet you do not know the least thing about what may happen tomorrow. What is the nature of your life? You are really but a wisp of vapor, a puff of smoke, a mist that is visible for a little while and then disappears into thin air."

Time is like a coin...

Upon reflection, I thought it wise to consider my longevity going back to my birth. Based upon Psalms chapter 90, verse 10 my remaining longevity could be less than 2,100 days by the time of this publication's release date. *I am convinced that if we were to treat the days of our lives as if they were one-dollar bills, realizing that we only have "twenty-five thousand, five hundred sixty eight dollars" to spend, our individual approaches to time spent would be considerably different.* An American writer, Carl Sandburg quoted the following...

> "Time is the coin of your life. It is the only coin you have and only you can determine how it is spent. Be careful lest you let other people spend it for you."

Each new day, a spiritual labyrinth...

If we were to quantify and rate each twenty-four hour period in our lives based upon receiving a reward at the end of each day, it would become clear that each new day is literally a *"spiritual labyrinth"* or *"maze"* that is placed before us for successful matriculation on a day-by-day basis. Webster's Dictionary states the following...

> "A maze is a confusing, intricate network of winding pathways, specifically with one or more blind alleys."

The American Heritage Dictionary states...

> "A maze is something made up of many confusing conflicting elements, a physical situation in which it is easy to get lost. A maze is intended by design to function like a difficult to solve puzzle that rewards the participant psychologically and otherwise for having accomplished the goal."

This description sounds strikingly similar to a common day in the lives of all humans, regardless of age, nationality, faith or ethnicity. I firmly believe that God places each day before us as a test filled with trials and obstacles that complicates and obstructs our passage as we journey toward the end of each day. The trials and obstacles have the desired effect of building a stronger and deeper spiritual foundation, while strengthening our spiritual character on a daily basis. The difficulties that confront us are purposed by design to strengthen our spiritual resolve in every area of our lives. Every temptation and challenge is a test of spiritual endurance, wherein God allows Satan to obstruct our paths to increase our faith in Him. The Apostle Paul stated that even Jesus was tested in all areas {Hebrews chapter 4, verse 15}...

> "For we do not have a high priest who is unable to sympathize with our weaknesses, but One who has been tested in every way as we are, yet without sin." {Holman's Christian Standard Version}

Life outside of Christ...

Unlike the rest of humanity, Jesus walked the Earth endowed with all knowledge and power during His earthly ministry, while operating as *Lord*, *Savior* and *Redeemer* of our lives. Humans do not possess the "VESTED POWER" or "SPIRITUAL AUTHORITY" to live the fullness of life outside of Christ, wherein we learn day-by-day to walk spiritually with God. We live in a state of sinful existence resulting from the *"Original Sin"* committed by Eve and passed down by Adam, when he alone violated the "FOUNDATIONAL COVENANT". Our challenge individually and collectively is to increase our resistance to Satan's snares and entrapments on a moment-by-moment basis until we mature into the "OVERCOMERS" that God the Father requires us to be. This is a mandatory requirement for receiving the gift of eternal life.

Disclosure of the Eternal Gift | 305

It is God's desire that all be empowered to withstand the trials and test of Satan and not stumble or perish. Salvation requires each of us to become a virtual *"spiritual pole-vaulter"* in the name of Jesus when confronted with the obstacles of temptations that Satan places before us on a daily basis. God's expectation for us is that we resist Satan on every level, until the bar of temptation has been elevated to its highest possible standard. The prophet Isaiah wrote the following in the book of Isaiah chapter 59, verse 19...

> *"So shall they fear The name of the LORD from the west, And His glory from the rising of the sun; When the enemy comes in like a flood, The Spirit of the LORD will lift up a standard against him."* {New King James Version}

It is to this end that God the Father allows the extended family of Adam to continue moving through the repetitive cycles of *death, birth and spiritual regeneration*. Life is a process of prolonged agony and sinful posterity, wherein we are afforded every opportunity to get our lives right prior to dying in sin and not preparing ourselves spiritually for the Lord's return. In fact, this is what mercy and grace is all about.

Jesus made lower than angels...

Christ was born from the womb of a woman and made lower than angels *(Hebrews 2:9)* in order for all to be granted the right to freely receive salvation from God the Father by the *"grace"* of His only begotten Son, Jesus. The following is recorded in the book of John chapter 1, verse 17, wherein the Apostle John writes... *"For the law was given by Moses, but grace and truth came by Jesus Christ."* The prophet Jeremiah goes on to write in the book of Lamentations chapter 3, verse 22... *"It is of the LORD's mercies that we are not consumed, because his compassions fail not."* It is by the *"mercy"* of God the Father and the *"grace"* of God the Son that each new day is placed before us in the form of a *"spiritual maze"*. Each new day is established upon the sacrifice of Jesus through the shedding of His blood on Calvary for our sins. Jesus is *"the Lamb slain from the foundation of the world"* and each new rising and setting of the sun is God's *"precious present"* to us in the form of... "A MAZE IN GRACE"!

The life or death question…

Satan uses sensory manipulation of our *sight, touch, feel, taste and hearing* as weapons of carnal enticement to confuse and intoxicate our physical senses with the goal of seducing our *"freewill"*. Satan dupes us into believing that our lives outside of Christ are overflowing with happiness and bliss while being free of penalty and judgment, when in fact all the days of our lives without Christ are just ticking time bombs of final destruction leading up to judgment day. When Christ returns on the *"day of judgment"* to receive the Church unto Himself, the Heavenly Father will weigh the deeds of each of our daily lives against the entries recorded in the *"Book of Life"* (Rev. 20:12 & 20:15) to determine the crucial answer to one *"life or death"* question…

> *Is the end-result of your day-by-day life sufficient to reward you with an after-life in eternity with Jesus Christ?*

A "God Day" dwarfs the solar measurement of time…

It is a well-known fact that the world has worked extremely hard at maintaining one of the *"greatest of all truths"* as a well-kept secret. The secret is that none of the days in the life of any one human, equals just one day that God has prepared and preserved for us in *"eternity"*. The Apostle Peter permanently shatters *"the official hourglass of man's earthly longevity"* when he states the following in the book of 2nd Peter chapter 3, verse 8…

> *"But do not forget this one thing, dear friends: With the Lord a day is like a thousand years, and a thousand years are like a day."*

Therefore, if a *"calendar day"* equates to *"24 hours"* to *"fallen man"*, then a *"God day"* according to the Apostle Peter would be equivalent to *"1,000 years"* in eternity to the *"redeemed man"*. Better yet, a calendar year that equates to 365 days to fallen man, would equate to 365,000 years in *"God years"* *(365 days x 1,000 years)* for the redeemed of God in eternity. Imagine looking back over the previous four seasons and reminiscing through 365,000 years of abundant life versus 365 calendar days of trials and tribulations that we have all grown accustomed. What an incredible thought to embrace

A "perceivably long", but very short life...

Consider this... Noah's grandfather, Methuselah lived 969 years before dying prior to the great flood. Methuselah lived longer than any man in the entirety of recorded history of humankind, and on its face, 969 years appears to be an extremely long period. This is particularly notable when compared to the 70 years average lifespan of man today. The scriptures state in Genesis chapter 5, verses 25 thru 27...

> *"Methuselah lived one hundred and eighty-seven years, and begot Lamech. After he begot Lamech, Methuselah lived seven hundred and eighty-two years, and had sons and daughters. So all the days of Methuselah were nine hundred and sixty-nine years; and he died." {King James Version}*

In hindsight, it is very clear that the lifespan of Methuselah was incredibly short in comparison to the length of life that awaits those of us who love the Lord and trust in His promises and provision.

In fact, <u>Methuselah's life was incredibly short</u> when considering he only lived 969 years before dying a very young death. I find it interesting that Methuselah is thought to have lived an extremely long life by most, but surprisingly he failed to live one full *"eternal day"* based upon the "God day" of 1,000 years referenced by Peter. Under the "FOUNDATIONAL COVENANT" also known as the "ADAMIC COVENANT", God granted Adam an endless life filled with the *"God days"* that are referenced by the Apostle Peter. When attempting to compare the days of Methuselah's life *(calendar days)* to just one moment in eternity is like trying to compare a stitch in the eternal fabric of existence to one breath of God and there is no comparison!

Time... The only God given provision belonging to man...

Time marks and punctuates the space that envelopes and cradles the entire universe! In fact, *time* is a byproduct of CREATION that will cease to exist as a functional measure of man's longevity when Christ returns. Time is without doubt the only *"God given provision"* that remains a "CONSTANT" until the time of death when it is required back. Unlike the other attributes received from God, time is the only one that does not undergo a diminishing capacity during the lifetime of humans.

All of the other God given assets and attributes received by humans between *"initial breath"* and *"physical death"* including sight, memory, energy, mobility, reproductive health, sexual health and fine motor skills, among others are required back in varying degrees during our lifetimes accept time. Time is man's only "SACRED PROVISION" in which God requires its use to be personally accounted for on the *"Day of Judgment"*. Every living and resurrected soul whose names are not written in the *"Lamb's Book of Life"* are required to give account of how their time was spent relative to *God's prescribed will, plan, and purpose for their lives*. <u>On that day, this will be the ultimate question...</u>

Did you use the time allocated to you to prepare yourself and others for the coming Kingdom of Jesus Christ our Lord?

Or, did you spend your life-long days in carnal mischief, being foolishly entertained and distracted by the wiles of Satan?

Disclosure of the Eternal Gift | 309

*O*ur days are so overwhelmingly dwarfed in comparison to God's *"eternal days"*, which are used to fill and blanket eternity that the Apostle James provides an astonishing comparison in the book of James chapter 4, verse 14 to provide contrast...

> *"You are really but a wisp of vapor, a puff of smoke, a mist that is visible for a little while and then disappears into thin air." {Amplified Version}*

I so love God in Whom we were created to serve, because *"God is not a man that he should lie" (Numbers 23:19)*. The Lord promised Adam that in *"the day"* that he ate of the *"tree of knowledge of good and evil"* that he would surely die.

> *"In the beginning God created the heaven and the earth. And the LORD God formed man of the dust of the ground, and breathed into his nostrils the breath of life; and man became a living soul. And the LORD God planted a garden eastward in Eden; and there he put the man whom he had formed. And out of the ground made the LORD God to grow every tree that is pleasant to the sight, and good for food; the tree of life also in the midst of the garden, and the tree of knowledge of good and evil. And the LORD God commanded the man, saying, Of every tree of the garden thou mayest freely eat: But of the tree of the knowledge of good and evil, thou shalt not eat of it: for in the day that thou eatest thereof thou shalt surely die."*
> {Genesis 1:1 & 2:7, 8, 9, 16, 17 (King James Version)}

*U*pon reviewing the life spans of countless humans born into the Earth beginning with Adam, we find that not one, even *"Methuselah"* lived the one "GOD DAY" of 1,000 years that is described by the Apostle Peter in the book of 2nd Peter Chapter 3, verse 8...

> *"Dear friends, don't let this one thing escape you: With the Lord one day is like a thousand years, and a thousand years like one day."*

*T*his observation should give us serious pause when comparing days lived based upon the *"rising and setting of the sun in the sky"* versus the *"setting and rising of the Son of God"* by way of His crucifixion and resurrection on Earth. When Jesus surrendered His spirit during His crucifixion on Calvary, *"Son Set"* and *"spiritual death"* occurred for Satan. When Jesus rose from the dead on the third day and ascended back into Heaven to be seated at the right hand of our Heavenly Father, *"Son Rise"* and *"everlasting life"* occurred for man.

Interestingly enough, Satan would have us believe that the days of our lives are long and rewardingly fruitful when we willfully agree to devote our lives to sin by living in accordance with the cultural standards, practices and traditions of this world. Satan's goal is to persuade us into adopting the worldly values of *"sin culture"* versus the godly attributes of *"Spirit culture"* that abounded in the Garden of Eden prior to Adam's transgression, and the Christian church is the only earthly alternative until Christ returns. The Holy Scriptures teaches us that all of the days of our lives were purchased with the blood of the *"Lamb slain from the foundation of the world"*. Our inheritance of faith through Abraham makes us heirs to the *"coming kingdom"* that is promised to the faithful whom love the Lord and believe He will return.

The penalty of the Law, versus the mercy of Grace...

There is a prevailing belief that is deeply rooted in the Christian Church concerning the law, wherein we are taught that the *"Law of the Ten Commandments"* was abolished at the time of Christ's resurrection and was replaced with *"grace"*. Merriam Webster's theological definition of *"day of grace"* is... *"The time of probation when sinners may obtain forgiveness."* Jesus stated the following... **"Do not think that I have come to abolish the law or the Prophets; I have not come to abolish them but to fulfil them."** *{Matthew 5:7}*

Therefore, when we examine the nature of the law, we find its characteristics to be totally opposite of grace. Grace for one is merciful and the law is not. Under Mosaic Law each sinful act carried a penalty of physical death. Unlike grace, wherein physical death for individual sin was abolished and replaced with the penalty of *"eternal separation from God"*, which will be determined on *"judgment day"*. No longer are we penalized with loss of life for *"individual sins"*, we are now judged for our *"body of sin"*, which is our *"condemnation"*. Romans chapter 5, verse 12 records... *"And the gift is not like the one man's sin, because from one sin came the judgment, **resulting in condemnation**, but from **many trespasses** came the gift, resulting in justification."*

Under Mosaic Law, *"physical death"* was the wage earned for sin, wherein the sinner received no opportunity for repentance unto redemption due to an abbreviated life. Yet under grace all are afforded a lifetime of opportunity to repent and accept Christ as their Lord and be redeemed. The Apostle Paul recorded the following in *Romans chapter 6, verse 23... "For the wages of sin is death, but the gift of God is eternal life through Jesus Christ our Lord."* Unlike grace, the penalty under the law was *"physical death"*, wherein under grace the penalty is the deferment of *"spiritual death"* until the *"Day of Judgment"*.

Under the law there was no deferment of penalty for sin, in fact the penalty was swift, immediate, unmerciful and without conditional consideration. Therefore, grace by its nature is capable of doing something that the law is incapable of doing, *which is to bring about "repentance", "redemption" and "forgiveness"*. In fact, we receive a higher standard of judgment under grace that provides a pathway into eternity.

The *"penalty of the law"* of the Ten Commandments was abolished, *not the actual law*. The law is the bedrock and foundation of grace *{Exodus 20:2-17}*, without the law, the need for grace would not exist.

~ The Ten Commandments ~

1. Thou shalt have no other gods before Me.
2. Thou shalt not make unto thee any graven image, nor bow down thyself to them, *nor serve them*.
3. Thou shalt not take the name of the LORD thy God in vain.
4. Remember the Sabbath day, to keep it holy.
5. Honor thy father and thy mother.
6. Thou shalt not kill.
7. Thou shalt not commit adultery.
8. Thou shalt not steal.
9. Thou shalt not bear false witness against thy neighbor.
10. Thou shalt not covet thy neighbor's house; nor anything that is thy neighbor's.

Grace simply grants an allowance for sin without regard for the type of sin committed until Christ returns, when <u>all will be individually judged by the same standard</u> for the sin nature inherited from Adam, instead of being judged at the time of the offense as it were under the law. It is to this end that the following Scripture was recorded in Romans chapter 5, verse 12... "<u>Wherefore, as by one man sin entered into the world, and death by sin; and so death passed upon all men, for that all have sinned:</u>" Without the law, there could be no grace, because there would not be a penalty for sin, wherein we are to be forgiven.

Upon careful examination of the *"nature of the law"* verses the *"nature of grace",* it is abundantly clear that the *"penalty of physical death under the law"* was suspended under grace and deferred until the *"Day of Judgment",* at which time it will be replaced with the *"ultimate penalty of spiritual death".* Grace provides an allowance for *"daily forgiveness",* which is granted in the Lord's prayer...**" <u>Give us day by day our daily bread. And forgive us our sins;...</u>" *{Luke 11:3-4}* Daily prayer is a provision of grace that prevents individual sin from growing back into a *"<u>body of sin</u>" {Rom 6:5-7},* due to *"daily prayer"* and *"daily forgiveness".* Grace by its nature grants us a series of second chances to get our lives right by receiving Jesus as our Lord and Savior, prior to physical death or Christ's return. The following Scripture serves as an open invitation... *"<u>There is therefore now no condemnation for those who are in Christ Jesus.</u>" {Rom. 8:1}*

The law, by its very nature levied a *"penalty of physical death"* for each sinful act committed, wherein there was no allowance for forgiveness of sin. Grace on the other hand, provides a *"<u>Spiritual pardon of physical death with penalty deferred</u>"* until the Lord returns, when the books of our deeds, along with the *"Book of Life"* will be opened on the Day of Judgment. Under Mosaic Law the penalty or wage for sin was very similar to a modern day cash transaction... *"<u>buy now and pay now with your life</u>".* Unlike grace, which is based on an accounting *"accrual process"* similar to purchasing with a credit card wherein... *"<u>you buy now and pay later, when the bill comes due upon the return of Christ</u>".* Grace allows us to *"<u>recognize sin without realizing the debt</u>",* because the payment for our debt is written off through the process of repentance and forgiveness by accepting Christ.

𝒰nfortunately, many believe there is no imminent judgment for their sins, due to the lack of immediate penalty under grace, believing there is no debt to be paid. Therefore, many have chosen not to have their debt of condemnation expunged by accepting Jesus as their Lord and Savior. Many continue to live in sin, because there is no immediate penalty and this in effect is an **"abuse of grace"**. When Jesus was crucified, our condemnation resulting from the deeds of the *"old creature" (dead body of sin)* was cut from our backs and we were reborn into a *"new creature" {2nd Cor. 5:17}* free of condemnation.

𝒥n order to gain a full understanding of the *"condemnation"* that was expunged by Christ, we need first understand the burden that Adam the *"original man"* put on us, starting in the Garden of Eden as the *"first fallen man of iniquity"*. The sin nature inherited from Adam by each of us at the time of our births has seeded our condemnation requiring 6 steps of transition in order for us to be restored, *requiring acknowledgment of our transgressions, repentance, withdrawal from sin, redemption, sacrifice and judgment*. Each of the Apostles, Paul, Luke, John, Timothy, and James used the word *"condemnation"* in their writings. However, Paul being born an Israelite and having dual citizenship as a Roman citizen was far more aware of Roman laws and customs than the other apostles were. Therefore, the Apostle Paul, a Roman citizen understood better than most that *"condemnation"* as a rule, preceded the *"penalty of judgment"* in Roman society. Therefore, Paul applied this term in his epistles in order for us to understand the terrible price paid by Jesus in crucifixion to expunge our indebtedness.

𝒲hen a crime was committed under Roman law the condemned person would undergo public humiliation and public shame following the sentencing phase prior to their punishment. This involved strapping the subject or object of the crime to the condemned person's back and parading them through the streets of Rome for all to see. If the convicted person had killed someone, the corpse was strapped to the back of the condemned person for public viewing, taunting, and humiliation as part of their punishment. This practice of public condemnation and public humiliation was a normal part of sentencing under Roman law, which explains why Jesus had to carry the cross on His back through the streets of Rome on His way to Golgotha Hill on Calvary. The carrying of the cross for public viewing signified *"Jesus' body of sin"* to the Romans, but more importantly it symbolized *"our body of sin"* being taken from our backs, wherein Jesus bore all of the sins of the world that were passed down from Adam to us and accumulated in each of our lives in the form of *"condemnation"*. Paul decidedly used this term in his epistles knowing its profound significance and social impact in Roman society and tradition. Paul wanted us to fully understand the price Jesus paid to take our *"body of sin"* from our *"spiritual backs"* by the shedding of His blood in crucifixion on the cross of Calvary *(Ephesians 2:8-9 & Romans 5:15)*. Scripture states… *"There is therefore now no condemnation for those who are in Christ Jesus, who walk not according to the flesh, but according to the Spirit." {Romans 8:1, 5:16, 1ˢᵗ Corinthians 11:34, 1ˢᵗ Timothy 3:6, Luke 23:40, John 5:24, James 3:1 & 5:12}*

Life's spiritual maze…

I truly believe each new day is divinely established upon the Lord's foundation of new mercies, which were paid for in full by Jesus when He surrendered His life and shed his blood on Calvary for our sins. The death and resurrection of Jesus made it possible for all to live righteous according to the Heavenly Father's riches in glory *(Philippians 4:19)*. It is by the *"mercy of God the Father"* and the *"grace of God the Son"* that we continue to live in the hopeful assurance of receiving eternal life, wherein all are blessed to accept Jesus Christ and reside in the presence of our Lord and Savior for eternity. Each new day is unique to all others and it is by the grace of Jesus that each new day is placed before us in the form of a *"spiritual maze"*. It is by the guidance of the Holy Spirit that the redeemed have been blessed to successfully navigate the spiritual mazes placed before each of us in our daily lives.

*M*any would be surprised to learn that their lives function as *"scales of balance"* from which our deeds are weighed and recorded in the presence of God the Father on a daily basis. If our deeds were not brought before our Heavenly Father each day Jesus would not have instructed His disciples to pray for forgiveness for their sins on a daily basis. When Jesus taught His disciples to pray the Lord's Prayer, the prayer included a *"daily request"* to our Heavenly Father for provision in the areas of <u>food</u>, <u>forgiveness</u>, <u>indebtedness</u> and <u>deliverance</u>...

> *"After this manner therefore pray ye: Our Father which Art in heaven, Hallowed be thy name. Thy kingdom come, Thy will be done in earth, as it is in heaven.*
>
> *Give us <u>this day</u> our daily bread. <u>And forgive us our debts, as we forgive our debtors</u>. And lead us not into temptation, but deliver us from evil: For thine is the kingdom, and the power, and the glory, forever. Amen." Matthew chapter 6, verses 9 thru 13 {King James Version}*

There are those among us who view their days in life as meaningless risings and settings of the sun, which could not be further from the truth. Prior to my accepting Christ into my life, God blessed me to have *"spirit filled Christians"* whose lives were lived as positive Christian examples. They shared an awesome knowledge and faith that one can only find in Jesus Christ. Their lives were living testimonies of how the Lord goes before us each day to order our steps. In Isaiah chapter 45, verses 2 thru 4 the Prophet Isaiah writes...

> *"<u>I will go before thee, and make the crooked places straight</u>: I will break in pieces the gates of brass, and cut in sunder the bars of iron:" {King James Version}*

It is here that we receive witness of the Lord going before us in the *"spiritual labyrinths of time and space"*, breaking down barriers, removing obstacles of obstruction and clearing a path for us as we meander through the mazes placed before us on a daily basis. Armed with the knowledge that each new day is my *"gift of grace"* from Christ, I press forward knowing that I have entered into a *"mystical maze"* constructed of God's perfect will toward me. I live with the peaceful assurance that the Lord has anointed me with "SALVATION" and "HIS POWER" to overcome all barriers and move past obstructions as He makes the winding paths straight each and every day of my life. I trust that God has placed each day before me as a maze overflowing with *anointed teachings, bountiful blessings* and *endless tranquility.*

The Heavenly Father will, desired in us...

To this glorious end, God desires us to be as little children in our motives toward one another. He desires that we view life as *"spiritual play"* lacking competition, with relationships void of malice, while living in a world filled with hatred, contention, madness and strife. God desires that all of our days be joyous as we traverse the corridors, twist, and turns of the spiritual mazes that He places before us. God's will toward us is that we humble ourselves and be grateful and thankful for the *"temporal blessings"* of daily provision that Jesus taught His disciples to pray for and cling to the *"Eternal Blessing"* of spiritual salvation, which is our eternal provision. King David states the following in the book of Psalms chapter 118, verse 24...

> *"Today is the day, which the Lord hath made;*
> *we will rejoice and be glad in it."*

It is God's intent that we traverse today's spiritual maze as little children and be not thoughtful of the traps and pitfalls of yesterday, nor mindful of the concerns of tomorrow. God's desire for each of us is that we live each day in a righteous state of peaceful co-existence, being in need of nothing. Jesus died that we might be justified in Him to live all of the days of our lives free of need, fear, worry, stress and anxiety. God's perfect will towards us is that we are not consumed by the trials of our past that have come upon us for the *"good of our futures"*. He wants *"today"* to be the very first day of the rest of our eternal lives, free of concern for need of provision, in that our Heavenly Father is Jehovahjireh *(Genesis 22:14); "The God of our provision"*. The Lord never ceases to amaze me with His mercy and His grace.

All of the days of my life have truly been *"A Maze in Grace"*. God in His infinite mercy, grace and wisdom finds new ways to amaze me every day. This is just one of the countless reasons that I cherish, honor and adore *our Heavenly Father, Jesus Christ* and the *Holy Spirit* for the abundant gifts and treasured blessings of abundant life. God has conferred this glorious knowledge upon us through the blessed light of His precious Son, Jesus.

Disclosure of the Eternal Gift | 317

Therefore, we come boldly unto Your throne of grace *(Hebrews 4:16)* offering praise and thanksgiving to You Holy Father in the name of Jesus, with the Holy Spirit as our Eternal Witness. We come into Your presence bowing down in Your mercy and grace giving thanks for all things, realizing that all things come from You and without You we would have nothing and be nothing in Heaven nor in Earth.

We thank You Holy Father for all of our TEMPORAL BLESSINGS of earthly provision and SPIRITUAL BLESSINGS of heavenly provision. We offer endless blessings of thanksgiving and praise for the price that Jesus paid when He surrendered His life for every human born of Adam in order for all to receive the ETERNAL BLESSING of everlasting life.

Dear Holy Father, we honor and adore You for being loving enough and merciful enough to dispatch Your only Son into the Earth to serve as a willing human sacrifice by surrendering His life on Calvary to restore Your *"amazing God-like character" in us.*

Dear Holy Father, Creator of the Universe, we praise You for manifesting our *"appointed purpose"* in Christ Jesus, in Whom *"Your will"* was done in Heaven and Earth for the purpose of modeling how Your will is to be done in us. Therefore, we boldly come before Your throne of grace giving thanks to You for granting us an *"extension of time"* through grace to study Your Word and diligently learn of You…

Grace informs us that the "wisdom of time", when viewed in light of "infinite existence", reveals "YESTERDAY'S FUTURE" to be "TOMORROW'S PAST".

Don't wait until the last grain of mortality sift through your hourglass. Enter this day into "THE ETERNAL NOW" with JesusChrist… Our "Anointed Gift of Eternal Blessing".

Jesus Christ is God's "Eternal Gift" to Humanity. Your doorway to salvation and eternal life awaits you… Choose Christ as your Lord & Savior this day!!!

*On behalf of Neo Nexus Publishing, LLC
I personally thank you for investing
your time, energy and resource
into the exploration of...*
"Our Heavenly Father's Manufacturer's Handbook :
Disclosure Of The Eternal Gift".
*I sincerely hope that you were spiritually enriched.
You are cordially invited to explore and enjoy
the future publications that are yet to come!*

Charles E. Dickerson

www.ingramcontent.com/pod-product-compliance
Lightning Source LLC
Chambersburg PA
CBHW071648090426
42738CB00009B/1457